The Best of

Children's Books

1964–1978
INCLUDING 1979 ADDENDA

Virginia Haviland
Chief of the Children's Literature Center
Library of Congress
and
Advisory Committees
of Children's Literature Specialists

UNIVERSITY PRESS BOOKS   1981
302 FIFTH AVENUE
NEW YORK, NY 10001

Title Index, Author Index, Illustrator Index,
Copyright © 1981 by University Press Books.

Illustrations by Debbie Dieneman
Copyright © 1981 by University Press Books.

First Clothbound Edition 1981
International Standard Book Number 0-8295-0289-0
Library of Congress Catalogue Card Number: 81-50534

Printed in the United States of America

Preface

A look at the past fifteen years of publishing and selecting children's books in the United States—titles originating in this country and others made available as translations or republications from abroad—reveals a reduction in the quantity published annually from above three thousand (a peak when government funding was available for institutional purchasing) to something over two thousand. Using the same general criteria each year for selection, the advisory committee for the compilation of a Library of Congress annual list, without having in mind a specific annual numerical aim, found, however, that they chose each year about two hundred titles. Here, from the accumulation of some three thousand books from those years, is a listing of top choices. It is to be noted that certain desirable titles could not be listed because they had gone out of print—a situation worsening to the point of about eight thousand titles reported disappearing in one unusual year. Happily, the paperback explosion has kept many important works alive when a sales/cost formula used by publishers showed reason for dropping their hardback editions.

The diminution of institutional budgets as the general economy became depressed naturally affected book publishing in other ways also. In efforts to keep prices from escalating more than necessary such steps were taken as the use of black-and-white illustration instead of full color in some picture books. At the same time, improved photographic illustration owing to new technology enabled enlarged close-ups, time-filming, and scanning electron micrographs with three-dimensional effects.

In the production of more books on more topics, with a style of writing that engages rather than overtly instructs the reader, came a hugely increased publishing of easy-to-read books in "beginner" series and nonfiction designed for lower and lower reading levels, to which the country's widely publicized drop in levels of literacy can be related. It called forth a need to apply critical standards carefully to this area as also to the enlarged spread of books available to meet a more serious awareness of human rights—books concerning the handicapped, minorities (for example, the Jewish experience in World War II), women, and the aged—and numerous social concerns related to divorce, drugs, alcoholism, death, energy, and ecology. Judicious consideration became necessary also for works on such popular pursuits as the occult, mind control (hypnotism), judo, and karate.

The committees saw a greater relaxation of language and subject taboos in fiction published for the young teenager, in tune with higher maturity levels at given ages. Book production reflected, as always in the past, the culture of the day, with TV, "the great leveler," creating sudden interests and attention to social issues. New terms—"human sciences" and "sociobiology"—came into use.

It is hoped that this selection from some three thousand works, which has resulted from a vast number of hours of reading and discussion by committee members, will serve helpfully to bring a broad range of outstanding titles to the attention of those who stand in various relationships to the reading needs and interests of children and young people. In each entry the International Standard Book Number (ISBN) follows the price and the Library of Congress card number appears at the end of the bibliographic information for each book. At the end of the annotation grade level is indicated.

Virginia Haviland
Chief, Children's Literature Center
Library of Congress

Dedicated to the Children of the World
Our Only Hope for the Future

Contents

Picture and Picture-Story Books

Aardema, Verna. *Who's in Rabbit's House?* Pictures by Leo and Diane Dillon. New York, Dial Press, 1977. [32] p. $7.95 ISBN 0–8037–9550–5 (lib. ed. $7.45 ISBN 0–8037–9551–3)   77–71514
A Masai tale from the reteller's now out-of-print *Tales for the Third Ear* (Dutton) has brilliant pictures by the Dillons (who have twice won the Caldecott Medal). (K–Gr 3)

Afanasev, Alexei. *Salt; a Russian Tale.* Adapted by Harve Zemach from a literal translation by Benjamin Zemach, of the Russian of Alexei Afanasev. With illus. by Margot Zemach. Chicago, Follett, 1965. 32 p. $7.95 Farrar, Straus & Giroux, New York. ISBN 0–374–36385–4   65–12312
The famous Russian tale of Ivan the Fool, whose exploits to win a princess are pictured with full humor. (Gr 1–3)

Alexander, Martha G. *Blackboard Bear.* New York, Dial Press, 1969. [32] p. $4.95 ISBN 0–8037–0651–0 (lib. ed. $4.58 ISBN 0–8037–0652–9)   69–17975
A little boy, denied the pleasure of playing with big brother and his friends, invents an enormous bear which only he may touch. Few words, subtle illustration. Followed by *Bobo's Dream* (ISBN 0–8037–0686–3; lib. ed. ISBN 0–8037–0687–1) and *Nobody Asked Me If I Wanted a Baby Sister* (ISBN 0–8037–6401–4; lib. ed. ISBN 0–8037–6402–2). (PreS–Gr 2)

Andersen, Hans Christian. *The Ugly Duckling.* Translated by R. P. Keigwin. Illustrated by Adrienne Adams. New York, Scribner, 1965. [48] p. $7.95 ISBN 0–684–12646–X (paper $1.25 ISBN 0–684–13037–8)   65–21364
A favorite fairy tale has fresh interpretation in this artist's subtle watercolors. (Gr 1–4)

Anno, Mitsumasa. *Anno's Alphabet; an Adventure in Imagination.* New York, Crowell, 1975. [64] p. $7.50 ISBN 0–690–00540–7 (lib. ed. $7.89 ISBN 0–690–00541–5)   73–21652
In this unusual alphabet book, large letters, painted to look like carved wood, have a three-dimensional, optically challenging appearance. Borders, embellished with plants and hidden creatures, surround the pictured letters and objects. (K–Gr 4)

———. *Anno's Counting Book.* New York, Crowell, 1977. [28] p. $6.95 ISBN 0–690–01287–X (lib. ed. $6.79 ISBN 0–690–01288–8)   76–28977
A distinctive, beautifully conceived counting book in which twelve full-color double-spreads show the same village and surrounding countryside during different hours (by the church clock) and months. (PreS–K)

———. *Topsy-Turvies; Pictures to Stretch the Imagination.* New York, Walker/Weatherhill, 1970. 27 p. $4.95 ISBN 0–8348–2004–8   71–96054
In pictures of deceptive simplicity, optical illusions form structures in which curious little men can go up stairs to get to a lower place, hang pictures on the ceiling, and walk on walls. (All ages)

Aruego, José. *Look What I Can Do.* New York, Scribner, 1971. [32] p. $6.95 ISBN 0–684–12493–9   73–158880
Two water buffalo bounce along from one wild dare to another—an almost wordless picture book in which the copycat nonsense builds up to a hilarious climax. (K–Gr 2)

Asch, Frank. *MacGooses' Grocery*. Pictures by James Marshall. New York, Dial Press, 1978. [32] p. $5.95 ISBN 0-8037-5237-7 (lib. ed. $6.46 ISBN 0-8037-5231-8)   77-86270
A domestic absurdity in which mother, father, Junior, and Sis find duty tedious and leave an unhatched chick to fend for itself. Marshall's pictorial embellishments, softly colored in blue and orange, extend the humor. (PreS–Gr 1)

————. *Moon Bear*. New York, Scribner, 1978. [32] p. $7.95 ISBN 0-684-15810-8   78-9444
Bear, who has fallen in love with the full moon, worries when it diminishes. Asch's stylized brown bear and solid yellow moon contrast sharply with minute black-and-white background details. (PreS–Gr 1)

Babbitt, Natalie. *Phoebe's Revolt*. New York, Farrar, Straus and Giroux, 1968. [40] p. $5.95 ISBN 0-374-035907-5   68-13679
A family special—for young listeners, a stubborn little girl; and for parents and grandparents, charming pictures of the gaslight era. (K–Gr 2)

Bangs, Edward. *Steven Kellogg's Yankee Doodle*. New York, Parents' Magazine Press, 1976. [38] p. $5.95 ISBN 0-8193-0833-1 (lib. ed. $5.41 ISBN 0-8193-0834-X)   75-19190
Kellogg's full-page paintings, crammed with activity, illustrate each line of a familiar old song. He includes the melody and introductory information about variations of the verses and Bang's eighteenth-century role in rearrangements. (PreS–Gr 3)

Baylor, Byrd. *Hawk, I'm Your Brother*. Illustrated by Peter Parnall. New York, Scribner, 1976. [46] p. $6.95 ISBN 0-684-14571-5   75-39296
An Indian boy, whose great desire is to fly, feels he almost does so when he frees his pet hawk and watches him soar. Peter Parnall's illustrations with southwestern desert and mountains add much to the dimensions of the story. (Gr 1–3)

Benchley, Nathaniel. *Oscar Otter*. Illustrated by Arnold Lobel. New York, Harper & Row, 1966. 64 p. $4.95 ISBN 0-06-020471-0 (lib. ed. $4.79 ISBN 0-06-020472-9)   66-11499
In his frolicsome mountainside play young Oscar is pursued by a fox, a wolf, and a lion. Jolly first reading. (K–Gr 2)

————. *Small Wolf*. Pictures by Joan Sandin. New York, Harper & Row, 1972. 64 p. (An I can read history book) $4.79 ISBN 0-06-020492-3   70-183170
As the white man's settlement on Manhattan expanded, Small Wolf and his Indian family were mercilessly forced to move again and again. (Gr 1–2)

Bodecker, N. M. *"It's Raining," Said John Twaining; Danish Nursery Rhymes*. Translated and illustrated by N. M. Bodecker. New York, Atheneum, 1973. [32] p. (A Margaret K. McElderry book) $6.95 ISBN 0-689-30316-5 (paper $1.95 ISBN 0-689-70437-2)   72-85912
Bright paintings develop the storytelling quality of these traditional rhymes remembered from the translator's childhood. (PreS–Gr 2)

Bonsall, Crosby N. *And I Mean It, Stanley*. New York, Harper & Row, 1974. 32 p. $4.95 ISBN 0-06-020567-9 (lib. ed. $4.79 ISBN 0-06-020568-7)   73-14324
There is a surprise ending to this suspense-filled city story, featuring a child, a cat, a pile of junk, and unknown Stanley behind the fence. An Early I Can Read Book, illustrated in color by the author. (Gr 1–2)

Breinburg, Petronella. *Shawn Goes to School*. With illustrations by Errol Lloyd. New York, Crowell, 1974. [26] p. $5.95 ISBN 0-690-00276-9 ($6.49 ISBN 0-690-00277-7)   73-8003
On his first day at nursery school Shawn suffers the usual fears and receives murmurs of reassurance from his mother and teacher, and from a sister who tells this brief story. Full-page eye-catching colored illustrations. (PreS–K)

Briggs, Raymond. *Father Christmas*. New York, Coward, McCann & Geoghegan, 1973. [32] p. $4.95 ISBN 0-698-20272-4   73-77885
In a fresh style of comic-strip frames the artist shows an overworked and disgruntled Santa Claus coping with the snow and cold on his annual rounds. (K–Gr 2)

————. *Jim and the Beanstalk*. Written and illustrated by Raymond Briggs. New York, Coward-McCann, 1970. [40] p. $5.89 ISBN 0-698-30203-6   77-111062
The artist has invented a sequel to "Jack and the Beanstalk" in which another curious climber finds the giant now beset with the inadequacies of old age and endeavors to fill his needs. (K–Gr 3)

————. *The Snowman*. New York, Random House, 1978. [32] p. $4.95 ISBN 0-394-83973-0 (lib. ed. $5.99 ISBN 0-394-93973-5)   78-55904
A wordless picture story captures the full beauty and atmosphere of a winter's night as it portrays the adventures of a boy and his snowman. (K–Gr 3)

The Bun; a Tale from Russia [by] Marcia Brown. New York, Harcourt Brace Jovanovich, 1972. [32] p. $6.95 ISBN 0–15–213450–6   75–167832
Pictures crammed with action enliven this old tale of the mischievous bun who fools the hare, the wolf, the bear—but, alas, not the fox. (K–Gr 2)

Burningham, John. *Come Away from the Water, Shirley.* New York, Crowell, 1977. $6.95 ISBN 0–690–01360–4 (lib. ed. $7.49 ISBN 0–690–01361–2)   77–483
Twice winner of England's Kate Greenaway Medal for illustration, Burningham again uses attractive watercolors and artistic inventiveness for an engaging story. A little girl uses her imagination to rise above all-too-familiar parental warnings at the beach. (K–Gr 2)

————. *Mr. Gumpy's Outing.* New York, Holt, Rinehart and Winston, 1971. [32] p. $5.95 ISBN 0–03–089733–5   77–159507
Humorous, softly colored cross-hatched drawings expand a very simple cumulative tale of the friendly boatman who takes all his animal friends for a ride on the river. With this book, the artist became the first to win Britain's Kate Greenaway medal a second time. Followed by *Mr. Gumpy's Motor Car* ($7.95 Crowell. ISBN 0–690–00798–1). (PreS–Gr 1)

Carle, Eric. *Do You Want to Be My Friend?* New York, Crowell, 1971. [33] p. $8.95 ISBN 0–690–24276–X   70–140643
The title furnishes the only text for this gay full-color picture book about a mouse seeking for a friend and following a series of tails—ingeniously drawn over consecutive pages. Other bright picture books are: *The Secret Birthday Message* ($4.50 ISBN 0–690–72347–4; lib. ed. $5.79 ISBN 0–690–72348–2) and *The Grouchy Ladybug* ($7.95 ISBN 0–690–01391–4; lib. ed. $7.89 ISBN 0–690–01392–2). (PreS–Gr 2)

Carlson, Natalie S. *Marie Louise's Heyday.* Pictures by José Aruego and Ariane Dewey. New York, Scribner, 1975. [32] p. $6.95 ISBN 0–684–14360–7   75–8345
Babysitting five obstreperous opossums is not exactly a heyday for the little mongoose, Marie Louise, but the next day offers more. Sprightly pastel drawings capture the Haitian setting and delightful details of the adventure. (K–Gr 3)

Caudill, Rebecca. *A Pocketful of Cricket.* Illustrated by Evaline Ness. New York, Holt, Rinehart and Winston, 1964. 48 p. $5.95 ISBN 0–03–089752–1 (paper $1.95 ISBN 0–03–086619–7)   64–12617

Six-year-old Jay took a cricket to school, but not in mischief; his first day was "goodbye" to the summer countryside. Effective picture-book illustration. (Gr 1–3)

————. *Did You Carry the Flag Today, Charley?* Illustrated by Nancy Grossman. New York, Holt, Rinehart, and Winston, 1966. 94 p. $5.95 ISBN 0–03–089753–X (paper $1.65 ISBN 0–03–086620–0)   66–11422
An imaginative, curiosity-filled little boy in an Appalachian school finally achieves *the* honor for good behavior in first grade. (K–Gr 2)

Charlip, Remy. *Arm in Arm, a Collection of Connections, Endless Tales, Restorations, and Other Echolalia.* New York, Parents' Magazine Press, 1969. [42] p. $5.95 ISBN 0–8193–0235–X (lib. ed. $5.41 ISBN 0–8193–0236–8)   69–12610
Circular rhymes and silly plays on words with nonsensical illustrations to match. (All ages)

————, *and* Burton Supree. *Harlequin and the Gift of Many Colors.* Design and paintings by Remy Charlip. New York, Parents' Magazine Press, 1973. [42] p. $5.95 ISBN 0–8193–0494–8 (lib. ed. $5.41 ISBN 0–8193–0495–6)   76–136999
The origin of Harlequin's patchwork costume is suggested in a story about a small boy's need for a carnival suit. Impressive panoramas show an Italian town filled with festival crowds. (K–Gr 2)

Chenery, Janet. *Wolfie.* Pictures by Marc Simont. New York, Harper & Row, 1969. [64] p. $4.95 ISBN 0–06–021261–6 (lib. ed. $4.79 ISBN 0–06–021264–0)   78–77950
A genuinely funny introduction to the arachnids emerges from this story of two little boys secreting their pet spider from a nosy little sister while they conduct their research on its habits. (Gr 1–3)

Clifton, Lucille. *The Boy Who Didn't Believe in Spring.* Pictures by Brinton Turkle. New York, Dutton, 1973. [32] p. $5.95 ISBN 0–525–27145–7 (paper $1.95 ISBN 0–525–45038–6)   72–89844
Skeptical King Shabazz and his friend Tony Polito explore their city neighborhood to see if spring really exists. Brinton Turkle's colorful pictures capture the delight of the two boys as they uncover evidence along the way. (K–Gr 2)

Clymer, Eleanor L. *Horatio.* Drawings by Robert Quackenbush. New York, Atheneum, 1974. 63 p. Paper $1.25 ISBN 0–689–70403–8   67–18999
Mrs. Casey's cross-looking, "middle-aged" cat, after his unsought experience of mothering two kitten waifs,

radiates a changed personality. Easy reading, illustrated with humor. (K–Gr 3)

Cohen, Miriam. *When Will I Read?* Pictures by Lillian Hoban. New York, Greenwillow Books, 1977. [32] p. $7.25 ISBN 0–688–80073–4 (lib. ed. $6.96 ISBN 0–688–84073–6)   76–28320
Impatient to read books, first-grader Jim is astonished to discover that being able to read signs is reading, too. Cheerfully illustrated in color. (PreS–Gr 1)

———. *Will I Have a Friend?* Pictures by Lillian Hoban. New York, Macmillan, 1967. [32] p. $5.95 ISBN 0–02–722790–1 (paper $1.95 ISBN 0–02–042620–8)   67–5219
In an integrated nursery school Jim succeeds in finding a friend—an answer to all his first-day fears. (PreS–Gr 1)

Crews, Donald. *Freight Train.* New York, Greenwillow Books, 1978. [24] p. $6.95 ISBN 0–688–80165–X (lib. ed. $6.67 ISBN 0–688–84165–1)   78–2303
All the colors of a new crayon box are represented in this graphic view of a freight train moving through tunnels and cities and over trestles. (PreS–Gr 1)

Dayrell, Elphinstone. *Why the Sun and the Moon Live in the Sky; an African Folktale.* Illustrations by Blair Lent. Boston, Houghton Mifflin, 1968. 26 p. Paper $1.95 ISBN 0–25381–0   68–14293
A Nigerian myth distinctively illustrated with richly colored masked figures in an African village setting. (Gr 1–3)

De Paola, Thomas A. *"Charlie Needs a Cloak."* Englewood Cliffs, N.J., Prentice-Hall, 1973. [32] p. $4.95 ISBN 0–13–128355–3 (paper $0.95. Scholastic, New York. ISBN 0–590–10241–9)   73–16365
The author's illustrations in three colors depict the making of a new cloak: Charles shears his sheep, cards and spins the wool, weaves and dyes the cloth, and sews a fine red garment. (PreS–Gr 1)

———. *The Clown of God; an Old Story.* New York, Harcourt Brace Jovanovich, 1978. [46] p. $8.95 ISBN 0–15–219175–5 (paper $3.95 ISBN 0–15–618192–4)   78–3845
Giovanni the juggler spent his life making people laugh, until, old and destitute, he was capable of only one last performance as a gift to the Holy Child. Illuminated with large and splendid color paintings. (K–Gr 2)

———. *Strega Nona; an Old Tale.* Englewood Cliffs, N.J., Prentice-Hall, 1975. [32] p. $6.95 ISBN 0–13–851600–6   75–11565

A household helper of Strega Nona, "Grandma Witch," inundates his Calabrian village with pasta from her magic pot—which he knows how to start but not to stop—until the imperturbable Strega Nona provides a discomforting solution. Droll illustration in soft pastel line and wash. (K–Gr 2)

De Regniers, Beatrice S. *May I Bring a Friend?* Illustrated by Beni Montresor. New York, Atheneum, 1964. 48 p. $6.95 ISBN 0–689–20615–1 (paper $1.95 ISBN 0–689–70405–4)   64–19562
Jolly verse and sparkling pictures depict the adventures of a little boy who brings an astonishing series of animal friends to call on the king and queen. (PreS–Gr 2)

Du Bois, William Pène. *Bear Circus.* New York, Viking Press, 1971. 48 p. $4.95 ISBN 0–670–15073–8   76–153665
The author's soft color line-and-wash drawings enhance his captivating story of the kangaroo rescue of koala bears—the "real teddy bears"—and the circus produced by the grateful creatures. (K–Gr 3)

Dumas, Philippe. *The Story of Edward.* New York, Parents' Magazine Press, 1977. 48 p. $5.95 ISBN 0–8193–0868–4 (lib. ed. $5.41 ISBN 0–8193–0869–2; paper $1.95 ISBN 0–8193–0905–2)   76–28720
A droll tale translated from the French recounts the adventures of Edward, a debonair and talented dancing donkey who seeks his fortune wearing his old master's clothes. Beguiling pictures by the author. (K–Gr 2)

Emberley, Barbara. *Drummer Hoff.* Illustrated by Ed Emberley. Englewood Cliffs, N.J., Prentice-Hall, 1967. [32] p. $6.95 ISBN 0–13–220822–9 (paper $1.95 ISBN 0–13–220855–5)   67–28189
Richly stylized woodcuts give graphic substance to the cumulative martial chant about soldiers who in ascending rank play their parts in assembling a cannon, to have "Drummer Hoff fire it off." (PreS–Gr 1)

———. *One Wide River to Cross.* Adapted by Barbara Emberley. Illustrated by Ed Emberley. Englewood Cliffs, N.J., Prentice-Hall, 1966. [32] p. $5.95 ISBN 0–13–636167–6   66–20703
Bold woodcuts on colored pages depict the animals as they file into the ark—snakes on roller skates, elephants doing tricks, and so on, one by one up to ten by ten. The music for this old folk song is included. (K–Gr 2)

Emberley, Ed. *Drawing Book of Animals.* Boston, Little, Brown, 1970. [32] p. $3.95 ISBN 0–316–23597–0   75–107232

Entertaining instruction in how to proceed from the dot with simple shapes, letters, and symbols to draw almost any animal. (Gr 1–3)

Ets, Marie Hall. *Just Me*. Illustrated by the author. New York, Viking Press, 1965. 32 p. $2.50 ISBN 0–670–41109–4 (paper $0.75 ISBN 0–670–05044–X) 65–13349
A small boy's imaginative imitation of animals is appealingly depicted in strong, simply designed illustrations and brief, rhythmic text. A truly childlike picture book. (PreS–Gr 1)

The Fat Cat; a Danish Folktale. Translated and illustrated by Jack Kent. New York, Parents' Magazine Press, 1971. [30] p. Paper $1.25. Scholastic. ISBN 0–590–02174–5 70–136992
The translator-artist's clean watercolor drawings enforce the humor in this cumulative tale of a greedy cat who devoured everything in sight. (K–Gr 3)

Feelings, Muriel L. *Jambo Means Hello; Swahili Alphabet Book*. Pictures by Tom Feelings. New York, Dial Press, 1974. [60] p. $5.95 ISBN 0–8037–4346–7 (lib. ed. $5.47 ISBN 0–8037–4350–5) 73–15441
An alphabet book detailing with distinctive double-spread drawings East African village life and customs. (Gr 1–4)

Fenton, Edward. *The Big Yellow Balloon*. Illustrated by Ib Ohlsson. Garden City, N.Y., Doubleday, 1967. [48] p. $5.95 ISBN 0–385–08580–X (lib. ed. $6.90 ISBN 0–385–08621–0) 67–15962
A gay, cumulative picture tale ends in a "TREMENDOUS BANG" as Tom the Cat, who thinks he can kill the sun and thus have continuous nighttime for hunting, catches up with Roger's big yellow balloon. (K–Gr 4)

Fife, Dale. *Who's in Charge of Lincoln?* Illustrated by Paul Galdone, New York, Coward-McCann, 1965. 61 p. $4.99 ISBN 0–698–30406–3 65–13286
A series of swiftly moving and funny events carries a likeable little boy named Lincoln all the way from New York City to Washington, D.C., and safely home again—in an unexpected, plausible chain of circumstances. (Gr 2–4)

Freeman, Don. *Corduroy*. Story and pictures by Don Freeman. New York, Viking Press, 1968. 32 p. $6.50 ISBN 0–670–24133–4 (paper $1.25 ISBN 0–14–050173–8) 68–160689
Appealing pictures tell the amusing story of a toy bear who almost missed his chance to belong to someone because of a button missing from his green corduroy overalls. (PreS–Gr 1)

———. *Dandelion*. Illustrated by the author. New York, Viking Press, 1964. 48 p. $6.50 ISBN 0–670–25532–7 (paper $1.25 ISBN 0–14–050218–1) 64–21472
A vain lion makes himself unrecognizable to his friends. Humorous pictures of barber shop and party scenes. (K–Gr 2)

Freschet, Berniece. *The Ants Go Marching*. Illustrated by Stefan Martin. New York, Scribner, 1973. [32] p. $6.95 ISBN 0–684–13250–8 72–11108
This picture book with rhythmic, repetitive text is a simple counting book, illustrated with a blend of woodcuts, wood engravings, and lino cuts in two colors. (PreS–K)

Galdone, Joanna. *The Tailypo; a Ghost Story*. Retold. Illustrated by Paul Galdone. New York, Seabury Press, 1977. [32] p. (A Clarion book) $7.50 ISBN 0–8164–3191–4 77–23289
Demanding his "tailypo," a strange, furry creature repeatedly haunts the old man who cut off his tail to eat for supper. Retold from American folklore, this scary-enough story has humorous, brightly colored, full-page pictures. (K–Gr 3)

Ginsburg, Mirra. *Mushroom in the Rain*. Adapted from the Russian of V. Suteyev. Pictures by José Aruego & Ariane Dewey. New York, Macmillan, 1974. [32] p. $4.95 ISBN 0–02–736240–X (paper $2.50 ISBN 0–02–043270–4) 72–92438
Bright, humorous, color pictures show how a conveniently enlarging mushroom shelters from the rain a hunted rabbit and fellow refugees who conceal him. (PreS–Gr 1)

Goble, Paul. *The Girl Who Loved Wild Horses*. Scarsdale, N.Y., Bradbury Press, 1978. [32] p. $8.95 ISBN 0–87888–121–2 77–20500
Handsome panoramic scenes, with vibrant color and action, illuminate the story of a Native American girl whose love of wild horses leads her to live among them. Winner of the 1979 Caldecott Medal. (Gr 1–4)

Goodall, John S. *The Adventures of Paddy Pork*. New York, Harcourt, Brace & World, 1968. [60] p. $4.95 ISBN 0–15–201589–2 68–26425
Both childlike and technically fascinating, this toy book without words has matching half pages alternating with full pages to increase action as they open doors or disclose a hiding villain. Also, *The Ballooning Adventures of Paddy Pork* (ISBN 0–15–205693–9) and *Paddy Pork's Holiday* (Atheneum. ISBN 0–689–50043–2). (PreS–Gr 2)

―――. *The Surprise Picnic.* New York, Atheneum, 1977. [56] p. (A Margaret K. McElderry book) $4.95 ISBN 0–689–50074–2   76–28455
A pleasant little island picnic turns into a harrowing experience for Mrs. Cat and her kittens, for a storm comes up and only by ingenious means do they make it back to safety. Richly colored paintings tell the story in a wordless picture book with half-pages to be turned. (PreS–K)

Graham, Lorenz B. *Song of the Boat.* Pictures by Leo and Diane Dillon. New York, Crowell, 1975. [40] p. $6.50 ISBN 0–690–75231–8 (lib. ed. $6.79 ISBN 0–690–75232–6)   74–5183
African motifs in distinctive woodcut illustration accompany this poetic story of a little Liberian boy and his father searching for the right tree from which to make a new canoe. (K–Gr 3)

Greenfield, Eloise. *She Come Bringing Me That Little Baby Girl.* Illustrated by John Steptoe. Philadelphia, Lippincott, 1974. [32] p. $6.95 ISBN 0–397–31586–4   74–8104
Kevin feels displaced until he holds his baby sister and tries out his new role of older brother. Rich illustrations complement the warmth of the story. (Gr 1–3)

Gretz, Susanna. *The Bears Who Stayed Indoors.* Written and illustrated by Susanna Gretz. Chicago, Follett, 1970. [31] p. $5.95 ISBN 0–695–80178–3 (lib. ed. $5.97 ISBN 0–695–40178–5)   76–118919
A rainy day is fun for five small lively bears whose names the reader soon discovers—in terms of their different colors. (K–Gr 2)

―――. *Teddy Bears 1 to 10.* Written and illustrated by Susanna Gretz. Chicago, Follett, 1968. [32] p. $5.95 ISBN 0–695–88460–3 (lib. ed. $5.97 ISBN 0–695–48460–5)   68–9563
A counting book with simple familiar situations, pictured in color, of an increasing company of teddy-bear toys. (PreS–K)

Grimm, Jakob L. K. *The Four Clever Brothers; a Story by the Brothers Grimm,* with pictures by Felix Hoffmann. New York, Harcourt, Brace & World, 1967. [32] p. $6.95 ISBN 0–15–229100–8 67–6007
Both the mood of wonder and the drama of an old tale from Grimm are vividly sustained on spacious pages of pictures, distinguished by beautiful design and color. Also, *Hans in Luck* (New York, Atheneum, 1975. $7.95 ISBN 0–689–50020–3). (K–Gr 2)

Hill, Elizabeth S. *Evan's Corner.* New York, Holt, 1967. [47] p. $5.95 ISBN 0–03–015056–6 (paper $1.45 ISBN 0–03–080123–0)   67–279

Working hard to establish his own corner in his family's crowded two rooms, Evan finds a way to enjoy both solitude and family fun. Merry pictures by Nancy Grossman suit this lighthearted but also poignant little story. (K–Gr 3)

Hoban, Lillian. *Arthur's Christmas Cookies.* Words and pictures by Lillian Hoban. New York, Harper & Row, 1972. 63 p. (An I can read book) $4.95 ISBN 0–06–022367–7 (lib. ed. $4.79 ISBN 0–06–022368–5)   72–76496
Pictorial fun shows Arthur and his accomplices—all monkeys—making Christmas cookies. Salt-filled by mistake and hard as clay, the cookies are inventively converted into Christmas tree decorations. Followed by *Arthur's Honey Bear* (ISBN 0–06–022369–3; lib. ed. ISBN 0–06–022370–7), *Arthur's Pen Pal* (ISBN 0–06–022371–5; lib. ed. ISBN 0–06–022372–3), and *Arthur's Prize Reader* (ISBN 0–06–022379–0; lib. ed. $5.79 ISBN 0–06–022380–4). (K–Gr 3)

Hoban, Russell. *Bread and Jam for Frances.* Illustrated by Lillian Hoban. New York, Harper & Row, 1964. 31 p. $5.95 ISBN 0–06–022359–6 (lib. ed. $5.79 ISBN 0–06–022360–X)   64–19605
The humorous tale of how Frances, a badger child, comes to recognize that a varied diet has more interest than her temporarily permissive feast of bread and jam. (K–Gr 2)

―――. *Dinner at Alberta's.* Pictures by James Marshall. New York, Crowell, 1975. [40] p. $5.50 ISBN 0–690–23992–0 (lib. ed. $6.49 ISBN 0–690–23993–9)   73–94796
Arthur Crocodile's table manners caused his family to despair until Alberta Saurian came to dinner. The illustrations of dressed-up animals, printed in soft sepia like the text, have a delightful childlike spirit. (PreS–Gr 1)

―――. *How Tom Beat Captain Najork and His Hired Sportsmen.* Illustrated by Quentin Blake. New York, Atheneum, 1974. [32] p. $7.95 ISBN 0–689–30441–2 (paper $1.95 ISBN 0–689–70444–5)   74–75573
Tom, who, to his aunt's distress, indulges in all kinds of fooling around—"low and muddy fooling around" and "high and wobby fooling around"—proves more than equal to those picked by his aunt to teach him a lesson. Witty color drawings match the text in free-wheeling nonsense. (K–Gr 2)

Hoban, Tana. *Count and See.* New York, Macmillan, 1972. [41] p. $6.95 ISBN 0–02–744800–2 (paper $1.50 ISBN 0–02–043640–8)   72–175597
In a visually exciting counting book, stunning photographs clarify concepts represented by common objects and events. (PreS–Gr 1)

————. *Look Again!* New York, Macmillan, 1971. 20 p. $6.95 ISBN 0–02–744050–8   72–127469

In this appealing invitation to visual awareness, tantalizing small glimpses of patterns in nature are viewed through cutout windows in the pages before the whole of a turtle or fish or sunflower is revealed. The black-and-white photographs are striking. (K–Gr 2)

————. *Push, Pull, Empty, Full; a Book of Opposites.* New York, Macmillan, 1972. [33] p. $6.95 ISBN 0–02–744810–X (paper $1.95 ISBN 0–02–043600–9)   72–90410

A turtle's head, in and out of the shell; rubber boots in a puddle and sneakered feet rustling dry leaves; these and other contrasting images, seen with childlike clarity through the camera's eye, give visual substance to opposing concepts. (PreS–Gr 1)

Hodges, Margaret. *The Wave.* Adapted from Lafcadio Hearn's *Gleanings from the Budda-fields.* Illustrated by Blair Lent. Boston, Houghton Mifflin, 1964. 48 p. $3.50 ISBN 0–395–06817–7 (lib. ed. $3.23 ISBN 0–395–06818–5)   63–14524

Dramatic prints in three shades of brown and gray bring to life the awesome climax of the Japanese tale of the wise grandfather whose quick and drastic act saves the people of his village. (Gr 3–5)

Hoffmann, Felix. *The Story of Christmas, a Picture Book.* New York, Atheneum, 1975. [32] p. (A Margaret K. McElderry book) $6.95 ISBN 0–689–50031–9   75–6921

A noted graphic artist interprets the Nativity in subtle lithographs of great beauty and feeling. Matched by his graceful retelling, these strong images make the familiar story seem freshly heard. (K–Gr 3)

Holl, Adelaide. *The Rain Puddle.* Pictures by Roger Duvoisin. New York, Lothrop, Lee & Shepard, 1965. [32] p. $6.96 ISBN 0–688–51096–5   65–22026

A nursery story about silly barnyard animals, told with a folk-tale simplicity and pictured amusingly in bright picture-book pages. (PreS–Gr 1)

Holland, Viki. *We Are Having a Baby.* Photographs by the author. New York, Scribner, 1972. [62] p. $6.95 ISBN 0–684–12809–8   70–179441

Revealing photographs and simple text graphically interpret the concerns of a little girl on the arrival of a first sibling. (K–Gr 2)

Hughes, Shirley. *David and Dog.* Englewood Cliffs, N.J., Prentice-Hall, 1978. [32] p. $7.95 ISBN 0–13–197301–0   77–27070

A heart-warming picture book that won the Greenaway Medal tells of a small boy who loses his beloved stuffed dog. Illustrated with color paintings full of action. (Gr 3–5)

Hush, Little Baby. [Illustrated by] Margot Zemach. New York, Dutton, 1976. [32] p. $6.95 ISBN 0–525–32510–7   76–5477

The familiar folk lullaby is depicted in large, bold, color illustrations which bring rustic characters comically to life. The music is included. (PreS–Gr 2)

Hutchins, Pat. *Changes, Changes.* New York, Macmillan, 1971. [30] p. $5.95 ISBN 0–02–745870–9 (paper $0.95 ISBN 0–02–043770–6)   70–123133

In bright, bold, primary colors this wordless story depicts a wooden doll couple rapidly rearranging a set of building blocks to suit emergencies that arise: they build a house, a fire engine when the house catches fire, a boat when the water creates a flood, and finally are back to a house. (PreS–Gr 1)

————. *Rosie's Walk.* New York, Macmillan, 1968. [32] p. $6.95 ISBN 0–02–745850–4 (paper $1.25 ISBN 0–02–043750–1)   68–12090

A humorously pictured barnyard escapade, with only one word to the page, that shows a predatory fox getting his comeuppance as he pursues Rosie the hen. (PreS–Gr 2)

Isadora, Rachel. *Max.* New York, Macmillan, 1976. [32] p. $5.95 ISBN 0–02–747450–7   76–9088

An avid little baseball player discovers that ballet exercises in his sister's dancing class make good warming-up exercises for his Saturday games. The author's soft-pencil drawings enrich the text. (Gr 2–3)

Jeffers, Susan. *Three Jovial Huntsmen.* Adapted and illustrated by Susan Jeffers. Scarsdale, N.Y., Bradbury Press, 1973. [32] p. $7.95 ISBN 0–87888–023–2   70–122739

Pen-and-ink drawings overlaid with clear oil colors interpret an old rhyme with new zest, humor, and a special beauty. Subtly hidden animals, peering at dull-witted, unobservant hunters provide finger-pointing fun for the young and a low-key message for the thoughtful. (PreS–Gr 1)

Jensen, Virginia A. *Sara and the Door.* Drawings by Ann Strugnell. Reading, Mass., Addison-Wesley, 1977. [32] p. $4.95 ISBN 0–201–03446–8 76–28987

Beguiling drawings capture the frustrations and eventual triumph of a small girl as she figures out how to free herself when her coat is caught in the door. (PreS–K)

Keats, Ezra Jack. *Whistle for Willie.* Illustrated by the author. New York, Viking Press, 1964. 33 p. $5.95 ISBN 0–670–76240–7 (paper $1.50. Penguin. ISBN 0–14–050202–5)   64–13595

Peter (of *The Snowy Day*) learns to whistle so that he can call his dog. Collage pictures in unusual colors are full of details of childlike play in the city. Followed by *Peter's Chair* ($6.95. Harper & Row. ISBN 0–06–023111–4; lib. ed. $6.79 ISBN 0–06–023112–2) and *Pet Show!* ($5.95. Macmillan. ISBN 0–02–749620–1; paper $1.25 ISBN 0–02–044070–7). (PreS–Gr 1)

Kellogg, Steven. *Can I Keep Him?* New York, Dial Press, 1971. [32] p. $4.95 ISBN 0–8037–0988–9 (lib. ed. $4.58 ISBN 0–8037–0989–7; paper $1.95 ISBN 0–8037–1305–3)   72–142453
Droll full-page pictures by the author serve as perfect contrasts to a mother's sensible answers to her young son as to why he cannot keep as pets the many animals he would like to bring home. (K–Gr 2)

Latham, Hugh, *tr. Mother Goose in French.* Illustrated by Barbara Cooney. New York, Thomas Y. Crowell, 1964. 42 p. $5.95 ISBN 0–690–56265–9 (lib. ed. $6.79 ISBN 0–690–56266–7)   64–10863
The old rhymes are transported to France in light and airy watercolor pictures, full of charming details of French daily life. (All ages)

Langstaff, John M. *Oh, A-Hunting We Will Go.* Pictures by Nancy Winslow Parker. New York, Atheneum, 1974. [32] p. (A Margaret K. McElderry book) $7.95 ISBN–689–50007–6   74–76274
Droll, colorful illustrations enliven this old folksong. Guitar and piano accompaniments are appended. (PreS–Gr 1)

Lewis, Thomas P. *Clipper Ship.* Pictures by Joan Sandin. New York, Harper & Row, 1978. 63 p. (An I can read history book) $4.95 ISBN 0–06–023808–9 (lib. ed. $5.79 ISBN 0–06–023809–7)   77–11858
Captain Murdock, on a clipper ship run from New York City to San Francisco, takes his wife and children along—fortunately, since his wife can take over when he becomes ill and the children can also help. Lively three-color drawings. (K–Gr 2)

Lionni, Leo. *Frederick.* New York, Pantheon Books, 1967. [32] p. $5.99 ISBN 0–394–91040–0 (paper $1.45 ISBN 0–394–82614–0)   66–6482
A reversal of the grasshopper-and-the-ant fable in which a mouse named Frederick upholds the theme that poetry is as important as material well-being. Entertaining collage illustration. (PreS–Gr 2)

Little red hen. *The Little Red Hen.* [Illustrated by] Paul Galdone. New York, Seabury Press, 1973. [40] p. $6.95 ISBN 0–8164–3099–3   72–97770
The familiar old nursery tale, reworked with an amusing pictorial interpretation of the industrious little hen and her lazy friends. (PreS–Gr 2)

Lobel, Anita. *King Rooster, Queen Hen.* New York, Greenwillow Books/Morrow, 1975. 48 p. $5.71 ISBN 0–688–84008–6   75–9787
Accompanied by a sparrow, duck, and crow as servants, King Rooster and Queen Hen set out for the city but encounter a fox with different plans for them. A Danish folktale in the simple prose of a Read Alone Book, with delightful illustration by the reteller. (K–Gr 3)

————. *The Pancake.* New York, Greenwillow Books, 1978. 48 p. (Greenwillow read-alone) $5.95 ISBN 0–688–80125–0 (lib. ed. $5.71 ISBN 0–688–84125–2)   77–24970
An easy-to-read version of the familiar folktale. Here the mother who bakes the runaway pancake invites her hungry children and others home for "an even better pancake." Sprightly illustrations in color. (Gr 1–3)

Lobel, Arnold. *Frog and Toad Are Friends.* New York, Harper & Row, 1970. 64 p. $4.95 ISBN 0–06–023957–3 (lib. ed. $4.79 ISBN 0–06–023958–1)   73–105492
Engaging pictures by the author bring their own distinction to this I Can Read Book, which can also serve as a delightful read-aloud for small children. Sequels are *Frog and Toad Together* (ISBN 0–06–023959–X; lib. ed. ISBN 0–06–023960–3) and *Frog and Toad All Year* (ISBN 0–06–023950–6; lib. ed. ISBN 0–06–023951–4). (K–Gr 2)

————. *Grasshopper on the Road.* New York, Harper & Row, 1978. 62 p. (An I can read book) $4.95 ISBN 0–06–023961–1 (lib. ed. $5.79 ISBN 0–06–023962–X)   77–25653
Softly colored, animated drawings follow Grasshopper who "wanted to go on a journey" as he meets a variety of creatures, from beetles to dragonflies. (K–Gr 2)

————. *Mouse Soup.* New York, Harper & Row, 1977. 63 p. (An I can read book) $4.95 ISBN 0–06–023967–0 (lib. ed. $3.79 ISBN 0–06–023968–9)   76–41517
Four captivating, easy-to-read stories, told by a mouse in Scheherazade fashion, save him from becoming a weasel's soup. Also, *Mouse Tales* (ISBN 0–06–023941–7). (K–Gr 2)

————. *Owl at Home.* New York, Harper & Row, 1975. 64 p. (An I can read book) $4.95 ISBN 0–06–023948–4 (lib. ed. $4.79 ISBN 0–06–023949–2)   74–2630
Owl's winter activities include an unsuccessful attempt to entertain Wind and the making of tear-water tea. Engaging three-color pictures in muted tones bring out the warmth of five chapter-stories. (PreS–Gr 2)

Low, Joseph. *Five Men under One Umbrella, and Other Ready-to-Read Riddles*. New York, Macmillan, 1975. 63 p. (A Ready-to-read book) $5.95 ISBN 0–02–761460–3   74–20615
Wackily illustrated in full color are twenty-nine pieces of nonsense for the beginning reader, including such riddles as "When is a girl like a small bucket?" and "Which flowers should be kept in a zoo?" (K–Gr 1)

McDermott, Gerald. *Arrow to the Sun; a Pueblo Indian Tale*. Adapted and illustrated by Gerald McDermott. New York, Viking Press, 1974. [42] p. $8.95 ISBN 0–670–13369–8 (paper $2.50. Penguin. ISBN 0–14–050211–4)   73–16172
A brief adaptation of the Pueblo Indian myth which explains how the spirit of the Lord of the Sun was brought to the world of men. Stylized pictures in dynamic colors. (Gr 2–4)

McGovern, Ann. *Black Is Beautiful*. With photographs by Hope Wurmfeld. New York, Four Winds Press, 1969. [40] p. Paper $0.95. Scholastic. ISBN 0–590–08777–0   69–17247
Simple verses combine with telling photographs in a book of new semantic significance as well as human importance. (K–Gr 2)

McLeod, Emile W. *The Bear's Bicycle.* Illustrated by David McPhail. Boston, Little, Brown, 1975. 31 p. (An Atlantic Monthly Press book) $4.95 ISBN 0–316–56203–3 (paper $1.75 ISBN 0–14–050230–0)   74–28282
A boy on an exciting bike ride demonstrates correct habits and safety practices while an enormous bear (the boy's toy bear, actually) on a miniscule bike does the very opposite—and suffers the consequences. (K–Gr 2)

Maiorano, Robert, *and* Rachel Isadora. *Backstage*. New York, Greenwillow Books, 1978. [32] p. $5.95 ISBN 0–688–80130–7 (lib. ed. $5.71 ISBN 0–688–84130–9)   77–21822
The glamour and vocabulary of the backstage scene for the *Nutcracker* ballet is illustrated by Rachel Isadora in two-color details which show a small girl finding her way to her mother's dressing room. (K–Gr 2)

Marshall, James. *George and Martha*. Boston, Houghton Mifflin, 1972. 46 p. $6.95 ISBN 0–395–16619–5 (paper $1.95 ISBN 0–395–19972–7)   74–184250
Human frailties of carelessness, curiosity, and straying from the truth are exemplified in the behavior of two hippo friends delightfully portrayed in the author's amusing, diminutive color pictures. Also,

George and Martha Encore (ISBN 0–395–17512–7; paper ISBN 0–395–25379–9). (PreS–Gr 1)

[Martin, Sarah C.] Mother Goose. *The Comic Adventures of Old Mother Hubbard and Her Dog*. Illustrated by Arnold Lobel. Englewood Cliffs, N.J., Bradbury Press, 1968. [32] p. $3.95 ISBN 0–87888–003–8   68–9052
The capers in this familiar story are made newly explicit with witty drawings in muted orange and olive green. (PreS–Gr 1)

————. *Old Mother Hubbard and Her Dog*. Illustrated by Evaline Ness. New York, Holt, Rinehart & Winston, 1972. 32 p. $4.95 ISBN 0–03–088369–5 (paper $1.45 ISBN 0–03–005721–3)   74–182788
Mother Hubbard's companion is a beguiling shaggy sheep dog who quite outshines his mistress in this fully pictured version of the old nursery rhyme. (PreS–Gr 1)

Mayer, Mercer. *A Boy, a Dog, and a Frog*. New York, Dial Press, 1967. [32] p. $3.50 ISBN 0–8037–0763–0 (lib. ed. $3.39 ISBN 0–8037–0767–3)   67–22254
In a tiny book without printed text, a complete story emerges from the pictures—of boy-and-dog companionship, and comedy with a surprise conclusion. Fun for prereaders. Followed by *Frog, Where Are You?* ($3.95 ISBN 0–8037–2737–2; lib. ed. $3.69 ISBN 0–8037–2732–1). (PreS–Gr 1)

Miles, Miska. *Nobody's Cat*. Illustrated by John Schoenherr. Toronto, Boston, Little, Brown, 1969. 43 p. $4.95 ISBN 0–316–56969–0   68–12351
A scruffy, independent city cat visits a school briefly but returns to his own familiar territory. Excellent depiction of cat and community in dramatic orange-and-black illustrations. (Gr 1–4)

Monjo, F. N. *The Drinking Gourd*. Pictures by Fred Brenner. New York, Harper & Row, 1970. 62 p. $4.95 ISBN 0–06–024329–5 (lib. ed. $4.79 ISBN 0–06–024330–9)   68–10782
An I Can Read History Book tells how mischievous Tommy is sobered in his new role of sharing his family's responsibility for a station in the underground railroad. (Gr 1–2)

Mosel, Arlene. *Tikki Tikki Tembo*. Retold. New York, Holt, Rinehart and Winston, 1968. [45] p. $5.95 ISBN 0–03–012711–4   68–11839
A story-hour favorite from classic oriental lore is enhanced by Blair Lent's illustrations showing the fate of the little boy with an impossibly long name. (K–Gr 2)

Mother Goose. *The Mother Goose Treasury*. [Illustrated by] Raymond Briggs. New York, Coward-McCann, 1966. 217 p. $9.99 ISBN 0–698–30243–5
66–12045
The English artist's rollicking, rambunctious, storytelling pictures on every page of this large collection bring new vitality to very old verses. (PreS–Gr 1)

Munari, Bruno. *The Circus in the Mist*. New York, World Pub. Co., 1969. [57] p. $5.95. Collins. ISBN 0–529–00756–8 (lib. ed. $5.91 ISBN 0–529–00757–6)
78–82766
Translucent pages and cut-out patterns give an exciting new dimension to the book, as the viewer moves through foggy city streets into the brilliant circus world and back through a mist-shrouded park. (K–up)

Nakatani, Chiyoko. *My Day on the Farm*. New York, Crowell, 1977. 29 p. $5.95 ISBN 0–690–01074–5 (lib. ed. $5.79 ISBN 0–690–01075–3)   75–33248
A small boy visiting a farm from milking time to milking time sees the feeding of cows and calf, sow and piglets, sheep and goats. Illustrated with the author's charming watercolors. (PreS–K)

———. *My Teddy Bear*. New York, Crowell, 1975. [28] p. $5.95 ISBN 0–690–01076–1 (lib. ed. $5.79 ISBN 0–690–01077–X)   75–34110
A simple story from Japan of a small boy and his teddy bear, who is his best friend. Color oil paintings on canvas convey the warmth of their close relationship. (PreS–Gr 1)

Ness, Evaline. *Sam, Bangs, and Moonshine*. New York, Holt, Rinehart and Winston, 1966. [36] p. $5.95 ISBN 0–03–012716–5 (paper $1.45 ISBN 0–03–080111–7)   66–7085
Bangs was a cat, Sam was a little girl, and *moonshine* was what her father called the stories Sam told before she learned the difference between them and truth. Strongly interpretative three-color woodcuts. (K–Gr 2)

Oakley, Graham. *The Church Mice and the Moon*. New York, Atheneum, 1974. [36] p. $6.95 ISBN 0–689–30437–4   74–75569
Sampson the Church Cat is back, with his brotherly love toward mice, and determines to rescue Arthur and Humphrey, leaders of the church mice, when they have been captured for Wortlethorpe's Municipal Moon Programme. The author's detailed paintings point up every element of humor and excitement in this British spoof. Also, *The Church Mice Spread Their Wings* ($7.95 ISBN 0–689–30496–X) and *The Church Mice Adrift* (ISBN 0–689–30562–1). (K–Gr 2)

Ormondroyd, Edward. *Theodore*. Illustrated by John M. Larrecq. Berkeley, Calif., Parnassus Press, 1966. 33 p. $4.75 ISBN 0–87466–056–4 (lib. ed. $4.59 ISBN 0–87466–028–9)   66–9502
Theodore Bear, made unnaturally clean by an accidental trip to the laundromat, has to prevail on colleagues to dirty him up so that his Lucy can recognize him again. The imaginative drawings supply as much fun as the text. (PreS–Gr 2)

Oxenbury, Helen. *Helen Oxenbury's ABC of Things*. New York, F. Watts, 1972. [55] p. $4.95 ISBN 0–531–02020–7   72–175022
A British prize-winning artist's alphabet book that is meaningful for young children has clear capital and small letters with four "things" for each. (PreS–Gr 1)

———. *Pig Tale*. New York, Morrow, 1973. [32] p. $6.96 ISBN 0–688–30092–8   73–6357
An amusing fable about two pigs whose discovery of buried treasure brings them luxury and ennui. The color pictures, by the author, are as jolly as the rhymed text. (PreS–Gr 1)

Parish, Peggy. *Mind Your Manners!* Illustrated by Marylin Hafner. New York, Greenwillow Books, 1978. 55 p. (Greenwillow read-alone guide) $5.95 ISBN 0–688–80157–9 (lib. ed. $5.71 ISBN 0–688–84157–0)   77–19096
An etiquette book for the new reader provides instruction for good manners in everyday situations—at home, at school, and on the telephone. Entertainingly illustrated in three colors. (Gr 2–3)

Paterson, Andrew B. *Mulga Bill's Bicycle; Poem*. Illustrated by Kilmeny & Deborah Niland. New York, Parents' Magazine Press, 1975. [30] p. $5.41 ISBN 0–8193–0778–5   74–12286
An Australian balladlike text in which the virtues of the horse are seen after Mulga Bill's calamity on a newfangled bicycle. A prizewinner for its zestful full-color art. (K–Gr 2)

A Peaceable Kingdom; the Shaker Abecedarius. Illustrated by Alice and Martin Provensen; afterword by Richard Meran Barsam. New York, Viking Press, 1978. [42] p. $8.95 ISBN 0–670–54500–7   78–125
A Shaker alphabet song has rhythmic sequences of words, such as "Alligator, Beetle, Porcupine, Whale," pictured in action-filled paintings with mellow colors and humorous details. (K–Gr 2)

Peppé, Rodney. *Odd One Out*. Illustrated by the author. New York, Viking Press, 1974. 32 p. $6.50 ISBN 0–670–52029–2 (paper $1.25 ISBN 0–670–05097–0)   73–17298

A color-filled picture book game for prereaders and beginning readers has an object in each double-spread to be identified as out of place and found in the next scene. (PreS–Gr 1)

Piatti, Celestino. *Celestino Piatti's Animal ABC*. English text by Jon Reid. New York, Atheneum, 1966. [26] p. $4.95 ISBN 0–689–20335–7   66–12851
A visually striking addition to animal ABC books, with bold page-filling illustrations executed in strong black outline and rich color. (PreS–Gr 1)

―――. *The Happy Owls*. Illustrated by the author. New York, Atheneum, 1964. 32 p. $7.95 ISBN 0–689–20337–3 (paper $1.95 ISBN 0–689–70445–3)   64–3620
A Swiss poster-artist's brilliantly produced fable about some scrappy barnyard fowl and two peaceful owls. (K–Gr 2)

Polushkin, Maria. *Who Said Meow?* Adapted from the Russian. Pictures by Giulio Maestro. New York, Crown, 1975. [36] p. $5.95 ISBN 0–517–51846–5   74–19500
Puppy investigates the other animals to find out who belongs to the "meow" that has awakened him from his nap. The simple text and large, realistic illustrations make an inviting book. (PreS–K)

Pomerantz, Charlotte. *The Piggy in the Puddle*. Pictures by James Marshall. New York, Macmillan, 1974. [30] p. $4.95 ISBN 0–02–774900–2 73–6047
Verbal fun and humorous drawings in color make this singsong tale of a family of pigs that enjoys a "muddy little puddle" a lighthearted success for the very youngest. (PreS–K)

Prelutsky, Jack. *The Terrible Tiger*. Pictures by Arnold Lobel. New York, Macmillan, 1970. [38] p. $4.95 ISBN 0–02–775130–9   75–89592
A picture-book romp in chanting verse with a great yellow tiger singing his way as he swallows one prey after another. (K–Gr 2)

Provensen, Alice, *and* Martin Provensen. *Our Animal Friends at Maple Hill Farm*. New York, Random House, 1974. [57] p. $3.95 ISBN 0–394–82123–8   74–828
Farm animals stand out as individuals within their groups in this unusual and amusing presentation. Large format and soft watercolor pictures. (PreS–Gr 2)

Raskin, Ellen. *And It Rained*. New York, Atheneum, 1969. [48] p. $6.95 ISBN 0–689–20587–2 69–18967
Three animal friends cannot have a proper tea party in their rain forest, since it rains every day at tea time, but they settle their problem with ingenuity. (K–Gr 2)

―――. *Nothing Ever Happens on My Block*. New York, Atheneum, 1966. [32] p. $5.95 ISBN 0–689–20588–0 (paper $0.95. Scholastic. ISBN 0–590–01612–1)   66–1794
Fun for parents and children together lies in discovering on these picture-book pages an endless amount of city activity going on around Chester while he sits deploring the boredom of his life. (K–Gr 2)

―――. *Spectacles*. New York, Atheneum, 1972. [48] p. Paper $1.95 ISBN 0–689–70317–1   68–12234
Amusingly pictured nightmare creatures are the people Iris sees until her doctor prescribes glasses and her world becomes sharply defined. (K–Gr 2)

Rayner, Mary. *Mr. and Mrs. Pig's Evening Out*. New York, Atheneum, 1976. [32] p. $7.95 ISBN 0–689–30530–3   76–4476
How doughty piglets manage to outwit evil Mrs. Wolf, their baby-sitter, and save their youngest brother from becoming her dinner is told in a neatly rounded fantasy adventure and illustrated with charming detail by the author. Followed by the equally engaging *Garth Pig and the Ice Cream Lady* ($8.95 ISBN 0–689–30598–2). (K–Gr 2)

Reiss, John J. *Shapes*. Scarsdale, N.Y., Bradbury Press, 1974. [32] p. $7.95 ISBN 0–87888–053–4 73–76545
Basic shapes—the square, triangle, circle, rectangle, and oval—in one, two, and three dimensions, are attractively shown in bright primary colors. (K–Gr 2)

Revius, Jacobus. *Noah's Ark*. Translated from the Dutch and illustrated by Peter Spier. Garden City, N.Y., Doubleday, 1977. [44] p. $6.95 ISBN 0–385–09473–6 (lib. ed. $7.90 ISBN 0–385–12730–8)   76–43630
A picture book of the Bible story which is special on two scores: its text is the artist's translation of a seventeenth-century Dutch poem, and its soft watercolor pictures draw the onlooker's eye to humorous, minute details in panoramas alive with activity. (K–Gr 3)

Rockwell, Anne F. *Albert B. Cub & Zebra; an Alphabet Storybook*. New York, Crowell, 1977. [32] p. $7.95 ISBN 0–690–01350–7 (lib. ed. $8.49 ISBN 0–690–01351–5)   76–54224
A luxurious alphabet book—large, fresh watercolor pictures depicting many objects from "Aa" to "Zz" with a running story of a bear searching for a zebra. (K–Gr 2)

Rojankovsky, Feodor. *Animals on the Farm*. New York, Knopf, 1967. [40] p. $5.99 ISBN 0–394–91875–4   67–18586
Common barnyard animals lovingly pictured with life and warmth and humor make an enticing first picture book for the youngest child. (PreS–Gr 1)

Ryan, Cheli D. *Hildilid's Night*. Illustrated by Arnold Lobel. New York, Macmillan, 1971. [30] p. $5.50 ISBN 0–02–777990–4 (paper $0.95 ISBN 0–02–044810–4)   75–146627
An amusing folktale-like story about an old lady who hates everything about night and tries by many ineffective means to chase it away. Handsomely illustrated. (K–Gr 2)

Sandburg, Carl. *The Wedding Procession of the Rag Doll and the Broom Handle and Who Was in It*. Pictures by Harriet Pincus. New York, Harcourt, Brace & World, 1967. [32] p. $6.50 ISBN 0–15–294930–5   67–2763
For this excerpt from *Rootabaga Stories* the illustrator has created sturdy personifications of the absurd, nonsensical characters. (K–Gr 3)

Schick, Eleanor. *City in the Winter*. New York, Macmillan, 1970. [32] p. Paper $0.95 ISBN 0–02–044940–2   69–18237
The hushed quiet of a snowy day, Jimmy's inventive play, and his fun plowing down to the store in grandma's footsteps are detailed evocatively in an unusually realistic picture book. (PreS–K)

Scott, Ann H. *On Mother's Lap*. Drawings by Glo Coalson. New York, McGraw-Hill, 1972. [39] p. $6.95 ISBN 0–07–055896–5 (lib. ed. $7.95 ISBN 0–07–055897–3)   76–39726
A reassuring book for the very young about a little boy who learns that there is room for two on mother's lap. Striking crayon drawings of an Eskimo family. (PreS–K)

Segal, Lore G. *Tell Me a Mitzi*. Pictures by Harriet Pincus. New York, Farrar, Straus & Giroux, 1970. [40] p. $4.95 ISBN 0–374–37392–2 (paper $1.50. Scholastic. ISBN 0–590–11907–9)   69–14980
The vagaries of childhood are delightfully captured in three funny, imaginative stories about a little girl named Mitzi. The artist's stolid, unprettified people, busily engaged in the details of daily living, are a perfect accompaniment to the text. (K–Gr 2)

Selsam, Millicent E. *Let's Get Turtles*. Drawings by Arnold Lobel. New York, Harper & Row, 1965. 62 p. $4.79 ISBN 0–06–025311–8   64–16656

A lively Science I Can Read Book to please beginners interested in keeping turtle pets. Followed by *Benny's Animals, and How He Put Them in Order* (ISBN 0–06–025311–8). (Gr 1–2)

Sendak, Maurice. *Hector Protector, and As I Went over the Water; Two Nursery Rhymes with Pictures*. New York, Harper & Row, 1965. [54] p. $6.95 ISBN 0–06–025485–8 (lib. ed. $6.79 ISBN 0–06–025486–6)   65–8256
A full-color pictorial expansion of two old rhymes shows a small boy dealing with some monstrous animals. (PreS–Gr 2)

————. *In the Night Kitchen*. New York, Harper & Row, 1970. [40] p. $6.95 ISBN 0–06–025489–0 (lib. ed. $6.79 ISBN 0–06–025490–4)   70–105483
Fantasy about a little boy's dream descent into the baker's night kitchen where he pummels the dough into an airplane for further adventuring. Illustrated in a fresh cartoonish style. (PreS–Gr 1)

Seuling, Barbara. *The Teeny Tiny Woman; An Old English Ghost Tale*. Retold. New York, Viking Press, 1976. [32] p. $5.95 ISBN 0–670–69505–X (paper $1.75. Penguin. ISBN 0–14–050266–1)   75–22160
The heroine of this Joseph Jacobs folktale becomes a cheerful and sturdy little character in cozy illustrations, which take a bit of the chill off a favorite old ghost story. Large type is a plus for the younger reader. (K–Gr 2)

Shub, Elizabeth. *Clever Kate*. Adapted from a story by the Brothers Grimm. Pictures by Anita Lobel. New York, Macmillan, 1973. [62] p. (Ready-to-read) $5.95 ISBN 0–02–782490–X   72–81063
In an I Can Read book format, this humorously illustrated traditional tale shows how a naive wife who loses her husband's treasure gains it back again. (Gr 1–3)

Shulevitz, Uri. *Dawn*. New York, Farrar, Straus & Giroux, 1974. [32] p. $6.95 ISBN 0–374–31707–0   74–9761
The author-artist's luminous paintings complement poetic words heralding the coming of dawn. (K–Gr 3)

————. *One Monday Morning*. New York, Scribner, 1967. [40] p. $6.95 ISBN 0–684–13195–1 (paper $0.95 ISBN 0–684–12781–4)   67–1069
A small boy's imagined adventure enlivens a dreary city tenement with lengthening processions of droll and colorful playing-card figures of royalty, who come (K–Gr 2)

————. *Rain Rain Rivers*. Words and pictures by Uri Shulevitz. New York, Farrar, Straus & Giroux, 1969. [32] p. $7.95 ISBN 0–374–36171–1 73–85370
Few words and action-filled drawings, washed in blues and greens and muted yellows, express the essence of water and its power over people and places. (K–Gr 2)

Sleator, William. *The Angry Moon*. Retold by William Sleator, with pictures by Blair Lent. Boston, Little, Brown, 1970. 45 p. $6.95 ISBN 0–316–79735–9 74–91230
An Alaskan Tlingit legend has inspired illustration in dynamic colors. (K–Gr 2)

————. *The Erie Canal*. Illustrated by Peter Spier. Garden City, N.Y., Doubleday, 1970. [36] p. $6.95 ISBN 0–385–06777–1 (lib. ed. $7.90 ISBN 0–385–05452–1; paper $1.95 ISBN 0–385–05234–0) 70–102055
Pictures lavish with color and rich in authentic detail document the canal journey from Albany to Buffalo in the 1850s, with vignettes of life in the wayside towns and hearty action on the bustling waterway; full historical notes and music of the old song are provided. (All ages)

Steig, William. *The Amazing Bone*. New York, Farrar, Straus & Giroux, 1976. [32] p. $7.95 ISBN 0–374–30248–0 (paper $1.95. Penguin. ISBN 0–14–050247–5) 76–26479
Steig's inimitable, sunny paintings show Pearl Pig, who "loves everything," dawdling home from school and finding a talking bone capable of magic. (K–Gr 2)

————. *Amos & Boris*. New York, Farrar, Straus & Giroux, 1971. [32] p. $6.95 ISBN 0–374–30278–2 (paper $1.95. Penguin. ISBN 0–14–050229–7) 72–165403
A lavishly produced story of the friendship between Amos, a seagoing mouse, and Boris, his whale rescuer, whose life in turn Amos later manages to save. Superb seascapes. (K–Gr 2)

————. *Roland, the Minstrel Pig*. New York, Windmill Books; distributed by Harper & Row, 1968. 32 p. $7.89 ISBN 0–06–025762–8 (paper $2.95. Dutton. ISBN 0–525–62330–2) 68–14923
An original fable of pig and fox ends with jaunty Roland as court singer. Jolly large pictures in full color. (K–Gr 2)

————. *Sylvester and the Magic Pebble*. New York, Windmill Books, 1969. [32] p. $6.95. Simon & Schuster. ISBN 0–671–66511–1 (lib. ed. $6.70 ISBN 0–671–66512–X; paper $2.95. Dutton. ISBN 0–525–62300–0) 69–14484

Crisis comes to the happy Duncans, a family of donkeys, when Sylvester accidentally turns himself into a stone. Winner of the 1970 Caldecott Medal. (K–Gr 2)

Steptoe, John. *Stevie*. New York, Harper & Row, 1969. [24] p. $5.95 ISBN 0–06–025763–6 (lib. ed. $5.79 ISBN 0–06–025764–4) 69–16700
Informal "language as children speak it" and strong paintings of urban life tell the story of Robert, who finds Stevie a bothersome guest but misses him when he is gone. (Gr 1–4)

Taylor, Mark. *Henry the Explorer*. Illustrated by Graham Booth. New York, Atheneum, 1976. 48 p. Paper $1.95 ISBN 0–689–70427–5 66–9534
A very young reader of books on exploration sets forth with his small Scottie dog on a day that turns into a blizzard. They are bent on discovering—and do meet some bears, in a cave. Lavishly pictured in full color. (PreS–Gr 2)

The Three Bears. *The Story of the Three Bears, a Picture Book* by William Stobbs. New York, Whittlesey House, 1965. 32 p. $6.95. McGraw. ISBN 0–07–061576–4 64–8142
Using Chinese red, green, and brown the artist derives from Norwegian folk art a manner bold and somewhat primitive in his pictures for this traditional tale. Also from Stobbs is *The Story of the Three Little Pigs* (1965) in equally striking style. (PreS–Gr 2)

Tom Thumb. *Tom Thumb; the Story by the Brothers Grimm*. With pictures by Felix Hoffmann. New York, Atheneum, 1973. [32] p. (A Margaret K. McElderry book) $7.95 ISBN 0–689–30318–1 72–85917
A Swiss artist has rendered in a fresh, rustic manner the German version of this favorite tale. (PreS–Gr 3)

Tresselt, Alvin R. *Hide and Seek Fog*. Illustrated by Roger Duvoisin. New York, Lothrop, Lee & Shepard, 1965. [32] p. $6.00 ISBN 0–688–41169–X 65–14087
Full watercolor paintings capture the feeling of a heavy three-day fog and of its gradual lifting to reveal a contrastingly brilliant sunlit coastal village. (K–Gr 2)

————. *The Mitten*. Illustrated by Yaroslava. New York, Lothrop, Lee & Shepard, 1964. 34 p. $6.00 ISBN 0–688–41169–X 64–14436
A Ukrainian folk tale about animals that crowd into the mitten a little boy loses in the snow. Simply retold and illustrated with authentic costumes and amusing details of action. (K–Gr 2)

Turkle, Brinton. *Deep in the Forest*. New York, Dutton, 1976. [32] p. $5.95 ISBN 0–525–28617–9
76–21691

In an animated reversal of *Goldilocks*, the author-artist has produced a graphically successful, wordless picture book about an impish bear cub who samples the porridge, tries the chairs, and bounces on the beds in a forest cabin. (PreS–Gr 1)

Uchida, Yoshiko. *Sumi's Prize*. Pictures by Kazue Mizumura. New York, Scribner, 1964. 48 p. $5.95 ISBN 0–684–13157–9
64–19650

"Just once Sumi wanted to win a prize"—and she did, at the New Year's Day kite-flying contest when she chased Mr. Mayor's top hat. Illustrations in black-and-red wash are in perfect harmony with the simplicity of the story. (Gr 2–3)

Ungerer, Tomi. *Zeralda's Ogre*. New York, Harper & Row, 1967. [32] p. $6.89 ISBN 0–06–026259–1
67–3113

Even the most horrendous child-eating ogre can reform—if he meets a pitying cook with little Zeralda's skill. (K–Gr 2)

Van Woerkom, Dorothy. *Becky and the Bear*. Illustrated by Margot Tomes. New York, Putnam, 1975. 42 p. $5.29 ISBN 0–399–60924–5
74–16628

A realistic vignette of period fiction set in colonial Maine. Very young Becky demonstrates courage and ingenuity when meeting a bear. (Gr 2–4)

Viorst, Judith. *Alexander, Who Used to Be Rich Last Sunday*. Illustrated by Ray Cruz. New York, Atheneum, 1978. [32] p. $6.95 ISBN 0–689–30602–4
77–1579

A humorous first lesson in economics shows how Alexander quickly loses his dollar gift, penny by penny, to easy attractions. (K–Gr 2)

———. *The Tenth Good Thing about Barney*. New York, Atheneum, 1971. 25 p. $6.95 ISBN 0–689–20688–7 (paper $1.95 ISBN 0–689–70416–X)
71–154764

A gentle picture book about a little boy who overcomes the sadness caused by the death of his pet cat Barney. Quiet sketches by Erik Blegvad perfectly reflect the mood of the story. (K–Gr 2)

Waber, Bernard. *An Anteater Named Arthur*. Boston, Houghton Mifflin, 1967. 46 p. $7.95 ISBN 0–395–20336–8 (paper $2.45 ISBN 0–395–25936–3)
67–20374

Five amusingly illustrated episodes in the life of a young anteater whose questions and problems mirror those of any little boy. (K–Gr 2)

———. *I Was All Thumbs*. Boston, Houghton Mifflin, 1975. 48 p. $6.95 ISBN 0–395–21404–1   75–11689

The amusing adventures of a young octopus who, having spent all his early life in Captain Pierre's laboratory, now faces an adjustment to life in the sea. Humorously illustrated by the author. (K–Gr 3)

Wahl, Jan. *Drakestail*. Adapted from a French folktale. Illustrated by Byron Barton. New York, Greenwillow Books, 1978. 55 p. (Greenwillow read-alone) $5.95 ISBN 0–688–80126–9 (lib. ed. $5.71 ISBN 0–688–84126–0)
77–24331

The classic French version of a universal folktale tells about the duck who sets forth to see a king who owes him money and winds up being crowned king himself. Brightly illustrated. (Gr 1–3)

Watson, Clyde. *Father Fox's Pennyrhymes*. Illustrated by Wendy Watson. New York, Crowell, 1971. 56 p. $6.95 ISBN 0–690–29213–9 (lib. ed. $6.79 ISBN 0–690–29214–7)
71–146291

Thirty imaginative rhymes in the style of traditional verses record the activities of Father Fox, his lively family of seventeen children, and friends—with ample, colorful illustration. (PreS–Gr 2)

Watson, Wendy. *Lollipop*. New York, Crowell, 1976. [26] p. $4.50 ISBN 0–690–01067–2 (lib. ed. $5.79 ISBN 0–690–00768–X; paper $1.95. Penguin. ISBN 0–14–050264–5)
75–26642

A small child—rabbit—steadfastly denied a lollipop before dinner, runs to the store with his piggybank penny. Failing to get attention there, he falls asleep. The emotions of the frustrated child and harried mother are perfectly captured in the author's simple three-color pictures. (PreS–K)

Weber, Alfons. *Elizabeth Gets Well*. Pictures by Jacqueline Blass. New York, Crowell, 1970. 28 p. $7.49 ISBN 0–690–25839–9
78–120996

The child psychiatrist of a Zurich hospital describes pleasantly and precisely little Elizabeth's hospital stay for an appendectomy; detailed, full-page color pictures appeal and reassure. (K–Gr 3)

Welber, Robert. *The Winter Picnic*. Pictures by Deborah Ray. New York, Pantheon Books, 1976. [25] p. $4.99 ISBN 0–394–90444–3
77–77418

Who says you can't have a picnic in the snow? A self-reliant little boy named Adam is sure it is possible. (PreS–Gr 2)

Wells, Rosemary. *Morris's Disappearing Bag; a Christmas Story*. New York, Dial Press, 1975. [40] p. $4.95 ISBN 0–8037–5441–8 (lib. ed. $4.58 ISBN 0–8037–5510–4; paper $1.95 ISBN 0–8037–5509–0)
75–9202

With the author's pastel drawings of dressed-up sibling rabbits, this little volume owes a debt to Beatrix Potter, but its Christmas squabbles about trading gifts and the appearance of a magic bag make it fresh and modern. (PreS–K)

———. *Stanley & Rhoda*. New York, Dial Press, 1978. [40] p. $6.95 ISBN 0–8037–8248–9 (lib. ed. $6.47 ISBN 0–8037–8249–7)   78–51874

Three humorously illustrated short stories reveal Stanley's aplomb and ingenuity in coping with his little sister's antics. (PreS–Gr 1)

Wildsmith, Brian. *Fishes*. New York, Watts, 1968. [34] p. $5.95 ISBN 0–531–01528–9   68–12046

A successor to this artist's *Animals and Birds*, with equally brilliant, action-filled scenes. (PreS–Gr 1)

———. *Python's Party*. New York, Watts, 1975. [32] p. $5.95 ISBN 0–531–02808–9   74–20303

Jungle animals, pictured with the artist's typical brilliance, succumb to Python's invitation to a trick-performing party—and near extinction in his long, dark prison. (K–Gr 3)

Williams, Barbara. *Albert's Toothache*. Illustrated by Kay Chorao. New York, Dutton, 1974. [32] p. $5.95 ISBN 0–525–25368–8   74–4040

Toothless Albert has trouble convincing his family that he really does have a toothache—in his toe. A very funny picture book enhanced by the illustrator's delightful details of a turtle household. (K–Gr 1)

Williams, Jay. *The Practical Princess*. Illustrated by Friso Henstra. New York, Parents' Magazine Press, 1969. 42 p. $5.95 ISBN 0–8193–0233–3 (lib. ed. $5.41 ISBN 0–8193–0234–1)   69–12606

An unusual treatment of the princess in distress and the charming prince, with striking illustrations. (K–Gr 3)

Wittman, Sally. *A Special Trade*. Pictures by Karen Gundersheimer. New York, Harper & Row, 1978. [32] p. $7.95 ISBN 0–06–026553–1 (lib. ed. $7.89 ISBN 0–06–026554–X)   77–25673

Kindly Mr. Bartholomew and his young neighbor Nelly exchange roles as he grows old and she becomes the helping hand. (PreS–K)

Yashima, Tarō, *pseud*. *Seashore Story*. New York, Viking Press, 1967. [44] p. $4.95 ISBN 0–670–62710–0   66–11914

The old Japanese folktale of Urashima is imaginatively presented in dreamlike, semiabstract illustrations and evocative brief text. (Gr 1–4)

Yeoman, John. *Mouse Trouble*. Pictures by Quentin Blake. New York, Macmillan, 1972. [30] p. $4.95 ISBN 0–02–793600–7 (paper $1.95 ISBN 0–02–045610–7)   72–85190

The wildly comic tale of an inept, mouse-catching cat and some delightfully knowing mice who join forces to outwit a stingy miller. Rich and lively illustrations. (PreS–Gr 2)

———. *Sixes and Sevens*. Pictures by Quentin Blake. New York, Macmillan, 1974. [29] p. $4.95 ISBN 0–02–793610–4 (paper $1.25 ISBN 0–02–045720–0)   79–147893

High comedy in words and watercolor scenes distinguishes this brief counting book in which Barnaby poles a raft downstream with a mounting assortment of animal passengers. (K–Gr 2)

Yolen, Jane H. *The Emperor and the Kite*. Pictures by Ed Young. Cleveland, World Pub. Co., 1967. [32] p. Reprint $6.91. Collins, New York. ISBN 0–529–00255–8   77–27309

In this traditional Chinese tale, handsomely pictured in old papercut style, it is the tiniest daughter who with her kiteflying rescues her imprisoned father. (K–Gr 2)

———. *The Girl Who Loved the Wind*. Pictures by Ed Young. New York, Crowell, 1972. [32] p. $6.95 ISBN 0–690–33100–2 (lib. ed. $7.49 ISBN 0–690–33101–0)   71–171012

A tale, created through a smooth storytelling style and paintings with Persian-miniature effect, of a rich oriental establishment where a merchant's daughter is protected from the world until the whispering wind rouses her curiosity and discontent. (Gr 1–3)

———. *Greyling; a Picture Story from the Islands of Shetland*. Cleveland, World Pub. Co., 1968. [32] p. $4.91. Collins, New York. ISBN 0–529–00543–3   68–28481

The spirit of the sea and the northern isles pervades this haunting legend of the seal people. Brilliant illustrations by William Stobbs. (Gr 1–3)

Zemach, Harve. *Duffy and the Devil; a Cornish Tale*. Retold by Harve Zemach. With pictures by Margot Zemach. New York, Farrar, Straus & Giroux, 1973. [40] p. $6.95 ISBN 0–374–31887–5   72–81491

This amusing version of "Rumpelstiltskin" as told in Cornwall is complemented by Margot Zemach's imaginative drawings, depicting the ridiculous behavior of a devil that had the last word. The 1974 Caldecott Medal winner. (K–Gr 2)

Zemach, Margot. *It Could Always Be Worse; a Yiddish Folk Tale*. Retold. New York, Farrar, Straus & Giroux, 1977. [32] p. $7.95 ISBN 0–374–33650–4
76–53895
The artist-reteller's delightfully robust drawings capture the absurdities of an old tale about a poor man and his quarrelsome family crammed into a one-room hut. (K–Gr 3)

Zion, Gene. *Harry by the Sea*. New York, Harper & Row, 1965. [32] p. $5.95 ISBN 0–06–026855–7 (lib. ed. $6.49 ISBN 0–06–026856–5; paper $1.95 ISBN 0–06–443010–3)
65–21302
Draped with seaweed, Harry, the spotted dog, is mistaken for a monster from the deep. A hilarious new adventure for this popular hero. (K–Gr 2)

Stories for the Middle Group

Aiken, Joan. *Arabel's Raven*. Illustrated by Quentin Blake. Garden City, N.Y., Doubleday, 1974. 118 p. $5.95 ISBN 0–385–07493–X (lib. ed. $6.90 ISBN 0–385–08675–X)   73–81120
Perhaps the most hilarious of this author's tales is this nonsense story about small Arabel and the raven she names Mortimer, who croaks "Never-more" on many occasions and shows signs of phenomenal cleverness. (Gr 4–6)

———. *Black Hearts in Battersea*. Illustrated by Robin Jacques. Garden City, N.Y., Doubleday, 1964. 240 p. $4.50 ISBN 0–385–07781–5 (paper $0.95. Dell. ISBN 0–440–40648–X)   64–20376
A lively spoof of historical novels for children, this is a vivid adventure with young Simon (of the *Wolves of Willoughby Chase*) in London getting mixed up in a plan to assassinate the Duke of Battersea and overthrow the fictitious King James III. (Gr 5–7)

———. *A Necklace of Raindrops, and Other Stories*. Illustrated by Jan Pienkowski. Garden City, N.Y., Doubleday, 1971. 94 p. Paper $0.95. Dell. ISBN 0–440–46400–5   69–15184
A read-aloud collection of eight humorous short fantasies, varied in their inventions of magic. (K–Gr 4)

Aleksin, Anatolii G. *Alik, the Detective*. Translation from the Russian by Bonnie Carey. New York, Morrow, 1977. 192 p. $7.25 ISBN 0–688–22117–3 (lib. ed. $6.96 ISBN 0–688–32117–8)   77–24121
A suspenseful and humorous account of the adventure that befalls six young members of a writer's club honoring a local author, as they visit the scene of the only mystery story the man had ever written. (Gr 5–7)

Alexander, Lloyd. *The Book of Three*. New York, Holt, Rinehart and Winston, 1964. 217 p. $5.95 ISBN 0–03–089821–8   64–18250
Inspired by the legends of ancient Wales, the author has created Prydain, an imaginary land peopled with kings and villains—in particular, a beautiful and unorthodox student enchantress, an engaging furry thing uncertain of his identity, and an Assistant Pig-Keeper who proves to be a hero.
Others in the series are: *The Black Cauldron* (ISBN 0–03–089687–8), *The Castle of Llyr* (ISBN 0–03–057610–5), *The Taran Wanderer* ($6.95 ISBN 0–03–089732–7), and *The High King* (ISBN 0–03–089504–9). (Gr 5–up)

———. *The First Two Lives of Lukas-Kasha*. New York, Dutton, 1978. 213 p. $8.50 ISBN 0–525–29748–0   77–26699
In a fantasy-adventure with hair-raising political escapades anti-hero Lukas turns hero after being carried by enchantment to Abadan and declared its king. (Gr 5–7)

———. *The Town Cats and Other Tales*. Illustrated by Laszlo Kubinyi. New York, Dutton, 1977. 126 p. $7.50 ISBN 0–525–41430–4   76–13647
Eight sparkling fairy tales by an ailurophile who portrays canny felines cleverly outwitting humans. (Gr 3–6)

Andersen, Hans Christian. *The Fir Tree*. Illustrated by Nancy Ekholm Burkert. New York, Harper & Row, 1970. 34 p. $7.95 ISBN 0–06–020077–4 (lib. ed. $7.49 ISBN 0–06–020078–2)   73–121800
Exquisitely detailed pictures, freshly colored or in an equally clear soft pencil, give distinction to a small volume presenting the classic tale. (Gr 3–up)

Babbitt, Natalie. *The Devil's Storybook: Stories and Pictures*. New York, Farrar, Straus & Giroux, 1974. 101 p. $5.95 ISBN 0–374–31770–4 (Paper $1.50. Bantam. ISBN 0–553–15012–X)   74–5488
In ten entertaining, well-told stories the Devil tries his luck in the world, sometimes with success and sometimes not. (Gr 5–8)

————. *Kneeknock Rise*. Story and pictures by Natalie Babbitt. New York, Farrar, Straus & Giroux, 1970. 117 p. $5.95 ISBN 0–374–34257–1
79–105622
Deft mystery-fantasy set in the village of Instep and fearsome Kneeknock Rise, where an unknown "Megrimum" terrifies all but the boy Egan—whose curiosity uncovers the secret. (Gr 3–5)

————. *The Search for Delicious*. New York, Farrar, Straus & Giroux, 1969. 167 p. $6.95 ISBN 0–374–36534–2   69–20374
A quest to determine the meaning of "delicious" sends a young man through a magic-ridden kingdom. Notably original, humorous, and attractive. (Gr 4–7)

————. *Tuck Everlasting*. New York, Farrar, Straus & Giroux, 1975. 141 p. $5.95 ISBN 0–374–37848–7 (Paper $1.75. Bantam. ISBN 0–553–15005–7)
75–33306
When the Tuck family, ever on the move, discovers that ten-year-old Winnie and a conniving stranger share their secret about a spring whose waters bestow immortality, the result is violence and questions about the implications of this gift. Exceptional in story quality and narration. (Gr 5–7)

Baker, Betty. *Walk the World's Rim*. New York, Harper & Row, 1965. 168 p. $6.49 ISBN 0–06–020381–1 (paper $1.25 ISBN 0–06–440026–3)
65–11458
Of Esteban the slave who traveled with Cabeza de Vaca in 1527 from Cuba to Mexico and there gave his life. (Gr 5–7)

Bawden, Nina. *Carrie's War*. Philadelphia, Lippincott, 1973. 159 p. illus. $7.95 ISBN 0–397–31450–7 (Paper $1.95. Penguin. ISBN 0–14–030689–7)
72–13253
Revisiting the small Welsh mining town to which she and her brother were evacuated during World War II, Carrie recalls vividly an eccentric household in which she lived and another home that provided comfort to two lonely, homesick children. (Gr 4–6)

————. *The Peppermint Pig*. Philadelphia, Lippincott, 1975. 191 p. $7.95 ISBN 0–397–31618–6 (Paper $1.50. Penguin. ISBN 0–14–030944–6)
74–26922

A runty pet pig named Johnnie helps Poll through difficult adjustments when her family is forced to live with relatives in a small Norfolk town while her father, wrongly accused of theft, seeks to make his fortune in America. A vivid turn-of-the-century period piece. (Gr 5–6)

Beatty, Patricia. *Just Some Weeds from the Wilderness*. New York, Morrow, 1978. 254 p. $7.95 ISBN 0–688–22137–8 (lib. ed. $7.63 ISBN 0–688–32137–2)   77–28433
A women's rights view of the late nineteenth century shows young Lucinda helping her aunt produce and market patent medicines to recoup the family fortune. (Gr 5–7)

Bellairs, John. *The House with a Clock in Its Walls*. Pictures by Edward Gorey. New York, Dial Press, 1973. 179 p. $6.95 ISBN 0–8037–3821–8 (lib. ed. $6.46 ISBN 0–8037–3823–4; paper $1.25. Dell. ISBN 0–440–43742–3)   72–7600
A breezy and pleasantly shivery excursion into the occult, with a likeable boy hero and a pair of benign and eccentric adults whose zany magic defeats a ghost. (Gr 4–6)

Berends, Polly B. *The Case of the Elevator Duck*. Illustrated by James K. Washburn. New York, Random House, 1973. 54 p. $5.99 ISBN 0–394–92115–1 (paper $0.95. Dell. ISBN 0–440–41290–0)
72–158380
Both entertaining and convincing is this chronicle of an eleven-year-old apartment dweller's efforts to find the owner of a stray duck. (Gr 3–5)

Bodker, Cecil. *The Leopard*. Translated by Gunnar Poulsen. New York, Atheneum, 1975. 186 p. $7.95 ISBN 0–689–30444–7   74–19314
A tale of increasingly taut adventure follows a young Ethiopian cowherd into a mesh of evils perpetrated by a cattle thief. Written in Ethiopia by a prize-winning Danish author for first publication there. (Gr 4–6)

Bond, Michael. *The Tales of Olga da Polga*. Illustrated by Hans Helweg. New York, Macmillan, 1973. 113 p. $4.95 ISBN 0–02–711730–8 (paper $0.95. Penguin. ISBN 0–14–030500–9   72–89048
Amusing tall tales of a compulsively talkative guinea pig, by the creator of Paddington Bear. (Gr 3–5)

Bond, Nancy. *A String in the Harp*. [Map and frontispiece drawing by Allen Davis] New York, Atheneum, 1976. 370 p. (A Margaret K. McElderry book) $9.95 ISBN 0–689–50036–8   75–28181

Present-day realism and the fantasy world of sixth-century Taliesin meet in an absorbing novel set in Wales. The story centers around the Morgans—Jen, Peter, Becky, and their father—their adjustment to another country, their mother's death, and, especially, Peter's bitter despair, which threatens them all. (Gr 6–8)

Boston, Lucy. *The Fossil Snake.* Illustrated by Peter Boston. New York, Atheneum, 1976. 53 p. (A Margaret K. McElderry book) $5.95 ISBN 0–689–50037–8   75–26997
In a unique tale of fantasy and reality, Rob revives a rare fossil reptile and provides a home for it under his warm radiator. (Gr 4–6)

———. *The Sea Egg.* Illustrated by Peter Boston. New York, Harcourt, Brace & World, 1967. 94 p. $4.95 ISBN 0–15–271050–7   67–3334
A sea triton hatches from a special egg-shaped stone, to the satisfied amazement of two little English school boys who find him a splendid companion in island adventure. (Gr 4–5)

———. *The Stones of Green Knowe.* Illustrated by Peter Boston. New York, Atheneum, 1976. 117 p. (A Margaret K. McElderry book) $6.95 ISBN 0–689–50058–0   75–44143
Sixth of the Green Knowe stories, this tale describes the building of the Manor and how young Roger, son of the builder, discovers ancient stones whose mysterious power enables him to step into the future where he encounters, in their times, children from the earlier books. (Gr 4–6)

Bradbury, Bianca. *Two on an Island.* Illustrated by Robert MacLean. Boston, Houghton Mifflin, 1965. 139 p. $6.95 ISBN 0–395–06651–4   65–12175
A brother and sister, stranded on a coastal island for three days' endurance of hunger and cold, develop a new understanding relationship. (Gr 4–6)

Briggs, Katharine M. *Hobberdy Dick.* New York, Greenwillow Books, 1977. 239 p. $7.25 ISBN 0–688–80079–3 (lib. ed. $6.96 ISBN 0–688–84079–5; paper $1.50. Penguin. ISBN 0–14–030551–3)   76–39896
A midsummer-night's dream fantasy, centering on a hobgoblin who, while protecting a seventeenth-century English country estate, supervises the finding of a treasure. (Gr 5–7)

Brown, Palmer. *Hickory.* New York, Harper & Row, 1978. 42 p. $6.95 ISBN 0–06–020887–2 (lib. ed. $7.49 ISBN 0–06–020888–0)   77–11849
A poignant little story of friendship develops as Hickory, a house mouse, takes to the outside world and meets a friendly grasshopper. Delicately colored, detailed illustrations reinforce the narrative. (Gr 1–3)

Bulla, Clyde R. *Shoeshine Girl.* Illustrated by Leigh Grant. New York, Crowell, 1975. 84 p. $5.95 ISBN 0–690–00758–2   75–8516
In simple vocabulary Bulla tells the story of lazy ten-year-old Sarah Ida's summer of growth working for Al at his shoeshine stand. (Gr 3–5) ·

Burch, Robert. *Queenie Peavy.* Illustrated by Jerry Lazare. New York, Viking Press, 1966. 159 p. $6.95 ISBN 0–670–58422–3   66–15649
She was a bright thirteen-year-old, and a thorny problem to herself and everyone else in her southern rural community. When she finally accepted the fact of her father's shiftlessness, she gave herself a chance. (Gr 4–7)

Byars, Betsy C. *The 18th Emergency.* Illustrated by Robert Grossman. New York, Viking Press, 1973. 126 p. $5.95 ISBN 0–670–29055–6   72–91399
A sharply observant, lightly told story about a day-dreaming, compulsive doodler. Eleven-year-old Mouse is an appealing anti-hero as he faces up to reality and openly confronts the bully whom he has dishonored. (Gr 4–6)

———. *The Midnight Fox.* Illustrated by Ann Grifalconi. New York, Viking Press, 1968. 157 p. $5.95 ISBN 0–670–47473–8   68–27566
A city boy discovers the unexpected fascination of wildlife after glimpsing a black fox on his aunt's farm. (Gr 4–6)

———. *The Pinballs.* New York, Harper & Row, 1977. 136 p. $5.95 ISBN 0–06–020917–8 (lib. ed. $5.79 ISBN 0–06–020918–6)   76–41518
Three lonely foster children, each scarred by parental abuse or neglect, come together in a supportive home where they begin to understand themselves and to care for one another. (Gr 5–7)

———. *The Summer of the Swans.* Illustrated by Tex CoConis. New York, Viking Press, 1970. 142 p. $5.95 ISBN 0–670–68190–3   72–106919
A convincing portrayal of Sara, who with her friend Joe searches for her ten-year-old retarded brother and thereby gains insights which change her discontent to new maturity and acceptance. (Gr 5–7)

Callen, Larry. *Pinch.* Illustrated by Marvin Friedman. Boston, Little, Brown, 1975. 179 p. (An Atlantic Monthly Press book) $5.95 ISBN 0–316–12495–8   75–25618
Exaggerated characters and events in a small Louisiana town highlight this tongue-in-cheek tale about the boy Pinch, his pig Homer, and the annual hunting-pig contest. Sequels include *The Deadly Mandrake* ($6.95 ISBN 0–316–12496–6). (Gr 5–7)

Cameron, Eleanor. *The Court of the Stone Children.* New York, Dutton, 1973. 191 p. $7.95 ISBN 0–525–28350–1   73-77451
Within this unusual time fantasy set in a San Francisco museum, Nina, with the aid of a young woman's journal from nineteenth-century France, solves a murder mystery dormant since Napoleon's day. The 1974 National Book Award. (Gr 5–7)

———. *A Room Made of Windows.* Illustrations by Trina Schart Hyman. Boston, Little, Brown, 1971. 271 p. $6.95 ISBN 0–316–12523–7 (paper $1.25. Dell, New York. ISBN 0–440–47523–6)   77-140479
Perhaps a bit autobiographical, this story of strong-willed Julia, growing up in Berkeley determined to be a writer, introduces a range of positive characters of all ages whose relationships make this a richer than usual picture of adolescent development.
Followed by *Julia and the Hand of God* (New York, Dutton. ISBN 0–525–32910–2). (Gr 5–7)

———. *Time and Mr. Bass; a Mushroom Planet Book.* Illustrated by Fred Meise. Boston, Little, Brown, 1967. $5.95. Atlantic Monthly Press. ISBN 0–316–12536–9   67-2905
Chuck and David go with Tyco Bass in his space ship to a mysterious mountain in Wales, where they find innocent men corrupted by a symbolic necklace and an ancient scroll. In the series opened by *The Wonderful Flight to the Mushroom Planet* (ISBN 0–316–12537–7). (Gr 4–5)

Caudill, Rebecca. *A Certain Small Shepherd.* With illus. by William Pène Du Bois. New York, Holt, Rinehart and Winston, 1965. 48 p. $6.95 ISBN 0–03–089755–6 (paper $1.95 ISBN 0–03–080107–9)   65-17604
A quiet and poignant tale of a small mute boy in Appalachia and the miracle wrought by his faith and joy in Christmas. Illustrations intensify the reality and impact of the story. (All ages)

Christopher, John. *The Pool of Fire.* New York, Macmillan, 1968. 178 p. $7.95 ISBN 0–02–718350–5 (paper $1.95 ISBN 0–02–042720–4)   68-142716
Completing the science-fiction trilogy begun with *The White Mountains*, this provocative story sees the forces of freedom succeed in their attack on the cities of the dictator tripods. (Gr 5–9)

Clapp, Patricia. *Jane-Emily.* New York, Lothrop, Lee & Shepard, 1969. 160 p. $6.00 ISBN 0–688–51019–1   69-14326
Jane's summer vacation with an aunt is troubled by an uncanny link with Emily, dead "before she had learned how to live." A tale that grows in Gothic eeriness. (Gr 5–7)

Clarke, Pauline. *The Return of the Twelves.* Illustrated by Bernarda Bryson. New York, Coward-McCann, 1963. 224 p. $7.95 ISBN 0–698–20117–5   63-15541
A perceptive boy discovers in an attic the lost toy soldiers of the young Brontës and in wonder-filled adventures helps them reach safety in their original home. An English prizewinner. (Gr 5–7)

Cleary, Beverly. *The Mouse and the Motorcycle.* Illustrated by Louis Darling. New York, Morrow, 1965. 158 p. $6.75 ISBN 0–688–21698–6 (lib. ed. $6.48 ISBN 0–688–31698–0)   65-20956
Original make-believe in a tale of friendship between the boy Keith and a mouse whose mania for Keith's toy motorcycle leads to reckless adventure.
Sequel, *Runaway Ralph* ($7.25 ISBN 0–688–21701–X; lib. ed. $6.96 ISBN 0–688–31701–4). (Gr 3–5)

———. *Ramona the Pest.* Illustrated by Louis Darling. New York, Morrow, 1968. 192 p. $6.75 ISBN 0–688–21721–4 (lib. ed. $6.48 ISBN 0–688–31721–9)   68-12981
With heartfelt, absolute candor, Ramona gives a spirited account of the trials of kindergarten life. Followed by *Ramona the Brave* (ISBN 0–688–22015–0; lib. ed. ISBN 0–688–32015–5) and *Ramona and Her Father* (ISBN 0–688–22114–9; lib. ed. ISBN 0–688–32114–3). (Gr 2–4)

———. *Ribsy.* Illustrated by Louis Darling. New York, Morrow, 1964. 192 p. $7.25 ISBN 0–688–21662–5 (lib. ed. $6.96 ISBN 0–688–31662–X)   64-13263
Both exciting and amusing, this sequel to other stories about Henry Huggins and his dog follows Ribsy through extraordinary experiences in being lost. (Gr 3–5)

Cleaver, Vera, *and* Bill Cleaver. *Queen of Hearts.* Philadelphia, Lippincott, 1978. 158 p. $8.95 ISBN 0–397–31771–9   77-18252
To oppose Granny in any way was dangerous, but twelve-year-old Wilma had to do this and thereby began to learn the meaning of growing old. (Gr 5–7)

Cohen, Barbara. *Thank You, Jackie Robinson.* Drawings by Richard Cuffari. New York, Lothrop, Lee & Shepard, 1974. 125 p. $6.00 ISBN 0–688–51580–0   73-17703
A moving story of how shared enjoyment of baseball creates deep friendship between a fatherless white boy and an old black man. (Gr 3–6)

Conford, Ellen. *Me and the Terrible Two.* Illustrated by Charles Carroll. Boston, Little, Brown, 1974. 117 p. $6.95 ISBN 0–316–15303–6 73–18393
Putting up with the identical twins Conrad and Haskell, who have moved into the house next door, is a trial for Dorrie until their working together on a successful Book Week project shows what friendship and cooperation can mean. Also, *Felicia the Critic* (ISBN 0–316–15295–1). (Gr 4–5)

Cooper, Susan. *Over Sea, under Stone.* Illustrated by Margery Gill. New York, Harcourt, Brace & World, 1966. 252 p. $6.25 ISBN 0–15–2590434–X 66–11199
At the start of their Cornwall holiday, three children find an old map and thereby are caught up in a pattern of ancient mystery, powerful magic, and Arthurian legend.
Followed by: *The Dark Is Rising* ($7.95. Atheneum. ISBN 0–689–30317–3), *Greenwitch* ($6.95 ISBN 0–689–30426–9), *The Grey King* (ISBN 0–689–50029–7), and *Silver on the Tree* ($7.95 ISBN 0–689–50088–2). (Gr 5–7)

Cresswell, Helen. *The Bongleweed.* New York, Macmillan, 1973. 138 p. $4.95 ISBN 0–02–725500–X 73–4057
The mysterious seed that Becky tricks her playmate into planting in an English formal garden turns into such an excessively growing weed that it threatens to take over everything. (Gr 4–6)

———. *Ordinary Jack.* New York, Macmillan, 1977. 195 p. (The Bagthorpe Saga, pt. 1) $6.95 ISBN 0–02–725540–9 77–5146
A zany tale of what befalls Jack, the one "ordinary" member of an extraordinarily gifted British family when he, with the assistance of Uncle Parker, develops second sight. Followed by *Absolute Zero* (ISBN 0–02–725550–6) and *Bagthorpes Unlimited* (ISBN 0–02–725430–5). (Gr 5–7)

Day, Veronique. *Landslide!* Translated by Margaret Morgan. Illustrated by Margot Tomes. New York, Coward-McCann, 1966. 158 p. Paper $1.25. Dell. ISBN 0–440–44630–9 63–15543
Five children from Paris, trapped in a cottage after a mountain landslide, survive for nine days with Crusoe-like ingenuity and courage. (Gr 5–7)

Dejong, Meindert. *Far Out the Long Canal.* Illustrated by Nancy Grossman. New York, Harper & Row, 1964. 231 p. $3.95 ISBN 0–06–021465–1 (lib. ed. $7.89 ISBN 0–06–021466–X) 64–20947
An indelible picture of a nine-year-old Dutch boy's intense desire to learn to skate, and of one festival day when a deep freeze sent everyone in the village of Weirum onto the frozen canals. (Gr 3–6)

———. *Journey from Peppermint Street.* New York, Harper & Row, 1968. 242 p. $7.95 ISBN 0–06–021488–0 (lib. ed. $7.89 ISBN 0–06–021489–9; paper $1.95 ISBN 0–06–440011–5) 68–27870
Set in the author's own Holland of the early 1900s, this is a sensitive story of a nine-year-old boy whose first adventures away from home involve him in a tornado and other dangers of the water-filled lowlands. Winner of the 1969 National Book Award. (Gr 3–5)

Drury, Roger W. *The Champion of Merrimack County.* Illustrated by Fritz Wegner. Boston, Little, Brown, 1976. 198 p. $6.95 ISBN 0–316–19349–6 76–6453
An entertaining account of a mouse called O Crispin, whose bike-riding rink is the rim of an antique bathtub. (Gr 3–5)

Erickson, Russell E. *A Toad for Tuesday.* Pictures by Lawrence Di Fiori. New York, Lothrop, Lee & Shepard, 1974. 63 p. $5.52 ISBN 0–688–51569–X 73–19900
In this pleasant fantasy, a skiing toad carrying beetle brittle to an aging aunt is captured by an owl who first views him as a birthday feast but later finds him too pleasant a friend to lose. (Gr 2–4)

Fitzhugh, Louise. *Harriet, the Spy.* Illustrated by the author. New York, Harper & Row, 1964. 298 p. $6.95 ISBN 0–06–021910–6 (lib. ed. $6.89 ISBN 0–06–021911–4) 64–19711
About the writing career of eleven-year-old Harriet, a precocious, uninhibited child of sophisticated New York society, whose classmates find the notebook in which she has entered her unflattering observations of all of them. (Gr 4–6)

Fleischman, Albert Sidney. *Humbug Mountain.* Illustrations by Eric von Schmidt. Boston, Little, Brown, 1978. 149 p. (An Atlantic Monthly Press book) $6.95 ISBN 0–316–28569–2 78–9419
In their search for Grandpa Tuggle and his staked-out "promised land," Wiley Flint and his family tussle with crooks and zany characters. (Gr 4–6)

———. *Jim Bridger's Alarm Clock, and Other Tall Tales.* Illustrated by Eric von Schmidt. New York, Dutton, 1978. 56 p. (A Unicorn book) $6.95 ISBN 0–525–32795–9 78–5854
Three spun-out farces about a "ramshackle, sharp-eyed" army scout who discovered the Great Salt Lake, the Petrified Forest, and a flat-topped mountain which became his alarm clock. (Gr 3–6)

———. *Jingo Django.* Illustrated by Eric von Schmidt. Boston, Little, Brown, 1971. 172 p. (An Atlantic Monthly Press book) $5.95 ISBN 0–316–28580–3 75–140481

Nineteenth-century skullduggery abounds in this tall-tale adventure of orphaned Jingo as he and Mr. Jeffrey Peacock-Hemlock-Jones, Gent., cross the country to Texas in search of a treasure, pursued by the formidable Mrs. Daggett and General Dirty-Face Jim Scurlock. (Gr 5–7)

Fox, Paula. *How Many Miles to Babylon?* Illustrated by Paul Giovanopoulos. New York, David White, 1967. 117 p. $5.95 ISBN 0–87250–415–8 (paper $0.75. Pocket Books. ISBN 0–671–29621–3)

67–19301

An inner-city story, stirring in James's fantasy about his hospitalized mother and her talk of Africa and dramatic in his forced involvement with a gang of dog thieves. (Gr 3–6)

———. *Maurice's Room.* Pictures by Ingrid Fetz. New York, Macmillan, 1966. 64 p. $5.95 ISBN 0–02–735730–9 (paper $1.50 ISBN 0–02–043200–3)

66–10167

Maurice, like many boys, thinks his room is perfect when it is cluttered with junk. His parents' bewilderment at his preferring junkyard treasures to expensive presents is an equally universal experience. (Gr 3–5)

Garner, Alan. *Elidor.* New York, Walck, 1967. 185 p. New ed. $7.95. Collins. ISBN 0–529–05417–5

78–18417

Evil forces from Elidor, once a bright and glorious world, pursue a family of children to their own home and neighborhood. A story of power and terror in which sturdy children fight for true values. (Gr 5–8)

Gauch, Patricia L. *This Time, Tempe Wick?* Illustrated by Margot Tomes. New York, Coward, McCann & Geoghegan, 1974. 43 p. $5.95 ISBN 0–698–20300–3

74–79706

In a story based on a New Jersey legend about the Revolutionary War, young Tempe Wick thwarts two mutinous Continental soldiers who seek to steal her horse. Margot Tomes's robust pictures sustain the lively text. (Gr 2–5)

Goble, Paul, *and* Dorothy Goble. *Lone Bull's Horse Raid.* Pictures by Paul Goble. Scarsdale, N.Y., Bradbury Press, 1973. [64] p. $8.95 ISBN 0–87888–059–3

73–76546

Lone Bull's first participation in a horse-stealing raid against the Crow Indians is described as if in his own simple, direct telling. Distinctive full-color paintings, full of movement, are stylized in the manner of Plains Indian art. (Gr 4–7)

Goffstein, M. B. *Two Piano Tuners.* New York, Farrar, Straus & Giroux, 1970. 65 p. $5.95 ISBN 0–374–38019–8

71–106399

Humorous illustrations by the author of this highly original period piece show how Debbie seeks to become a master piano tuner like her grandfather. (Gr 2–4)

Greene, Bette. *Philip Hall Likes Me, I Reckon Maybe.* Pictures by Charles Lilly. New York, Dial Press, 1974. 135 p. $5.95 ISBN 0–8037–6098–1 (lib. ed. $5.47 ISBN 0–8037–6096–5; paper $1.25. Dell. ISBN 0–440–45755–6)

74–2887

In a small Arkansas town, bright, likable Beth is a natural leader who commands the respect not only of the girls but also of Philip, who enjoys her friendship even when she bests him as top student. (Gr 4–6)

Greene, Constance C. *Beat the Turtle Drum.* Illustrated by Donna Diamond. New York, Viking Press, 1976. 120 p. $5.95 ISBN 0–670–15241–2 76–14772

In a perceptive story that centers on Joss—who finally has her eleventh birthday gift, the rental of a horse for a week—the author movingly describes the tragedy of Joss's death and its effect on her sister, parents, and others. (Gr 4–6)

———. *A Girl Called Al.* Illustrated by Byron Barton. New York, Viking Press, 1969. 127 p. $5.95 ISBN 0–670–34153–3

69–18255

Stories of Al, "a little on the fat side," and her never-named companion who describes their shared frustrations at school and at home, and their needed friendship with Mr. Richards, "sort of the assistant superintendent" of their apartment house. Followed by *I Know You, Al* ($6.95 ISBN 0–670–39048–8). (Gr 5–8)

Hamilton, Virginia. *The House of Dies Drear.* Illustrations by Eros Keith. New York, Macmillan, 1968. 246 p. $7.95 ISBN 0–02–742500–2 68–23059

A former underground railroad station in Ohio becomes for young Thomas, a Negro boy from the South, not only his new home and a fascinating piece of the history of his people but a source of mystery and drama. (Gr 5–7)

———. *Zeely.* Illustrated by Symeon Shimin. New York, Macmillan, 1967. 122 p. $6.95 ISBN 0–02–742470–7 (paper $1.50 ISBN 0–02–043510–X)

66–31616

Geeder's summer at her uncle's farm is made special because of her adoration of a regal neighbor who raises hogs and who closely resembles the magazine photograph of a Watusi queen. (Gr 6–9)

Heide, Florence P. *The Shrinking of Treehorn.* Drawings by Edward Gorey. New York, Holiday House, 1971. [32] p. $4.95 ISBN 0–8234–0189–8

78–151753

The comic results of a small boy's involuntary shrinking are vividly suggested by the artist's line drawings. (Gr 2–4)

Holman, Felice. *Slake's Limbo*. New York, Scribner, 1974. 117 p. $5.95 ISBN 0–684–13926–X (paper $1.25. Dell. ISBN 0–440–97943–9)   74–11675
A fast-paced survival story describes how young Slake, made desperate by fear, manages to eke out an existence underground in a Manhattan subway cave. (Gr 5–9)

Houston, James A. *Tikta'liktak; an Eskimo Legend*. Illustrated by [the author] New York, Harcourt, Brace & World, 1965. 63 p. $6.25 ISBN 0–15–287745–2   65–21696
In vivid, spare prose are recounted the heroic adventures of an Eskimo whose brave seeking of food for his people sets him adrift on an Arctic ice pan. Also, *The White Archer; an Eskimo Legend*. ($6.50 ISBN 0–15–295851–7). (Gr 4–7)

How Djadja-em-ankh Saved the Day; a Tale from Ancient Egypt. Translated from the original hieratic with illustrations and commentary by Lise Manniche. New York, Crowell, 1977. [19] p. $5.95 (folded in slipcase) ISBN 0–690–01280–2; $8.95 (rolled in tube) ISBN 0–690–01281–0   76–26919
An Egyptologist's translation of a tale of a king and his magician thousands of years ago is accompanied by commentary on the life of the time and on the ancient writing called hieroglyphs. Illustrated impressively by reproductions of ancient drawings, and with the original hieroglyphic text reprinted. (Gr 4–6)

Hughes, Ted. *The Iron Giant; a Story in Five Nights*. Drawings by Robert Nadler. New York, Harper & Row, 1968. 56 p. $6.89 ISBN 0–06–022658–7   68–3551
An English poet's tall-tale invention, with an outsize iron hero who saves the world from a monstrous, hungry "space-bat-angel-dragon." (Gr 4–6)

Jansson, Tove. *Comet in Moominland*, written and illustrated by Tove Jansson. Translated by Elizabeth Portch. New York, Walck, 1975. 192 p. Paper $1.25. Avon. ISBN 0–380–00436–4   68–726
Young Moomintroll and Sniff make "an expedition of discovery" to learn about a comet threatening their valley—with more fantastic adventures to please readers of Moomintroll make-believe. Followed by *Moominpappa at Sea* (ISBN 0–380–01726–1), *Moominvalley in November* (ISBN 0–380–00763–0), and *Tales from Moominvalley* (ISBN 0–380–00911–0). (Gr 4–6)

Jarrell, Randall. *Animal Family*. New York, Pantheon, 1965. 180 p. $6.95 ISBN 0–394–81043–0   65–20659
A lyric writer has created a poetic idyll with unusual detail in the invention of a timeless seaside world and a lonely man who acquires a family—a mermaid, bear, lynx, and little boy. (Gr 4–up)

Jeffries, Roderic. *Against Time!* New York, Harper & Row, 1973. 151 p. Paper $1.25. Scholastic Book Service. ISBN 0–590–02552–X   63–14369
A breathless twenty-two hour search, using the resources of Scotland Yard, follows the kidnaping of Peter Dunn, son of a British detective inspector. (Gr 5–7)

Jones, Diana Wynne. *The Ogre Downstairs*. New York, Dutton, 1975. 191 p. $6.95 ISBN 0–525–36315–7   74–23745
Natural problems arise when an inflexible widower with two boys marries a widow with three children. Family adjustments become still more complicated as two magic chemistry sets cause fantastic happenings. (Gr 4–6)

Kaplan, Bess. *The Empty Chair*. New York, Harper & Row, 1978. 243 p. $7.95 ISBN 0–06–023092–4 (lib. ed. $7.89 ISBN 0–06–023093–2)   77–11852
Becky views with growing apprehension her Jewish relatives' plans for her father's remarriage, but her new stepmother gradually wins Becky to her and helps her lose her sense of betrayal to her mother's memory. (Gr 5–7)

Kerr, Judith. *When Hitler Stole Pink Rabbit*. Illustrated by the author. New York, Coward, McCann & Geoghegan, 1972. 191 p. $6.50 ISBN 0–698–20182–5 (paper $1.25. Dell. ISBN 0–440–49017–0)   71–185765
When her family escapes from Hitler's Germany, Anna finds that learning to be a refugee can be an adventure. In this engrossing story places, personalities, and details of adjustment to a new home, language, school, and friends are vividly recalled from the author's childhood. Also, a sequel *The Other Way Round* ($7.95 ISBN 0–698–20335–6). (Gr 4–7)

Key, Alexander. *The Forgotten Door*. Philadelphia, Westminster, 1965. 126 p. $6.75 ISBN 0–664–32342–1   65–10170
Falling onto earth from another planet, little Jon meets not only sympathy and understanding but also suspicion and hostility. (Gr 5–7)

Konigsburg, E. L. *From the Mixed-Up Files of Mrs. Basil E. Frankweiler*. New York, Atheneum, 1967.

162 p. $6.95 ISBN 0–689–20586–4 (paper $1.95 ISBN 0–689–70308–2)   67–18988

A delightfully enterprising sister and brother run away from their suburban home to camp out in the Metropolitan Museum of Art. A funny, original story to be enjoyed along with the author's first book, *Jennifer, Hecate, Macbeth, William McKinley and Me, Elizabeth* (ISBN 0–689–30007–7). (Gr 4–6)

Kooiker, Leonie. *The Magic Stone*. Translation from the Dutch by Richard and Clara Winston. Illustrated by Carl Hollander. New York, Morrow, 1978. 224 p. $6.95 ISBN 0–688–22143–2 (lib. ed. $6.67 ISBN 0–688–32143–7)   78–1713

Fantastic adventures of a boy in Holland who finds a magic stone that leads him to a coven of witches and membership in their association. (Gr 3–6)

Kurelek, William. *A Prairie Boy's Winter*. Boston, Houghton Mifflin, 1973. 47 p. $7.95 ISBN 0–395–17708–1   72–8913

Eloquent paintings by the author evoke the cold sky and space of winter on the prairies of Manitoba. Together with a brief unsentimental text they recreate the unique joys and hardship of his boyhood work and play. An ageless book for sharing, perhaps alongside the Wilder books. Also, *A Prairie Boy's Summer* (ISBN 0–395–20280–9). (Gr 2–up)

Levoy, Myron. *The Witch of Fourth Street, and Other Stories*. Pictures by Gabriel Lisowski. New York, Harper & Row, 1972. 110 p. Paper $1.25 ISBN 0–06–440059–X   74–183174

An old pencil-lady turned into a witch, a roller-skating boy and an injured pigeon, a peddler and his ancient horse—these are some of the perceptively drawn characters in eight wistful, imaginative stories of New York immigrant life in the 1920s. (Gr 3–6)

Lexau, Joan M. *Striped Ice Cream*. Illustrations by John Wilson. Philadelphia, Lippincott, 1968. 95 p. $6.95 ISBN 0–397–31046–3 (paper $0.95. Scholastic Book Service. ISBN 0–590–04506–7)   68–10774

A warm, poignant story about the birthday hopes and worries of Becky, youngest child in a large, hardworking family. (Gr 3–5)

Little, Jean. *From Anna*. Pictures by Joan Sandin. New York, Harper & Row, 1973. 201 p. $6.79 ISBN 0–06–023912–3 (paper $1.95 ISBN 0–06–440044–1)   72–76505

An understanding interpretation of acutely nearsighted Anna, for whom glasses introduce a startling new world, and of her and her family's adjustment to a new life in Canada as political refugees from Germany. (Gr 4–6)

Lively, Penelope. *The Ghost of Thomas Kempe*. Illustrations by Anthony Maitland. New York, Dutton, 1973. 186 p. $6.95 ISBN 0–525–30495–9 73–77456

When the ghost of a seventeenth-century sorcerer emerges as a poltergeist and attempts to make young James his apprentice, the boy must learn how to exorcise it. A story rich in surprises, mystery, and humor. (Gr 4–7)

Macdonald, George. *The Light Princess*. With pictures by Maurice Sendak. New York, Farrar, Straus & Giroux, 1969. 110 p. $5.95 ISBN 0–374–34455–8   69–14981

The artist's new interpretation, in fine-line drawings, fully conveys the magic of the story about a princess who "lost her gravity," giving new life to this classic. (All ages)

McIlwraith, Maureen M. H. M. *A Stranger Came Ashore*. By Mollie Hunter [*pseud.*] New York, Harper & Row, 1975. 192 p. $5.95 ISBN 0–06–022651–X (lib. ed. $6.89 ISBN 0–06–022652–8; paper $1.50 ISBN 0–06–440082–4)   75–10814

A haunting tale of the great Selkie, a giant bull seal of the Shetlands, who takes the form of a ship-wrecked sailor, comes ashore, and lures a pretty young girl to his underwater palace.

Earlier books dealing with Scottish folklore are *The Wicked One; a Story of Suspense* (ISBN 0–06–022647; lib. ed. ISBN 0–06–022648–X) and *The Haunted Mountain* (lib. ed. ISBN 0–06–022667–6; paper ISBN 0–06–440041–7). (Gr 4–6)

The Magic Umbrella and Other Stories for Telling. With notes on how to tell them by Eileen Colwell. Drawings by Shirley Felts. New York, McKay, 1977. 159 p. $6.95. Walck. ISBN 0–8098–0004–7   76–53970

An attractive balance of folktales and modern fairy tales, some of them likely to be unfamiliar, compiled by a widely recognized storyteller-anthologist. (Gr 4–up)

Mathis, Sharon Bell. *The Hundred Penny Box*. Illustrated by Leo and Diane Dillon. New York, Viking Press, 1975. 47 p. $6.95 ISBN 0–670–38787–8   74–23744

Aunt Dew's prized possession is a big old wooden box containing 100 pennies, one for each year of her long life. Young Michael, who loves playing with the pennies while his great-great-aunt relates her stories, defends her need to keep the old box. (Gr 3–5)

Merrill, Jean. *The Pushcart War*. Illustrated by Ronni Solbert. New York, W. R. Scott, 1964. 223 p. $6.95. Addison-Wesley, Reading, Mass. ISBN 0–201–09313–8   64–13581

A psuedo-serious history of a fictional war in 1976 between New York City's truck drivers and pushcart peddlers, this satirizes many facets of contemporary urban life in a fresh and original manner. (Gr 5–up)

———. *The Toothpaste Millionaire.* Prepared by the Bank Street College of Education. Boston, Houghton Mifflin, 1974. 90 p. $6.95 ISBN 0–395–18511–4   73–22055
In an exposé of overpricing, the author of *The Pushcart War* narrates the story of Rufus Mayflower and his classmates who successfully manufacture and market a toothpaste at low cost. (Gr 3–6)

Miles, Miska. *Annie and the Old One.* Illustrated by Peter Parnall. Boston, Little, Brown, 1971. 44 p. $5.95 ISBN 0–316–57117–2   79–129900
Annie, a little Navajo girl, learns that she cannot forestall the approaching death of "the Old One," her dearly beloved grandmother. (K–Gr 2)

Monjo, F. N. *The Secret of the Sachem's Tree.* Illustrated by Margot Tomes. New York, Coward, McCann & Geoghegan, 1972. 60 p. $4.69 ISBN 0–698–30446–2 (paper $0.95. Dell. ISBN 0–440–40763–X)   72–76699
Told in rhythmic, free, easy-to-read verse are the mysterious events of Halloween 1687, when King James ordered an agent to seize the Connecticut charter. Attractively illustrated. (Gr 1–4)

Morey, Walter. *Gentle Ben.* Illustrated by John Schoenherr. New York, Dutton, 1965. 191 p. $6.95 ISBN 0–525–30429–0   65–21290
Convincing story of the friendship between a boy and an enormous brown bear whose lives and fluctuating fortunes are interwoven. Set in a small fishing community in prestatehood Alaska. (Gr 5–7)

Moskin, Marietta D. *Lysbet and the Fire Kittens.* Illustrations by Margot Tomes. New York, Coward, McCann & Geoghegan, 1974. 46 p. (A break-of-day book) $4.49 ISBN 0–698–30522–1   72–97315
Small Lysbet, left to watch over cat and hearth fire in New Amsterdam of 1662, has unexpected adventures when she is alone for the night as well. (Gr 1–3)

Newman, Robert. *The Case of the Baker Street Irregulars; a Sherlock Holmes Story.* New York, Atheneum, 1978. 216 p. $7.95 ISBN 0–689–30641–5   77–15463
A skillful, fast-paced narrative: Andrew Craigie, alone in London after his guardian is kidnapped, becomes involved with Sherlock Holmes's famous "irregulars," Baker Street children who serve the great detective. (Gr 4–6)

O'Brien, Robert C. *Mrs. Frisby and the Rats of NIMH.* Illustrated by Zena Bernstein. New York, Atheneum, 1971. 233 p. $6.95 ISBN 0–689–20651–8   74–134818
An ingenious and original tale of the gentle field mouse, Mrs. Frisby, whose housing problems are solved by a colony of rats, escapees from the NIMH laboratory where training and injections have made them wise and inventive. (Gr 4–9)

O'Dell, Scott. *Zia.* Boston, Houghton Mifflin, 1976. 179 p. $7.95 ISBN 0–395–24393–9   75–44156
In a compelling sequel to *Island of the Blue Dolphins,* Zia, the fourteen-year-old niece of Karana, plays a role in the rescue of her aunt. With her strength, determination, and quiet dignity, Zia is a worthy successor to Karana. (Gr 5–7)

Paterson, Katherine. *Bridge to Terabithia.* Illustrated by Donna Diamond. New York, Crowell, 1977. 128 p. $7.95 ISBN 0–690–01359–0   77–2221
Jess finds a rich friendship with Leslie, a newcomer to his rural Virginia community. Together they create Terabithia, a private kingdom where all is well—until Leslie is drowned. The 1978 Newbery Award. (Gr 5–7)

———. *The Great Gilly Hopkins.* New York, Crowell, 1978. 148 p. $6.95 ISBN 0–690–03837–2 (lib. ed. $6.79 ISBN 0–690–03838–0)   77–27075
Bright, gutsy Galadriel Hopkins, determined to care for no one, finds she is up against two adults she cannot manage: a semiliterate foster mother and a black teacher whose cool is unshakeable. A moving and often funny story. National Book Award, 1978. (Gr 5–7)

Paton Walsh, Jill. *Children of the Fox.* Pictures by Robin Eaton. New York, Farrar, Straus & Giroux, 1978. 115 p. $7.95 ISBN 0–374–31242–7 78–8138
Two girls and a boy, each in a separate story, heroically serve the Greek leader Themistokles, "the fox," during the Persian wars. (Gr 4–6)

Peck, Richard. *The Ghost Belonged to Me.* New York, Viking Press, 1975. 183 p. $6.95 ISBN 0–670–33767–6   74–34218
Alexander with his special gift for seeing the unseen discovers an old mystery and becomes a real hero in the Midwest of the early 1900s. Followed by *Ghosts I Have Been* ($7.95 ISBN 0–670–33813–3). (Gr 5–7)

Pinkwater, Daniel Manus. *Lizard Music.* Written and illustrated by D. Manus Pinkwater. New York, Dodd, Mead, 1976. 157 p. $4.95 ISBN 0–396–07357–3   76–12508

The sudden appearance of real lizards playing regular musical instruments on a television program launches an eleven-year-old Walter Cronkite addict on a zany adventure, with the Chicken Man and Claudia, a hen, as companions. More fantastic fun is relayed in *The Hoboken Chicken Emergency* ($5.95 ISBN 0–13–392514–5) and *Fat Men from Space* ($5.50 ISBN 0–396–07461–8). (Gr 3–6)

Rabe, Berniece. *Naomi.* Nashville, Nelson, 1975. 192 p. $6.95 ISBN 0–8407–6444–8 (paper $1.25. Bantam, New York. ISBN 0–553–02762–X)
77–4599
Seared by a fortune-teller's sober prophecy, Naomi finally learns that she can listen to her own voice and set her own goals. Vivid characterizations and natural dialogue mark this intensely real picture of a poor rural family in Missouri in the 1930s. (Gr 5–7)

Reiss, Johanna. *The Upstairs Room.* New York, Crowell, 1972. 196 p. $6.95 ISBN 0–690–85127–8
77–187940
From childhood memories comes an achingly real story of a young Jewish girl hidden in the upper room of a Dutch farmhouse during World War II. The vivid and moving story is an affirmation of a child's complex feelings and of the sustaining power of human love. (Gr 4–6)
For a slightly older child is *Journey Back* (ISBN 0–690–01252–7). (Gr 5–7)

Robertson, Keith. *Henry Reed's Baby-Sitting Service.* Illustrated by Robert McCloskey. New York, Viking Press, 1966. 204 p. $5.95 ISBN 0–670–36825–3 (paper $1.50. Dell. ISBN 0–440–43565–X)
66–2876
The ingenious entrepreneur of *Henry Reed, Inc.,* goes into the baby-sitting business—with hilarious results. Amusingly illustrated. Followed by *Henry Reed's Big Show* ($5.50 ISBN 0–670–36839–3; paper $0.95. Grosset & Dunlap. ISBN 0–448–05434–5). (Gr 5–6)

Robinson, Barbara. *The Best Christmas Pageant Ever.* Illustrated by Judith Gwyn Brown. New York, Harper & Row, 1972. 80 p. $5.95 ISBN 0–06–025043–7 (lib. ed. $5.79 ISBN 0–06–025044; paper $1.25. Avon. ISBN 0–380–40394–3)   72–76501
A lively, entertaining story revolves around a church's Christmas pageant and one family of outlandish, unrestrained children who take it over. (Gr 4–6)

Rodgers, Mary. *Freaky Friday.* New York, Harper & Row, 1972. 145 p. (Harpercrest) $5.95 ISBN 0–06–025048–8 (lib. ed. $5.79 ISBN 0–06–025049–6; paper $1.50 ISBN 0–06–440046–8)   74–183158

A funny, subtle story in which rebellious thirteen-year-old Annabel learns some unexpected things about herself during the preposterous experience of being turned into her mother. Also, *A Billion for Boris* ($4.95 ISBN 0–06–025047–X; paper $1.95 ISBN 0–06–440075–1). (Gr 5–7)

Rounds, Glen. *Mr. Yowder and the Giant Bull Snake.* New York, Holiday House, 1978. [48] p. $5.95 ISBN 0–8234–0311–4   77–24136
A tongue-in-cheek tall tale recounts curious adventures that befall Mr. Yowder after he and Knute, the giant bull snake, become partners. Wryly humorous line drawings. (Gr 3–5)

Sachs, Marilyn. *Dorrie's Book.* Drawings by Anne Sachs. Garden City, N.Y., Doubleday, 1975. 136 p. $5.95 ISBN 0–385–03350–8 (lib. ed. $6.90 ISBN 0–385–03213–7)   74–33688
Dorrie, whose privileged only-child status is upset by the arrival of triplets in her family, writes about her trials for a school assignment. Her story is utterly realistic, refreshing, and frequently humorous. (Gr 4–6)

————. *Veronica Ganz.* Illustrated by Louis Glanzman. Garden City, N.Y., Doubleday, 1968. 156 p. $5.95 ISBN 0–385–01436–8 (paper $1.25. Pocket Books. ISBN 0–671–29564–0)   68–11813
Thirteen-year-old Veronica Ganz fights back at life's aggravations by being a bully, until she discovers that she is happier just being a girl. Also, *Peter and Veronica* ($6.95 ISBN 0–385–06639–2; paper. Dell. ISBN 0–440–48847–8) and *Marv* (ISBN 0–385–00009–X; paper $0.75 ISBN 0–440–45472–7). (Gr 4–6)

Sendak, Maurice. *Higglety Pigglety Pop, or There Must Be More to Life.* New York, Harper & Row, 1967. 69 p. $4.95 ISBN 0–06–025487–5 (lib. ed. $5.79 ISBN 0–06–025488–2)   67–3810
A fantasy, possibly symbolical, about discontented Jennie, a much-indulged Sealyham terrier who feels there must be more to life than having everything. She finds the "experience" she seeks, performing in the new World Mother Goose Theater production of "Higglety Pigglety Pop!" Fine-line drawings illuminate the nonsense. (Gr 2–3)

Shulevitz, Uri. *The Magician.* An adaptation from the Yiddish of I. L. Peretz. New York, Macmillan, 1973. 32 p. $7.95 ISBN 0–02–782510–8 (paper $1.95 ISBN 0–02–045320–5)   72–85186
A legend about the prophet Elijah who appears in the guise of a traveling magician bringing a Passover Eve feast to a poor old couple. The brevity and direct-

ness of telling and the rich atmosphere of small pen-and-ink drawings bring a traditional tale to life. (Gr 1–3)

Slote, Alfred. *Jake.* Philadelphia, Lippincott, 1971. 155 p. $4.95 ISBN 0–397–31414–0 (paper $2.50 ISBN 0–397–31327–6)   72–151469
Little League baseball from the point of view of Jake, who says, "I don't care about anything but baseball"; he never knew his father, and his mother deserted him, but his Uncle Lenny knows how to be a good baseball companion. (Gr 5–6)

Smith, Emma. *No Way of Telling.* New York, Atheneum, 1972. 256 p. map. (A Margaret K. McElderry book) $5.50 ISBN 0–689–30311–4
74–190560
A cozily detailed picture of Welsh cottage life adds conviction to a compelling mystery centered on snow-bound Amy and her grandmother, who are confronted by a huge inarticulate intruder and two other men on skis who claim to be policemen. (Gr 4–7)

Snyder, Zilpha K. *The Egypt Game.* Drawings by Alton Raible. New York, Atheneum, 1967. 215 p. $7.95 ISBN 0–689–300006–9 (paper $1.95 ISBN 0–689–70297–3)   67–10467
In a deserted storage yard behind an antique shop imaginative children play-act the pomp and symbolism of ancient Egypt—interrupted when the reality of the outside world crashes through with near tragedy. (Gr 5–6)

————. *The Headless Cupid.* Illustrated by Alton Raible. New York, Atheneum, 1971. 203 p. $6.95 ISBN 0–689–20687–9 (paper $1.95 ISBN 0–689–70414–3)   78–154763
Imaginative Amanda, a "student" of the occult who resents her mother's remarriage, stirs up her new family in a series of mysterious happenings, including a believable poltergeist. (Gr 4–6)

Southall, Ivan. *Ash Road.* Illustrated by Clem Seale. New York, St. Martin's Press. 1978. 154 p. $6.95. Greenwillow. ISBN 0–688–80135–8 (lib. ed. $6.67 ISBN 0–688–84135–X)   77–15063
A graphic story in which three boys on a trip into the tinder-dry Australian bush country face the disaster of fire after a camping accident. Characters of many ages have been well portrayed. (Gr 5–7)

Spykman, Elizabeth C. *Edie on the Warpath.* New York, Harcourt, Brace & World, 1970. 191 p. Paper $1.45 ISBN 0–15–627650–X   66–14797
Eleven-year-old Edie's "warpath," in suffragette days of 1907, is her personal resistance to restrictions imposed because she is a girl. Her ingenuity, one of

many lovable traits, creates hilarious episodes. (Gr 4–6)

Steig, William. *Abel's Island.* New York, Farrar, Straus & Giroux, 1976. 117 p. $5.95 ISBN 0–374–30010–0 (paper $1.75. Bantam. ISBN 0–553–15019–7)   75–35918
Animated by the author's line-and-gray wash drawings, this Robinson Crusoe-like tale describes the adventures of the gallant mouse Abelard Hassam di Chirico Flint, who is swept from his wife's side in a torrential storm and marooned on a desert island for a year. (Gr 4–6)

————. *Dominic.* New York, Farrar, Straus & Giroux, 1972. 145 p. $6.95 ISBN 0–374–31822–0 70–188272
A hound dog who has set out on the road to adventure heroically aids a variety of animal friends, overcomes the wicked Doomsday Gang, and wins his heart's desire. Line drawings by the author are filled with action and emotion. Also, *The Real Thief* ($4.95 ISBN 0–374–36217–3). (Gr 3–5)

Stevenson, William. *The Bushbabies.* Illustrated by Victor Ambrus. Boston, Houghton Mifflin, 1965. 278 p. $8.95 ISBN 0–395–07116–X   65–22509
All the magical beauty and appeal of primitive Africa is here in the story of a young girl's journey to save her bushbaby pet. (Gr 4–7)

Stolz, Mary. *Cat in the Mirror.* New York, Harper & Row, 1975. 256 p. $6.95 ISBN 0–06–025832–2 (lib. ed. $6.79 ISBN 0–06–025833–0)   75–6307
A fresh style of time-slip story in which a New York City child of today, suffering from a concussion, lives out a parallel family life 3,000 years earlier in Egypt. (Gr 5–7)

Taylor, Mildred D. *Roll of Thunder, Hear My Cry.* Frontispiece by Jerry Pinkney. New York, Dial Press, 1976. 276 p. $7.95 ISBN 0–8037–7473–7
76–2287
A sequel to *Song of the Trees,* this compelling story of the Depression is narrated with the realism of the firsthand experience of Cassie and her family in Mississippi, accepting deprivations in a low-grade black school and doggedly holding on to their farm. (Gr 5–7)

Taylor, Sydney. *All-of-a-Kind Family Downtown.* Illustrations by Beth and Joe Krush. Chicago, Follett Pub. Co., 1972. 187 p. $4.95 ISBN 0–695–80308–5 (lib. ed. $4.98 ISBN 0–695–40308–7; paper $1.25. Dell. ISBN 0–440–42032–6)   70–184789
More childlike fun and mischief with the five little girls and their adored baby brother at the turn of the century on New York's Lower East Side. (Gr 3–6)

Taylor, Theodore. *The Cay*. Garden City, N.Y., Doubleday, 1969. 137 p. $5.95 ISBN 0–385–07906–0 (lib. ed. $6.90 ISBN 0–385–08152–9)   69–15161
Shipwrecked during World War II and stranded on an isolated coral cay, a young white boy of eleven, blinded and helpless, learns human values from his companion in disaster, an elderly West Indian Negro. (Gr 5–9)

Waber, Bernard. *Nobody Is Perfick*. Boston, Houghton Mifflin, 1971. 128 p. $6.95 ISBN 0–395–15991–1
75–161646
In a series of verbal vignettes there is fun with a secret diary, a variety of random nonsense, and jolly revenge on the anti-hero Peter Perfect. Amusing sketches by the author complete an entirely childlike invention. (Gr 1–3)

White, Elwyn B. *The Trumpet of the Swan*. [By] E. B. White. Pictures by Edward Frascino. New York, Harper & Row, 1970. 210 p. $5.95 ISBN 0–06–026397–0 (lib. ed. $5.79 ISBN 0–06–026398–9; paper $1.95 ISBN 0–06–440048–4)   72–112484
A mute young trumpeter swan finds a voice—a fantastic story which blends fresh make-believe and clear knowledge of wildlife, as only the author of *Charlotte's Web* could manage to do. (Gr 3–6)

Wrightson, Patricia. *The Nargun and the Stars*. New York, Atheneum, 1974. 184 p. (A Margaret K. McElderry book) $6.95 ISBN 0–689–30432–3
73–85323
In this absorbing Australian fantasy, Simon and his cousins find themselves menaced by a primeval monster, driven from its original home by encroaching civilization. (Gr 5–up)

———. *A Racecourse for Andy*. Illustrated by Margaret Horder. New York, Harcourt, Brace & World, 1968. 156 p. $5.95 ISBN 0–15–265080–6 68–11507
A mentally retarded boy believes he has bought a race track for three dollars; until a solution to the problem can be found, only the patience and understanding of loyal friends keep him from being hurt. (Gr 4–6)

Zei, Al'ki. *Wildcat under Glass*. Translated from the Greek by Edward Fenton. New York, Holt, Rinehart and Winston, 1968. 177 p. $4.50 ISBN 0–03–089512–X   68–11835
A vivid story with deep implications, set on a small Greek island under prewar German occupation. Also, *Petros' War* ($7.50. Dutton. ISBN 0–525–36962–7). (Gr 5–7)

Stories for Older Boys and Girls

Adams, Richard G. *Watership Down*. New York, Macmillan, 1974. 429 p. maps. $10.95 ISBN 0–02–700030–3   73–6044

An allegorical fantasy of almost epic proportions, set in a world of rabbits in which one group searches to establish a new warren where it can live in peace and safety. Twice a British award-winner. (Gr 6–up)

Aiken, Joan. *Midnight Is a Place*. New York, Viking Press, 1974. 287 p. $6.95 ISBN 0–670–47483–5   74–760

In a Dickensian tale of nineteenth-century England, Lucas and Anna-Marie are caught up in brooding mystery and exploitation in a carpet factory. (Gr 6–up)

Almedingen, Martha E. *Anna (Anna Khlebnikova de Poltoratzky, 1770–1840)*. New York, Farrar, Straus & Giroux, 1972. 180 p. $5.95 ISBN 0–374–30361–4   71–175823

A first-person account of Anna Poltoratzky (great-grandmother of the author) as she grew up. The daughter of a wealthy Moscow merchant, she was educated far above the accepted eighteenth-century standard for women. (Gr 7–9)

———. *Young Mark; the Story of a Venture* [by] E. M. Almedingen. Illustrated by Victor G. Ambrus. New York, Farrar, Straus & Giroux, 1968. 177 p. $3.75 ISBN 0–374–38745–1   68–13675

Using facts from her great grandfather's journal, the author describes in fictional form young Mark's long journey on foot from the Ukraine to St. Petersburg, where his beautiful voice won him fame and royal favor. (Gr 7–9)

Armstrong, William H. *Sounder*. Illustrations by James Barkley. New York, Harper & Row, 1969. 116 p. $5.95 ISBN 0–06–020143–6 (lib. ed. $5.79 ISBN 0–06–020144–4)   70–85030

Courage comes slowly to a young Negro boy humiliated and angry in the course of his father's unjust jail sentence, but learning to read brings new hope. (Gr 5–7)

Benchley, Nathaniel. *Bright Candles; a Novel of the Danish Resistance*. New York, Harper & Row, 1974. 256 p. $6.95 ISBN 0–06–020461–3 (lib. ed. $6.79 ISBN 0–06–020462–1)   73–5477

In this well-researched and gripping story sixteen-year-old Jens Hansen becomes deeply involved in the Danish resistance during the German occupation in World War II. (Gr 7–9)

Brancato, Robin F. *Winning*. New York, Knopf, 1977. 213 p. $7.95 ISBN 0–394–83581–6   77–5632

In a realistic portrayal of dealing with a physical handicap, Gary's paralysis due to a football injury deeply affects his family and his friends. When he confides his sense of hurt to his widowed English teacher, they both come to learn what "winning" means. (Gr 7–up)

Burnford, Sheila E. *Bel Ria*. Boston, Little, Brown, 1978. 215 p. (An Atlantic Monthly Press book) $7.95 ISBN 0–316–77139–2   77–21082

A poignant novel with appeal for both children and adults describes the amazing adventures of a performing dog rescued by a British soldier during the evacuation of Dunkirk. (Gr 6–up)

Burton, Hester. *In Spite of All Terror*. Illustrated by Victor G. Ambrus. Cleveland, World Pub. Co., 1969. 203 p. $5.91. Collins, New York. ISBN 0–529–00611–1   69–13060

An engrossing story of fifteen-year-old Liz, a courageous Cockney orphan who discovers new meaning to life while exiled to the country during World War II. (Gr 6–9)

Catherall, Arthur. *The Strange Intruder*. New York, Lothrop, Lee & Shepard, 1964. 160 p. $6.00 ISBN 0–688–41455–9   65–13393

An engrossing adventure unfolds on the remote Faroes island of Mykines where a shipwreck and a marauding polar bear test the ingenuity of sixteen-year-old Sven. (Gr 5–8)

Christopher, John. *The White Mountains*. New York, Macmillan, 1967. 184 p. $6.95 ISBN 0–02–718360–2   67–3794

Science fiction about a future dictatorship when present cities lie destroyed and weird Tripod creatures pursue boys escaping to an outpost of freedom in the Alps. Sequels: *City of Gold and Lead* (ISBN 0–02–718380–7) and *The Pool of Fire* (ISBN 0–02–718350–5). (Gr. 6–9)

Clapp, Patricia. *Constance; a Story of Early Plymouth*. New York, Lothrop, Lee & Shepard, 1968. 255 p. $6.48 ISBN 0–688–51127–9   68–14064

Realistic details of the life and loves of a pretty young girl in early Plymouth Colony flavor this substantial but lively chronicle, told by the heroine herself. (Gr 6–8)

————. *I'm Deborah Sampson; a Soldier in the War of the Revolution*. New York, Lothrop, Lee & Shepard, 1977. 176 p. $6.75 ISBN 0–688–41799–X (lib. ed. $6.48 ISBN 0–688–51799–4)   76–51770

Biographical fiction about courageous and strong Deborah Sampson, who enlists and serves in the Continental Army to honor the memory of the soldier she loved. Particularly entertaining is the way she conceals her sex. (Gr 7–up)

Cleaver, Vera, *and* Bill Cleaver. *Where the Lilies Bloom*. Philadelphia, Lippincott, 1969. 128 p. $7.95 ISBN 0–397–31111–7   75–82402

A memorable story set in Appalachia, of fourteen-year-old Mary Call and her struggle to keep her motherless family together—and fed—after her father's death. Sequel, *Trial Valley* (ISBN 0–397–31722–0). (Gr 6–8)

Cohen, Barbara. *Bitter Herbs and Honey*. New York, Lothrop, Lee & Shepard, 1976. 159 p. $6.25 ISBN 0–688–41772–8 (lib. ed. $6.00 ISBN 0–688–51772–2)   76–18132

Teenaged Becky, sometimes socially a minority of one in her New Jersey community in 1916 because of her loyalty to her family's Jewish traditions, ends a relationship with an attentive gentile but also refuses an arranged marriage and goes her own way to college. (Gr 6–8)

Collier, James Lincoln, *and* Christopher Collier. *My Brother Sam Is Dead*. New York, Four Winds Press, 1974. 216 p. illus. $6.95 ISBN 0–590–07339–7   74–8350

A grim view of the Revolution in Connecticut, as seen by Tim Meeker, who is unable to accept either the convictions of his Tory parents or those of his "rebel" brother Sam. (Gr 6–9)

Collier, James L. *The Teddy Bear Habit*. New York, Norton, 1967. 177 p. Paper $0.95. Dell. ISBN 0–440–48560–6   67–10317

The young guitar-playing hero of this comic novel, about a mad pursuit and escape in New York City, unknowingly carries stolen jewels inside the toy bear he keeps in his guitar to give him confidence. (Gr 6–8)

Corbett, Scott. *The Discontented Ghost*. New York, Dutton, 1978. 180 p. (A Unicorn book) $7.95 ISBN 0–525–28775–2   78–18013

In Corbett's witty retelling of Oscar Wilde's classic "The Canterville Ghost," the maligned ghost gives his version of what took place at Centerville Chase after the American ambassador and his family moved into this stately old home. (Gr 6–8)

Cormier, Robert. *I Am the Cheese; a Novel*. New York, Pantheon Books, 1977. 233 p. $6.95 ISBN 0–394–83462–3   76–55948

In this chilling indictment of government agencies that use mind control as an acceptable operational activity, fourteen-year-old Adam relives the events of a threatened childhood through a series of taped interviews with a faceless "Brint"—a psychiatrist? or a hostile interrogator? Suspenseful fiction, deftly constructed. (Gr 8–up)

Cresswell, Helen. *The Winter of the Birds*. New York, Macmillan, 1976. 244 p. $8.95 ISBN 0–02–725510–7   75–34278

In an arresting tale of fantasy and realism, the appearance of Patrick Finn affects the lives of young Edward Flack, who dreams of heroes and longs to be one, of elderly Mr. Rudge, who envisions menacing steel birds, and of Uncle Alfred, who at last finds joy after despairing of it. (Gr 5–7)

Degens, T. *Transport 7–41–R*. New York, Viking Press, 1974. 171 p. $5.95 ISBN 0–670–72429–7 (paper $1.25. Dell. ISBN 0–440–99003–3)
74–10930
On a repatriation train running from East Germany to Cologne in 1946, a thirteen-year-old girl, sent away by her family, finds herself enmeshed in the problems of an old grocer who is taking his equally old wife home to die. Powerful and unsentimental. (Gr 6–up)

Dickinson, Peter. *Annerton Pit*. Boston, Little, Brown, 1977. 175 p. (An Atlantic Monthly Press book) $6.95 ISBN 0–316–18430–6
77–9885
It is blind, thirteen-year-old Jake who manages to free his elder brother, his ghost-hunting grandfather, and himself from haunted Annerton Pit and the revolutionaries who hold them prisoners. A thriller. (Gr 5–8)

———. *The Blue Hawk*. Boston, Little, Brown, 1976. 229 p. (An Atlantic Monthly Press book) $8.95 ISBN 0–316–18429–2
76–1857
Set in a mythical kingdom, this engrossing story concerns Tron, an acolyte who breaks a sacred ritual by rescuing a sacrificial hawk and thus causes his king to die. (Gr 8–up)

———. *The Dancing Bear*. Illustrated by David Smee. Boston, Little, Brown, 1973. 244 p. $5.95 ISBN 0–316–18426–8
72–11530
A tale of Byzantium in A.D. 558: when raiding Huns steal fourteen-year-old Lady Ariadne, the slave Silvester (her childhood playmate) gives determined chase, with his engaging trained bear in tow. High adventure, some history, and much fun. (Gr 5–up)

Eckert, Allan W. *Incident at Hawk's Hill*. With illustrations by John Schoenherr. Boston, Little, Brown, 1971. 173 p. $6.95 ISBN 0–316–20866–3 77–143718
"A slightly fictionalized version" of a six-year-old boy's experiences when he was lost on the prairie near Winnipeg in 1870 and protected by a female badger. A compelling story enriched by the vivid details of wildlife. (Gr 5–up)

Engdahl, Sylvia L. *This Star Shall Abide*. Drawings by Richard Cuffari. New York, Atheneum, 1972. 247 p. $6.95 ISBN 0–689–30026–3
79–175553
In another world and another time, Noren, accused of heresy for questioning the "system" and punished by Scholars in the Walled City, is forced to recant and is left with a heavy weight of knowledge. Followed by *Beyond the Tomorrow Mountains* ($7.95 ISBN 0–689–30084–0). (Gr 6–9)

Farmer, Penelope. *Castle of Bone*. New York, Atheneum, 1972. 152 p. (A Margaret K. McElderry book) $4.95 ISBN 0–689–30313–0   78–190553
In a taut, original fantasy, strange, recurring dreams of a castle and the possession of a cupboard capable of reducing anything put in it to an early stage of development plunge two boys and two girls into a complexity of incidents that are amusing and then frightening, when Penn suffers a magical transformation. (Gr 5–8)

Forman, James. *Ring the Judas Bell*. New York, Farrar, Straus & Giroux, 1965. 218 p. $4.95 ISBN 0–374–36304–8 (paper $1.25. Dell. ISBN 0–440–974887)
65–11619
Nicholas and his sister, with other Greek children, are taken by guerilla forces to an internment camp after World War II. A moving story which reveals the horrors of war while it also expresses belief in the power of love. For mature readers. (Gr 8–up)

Fox, Paula. *The Slave Dancer; a Novel*. With illustrations by Eros Keith. Scarsdale, N.Y., Bradbury Press, 1973. 176 p. $8.95 ISBN 0–87888–062–3
73–80642
The harrowing experiences of an ill-fated voyage from Africa when a young New Orleans flute player impressed aboard the evil slave ship must "dance" the imprisoned Africans to give them daily exercise. The 1974 Newbery Medal winner. (Gr 7–9)

Fritz, Jean. *Early Thunder*. Illustrated by Lynd Ward. New York, Coward-McCann, 1967. 255 p. $7.95 ISBN 0–698–20036–5
67–24217
Salem, Massachusetts, and events leading actively to the Revolution provide fresh background for this story of a clear-thinking boy who saw both the Tory and Patriot sides, and took a stand apart from his family. (Gr 6–9)

Gardam, Jane. *A Long Way from Verona*. New York, Macmillan, 1972. 190 p. $4.95 ISBN 0–02–735780–5 (paper $1.25 ISBN 0–02–043220–8)   76–171923
The sensitive portrayal, in a first-person narrative, of Jessica's efforts to be herself and to believe in her ability to write, during a bleak Second World War Yorkshire childhood. (Gr 6–8)

———. *Bilgewater*. New York, Greenwillow Books, 1977. 212 p. $7.25 ISBN 0–688–80108–0 (lib. ed. $6.96 ISBN 0–688–84108–2)   77–2890
Being the only girl living in a boys' boarding school is not easy, especially for someone like Bilgewater ("Bill's daughter") who thinks she is as ugly as her name implies. A funny, poignant story of adolescence. (Gr 8–up)

———. *Smith*. Pictures by Anthony Maitland. New York, Pantheon Books, 1967. 224 p. $5.69 ISBN 0–394–91641–7   67–4223

He was twelve years old, an adept pickpocket in the sordid world of eighteenth-century London's criminals, and his hero was a highwayman. Witnessing a murder did not help matters—but his ingenuity and his courage did. (Gr 6–8)

George, Jean C. *Julie of the Wolves*. Pictures by John Schoenherr. New York, Harper & Row, 1972. 170 p. $5.95 ISBN 0–06–021943–2 (lib. ed. $5.79 ISBN 0–06–021944–0; paper $1.50 ISBN 0–06–440058–1)   72–76509

While running away from an unwanted marriage, a thirteen-year-old Eskimo girl becomes lost on the North Slope of Alaska and is befriended by a wolf pack. The 1973 Newbery Medal winner. (Gr 6–9)

Greene, Bette. *Summer of My German Soldier*. New York, Dial Press, 1973. 230 p. $6.95 ISBN 0–8037–8321–3 (paper $1.75. Bantam. ISBN 0–553–10192–7)   73–6025

Sheltering an escaped German prisoner of war is the beginning of shattering experiences for twelve-year-old Patty Bergen. (Gr 5–7)

Guy, Rosa. *The Friends*. New York, Holt, Reinhart and Winston, 1973. 203 p. $5.95 ISBN 0–03–007876–8   72–11068

An intense, probing picture of problems of adjusting to life in Harlem for Phyllisia Cathy from the West Indies. (Gr 7–9)

Hamilton, Virginia. *Arilla Sun Down*. New York, Greenwillow Books/Morrow, 1976. 249 p. $8.25 ISBN 0–688–80058–0 (lib. ed. $7.92 ISBN 0–688–84058–2)   76–13180

Arilla, twelve years old and from an Amerind-black family, tells her story, sometimes in flashback remembrances expressed in partial sentences. She relates her devotion to her parents, her love-hate feelings for her arrogant older brother Sun Run who stresses his Indian heritage, and her gropings for identity. (Gr 8–up)

———. *M. C. Higgins, the Great*. New York, Macmillan, 1974. 278 p. $7.95 ISBN 0–02–742480–4   72–92439

As a slag heap from strip mining creeps closer to his house in the Ohio hills, M. C., a totally engaging young hero, is torn between trying to get his family away and fighting for the home they love. The 1975 Newbery Medal winner. (Gr 6–8)

———. *The Planet of Junior Brown*. New York, Macmillan, 1971. 210 p. $7.95 ISBN 0–02–742510–

X (paper $0.95 ISBN 0–02–043530–4) 71–155264

A strong story, of a city black boy's struggle to care for abandoned children in an underground world of the homeless. Realism and fantasy create a book which may be read on two levels. (Gr 6–9)

Haugaard, Erik C. *The Little Fishes*. Illustrated by Milton Johnson. Boston, Houghton Mifflin, 1967. 214 p. $6.95 ISBN 0–395–06802–9   67–1065

A moving story about abandoned Italian children, the "little fishes," caught between armies in World War II. (Gr 6–8)

Hinton, S. E. *The Outsiders*. New York, Viking Press, 1967. 188 p. $6.50 ISBN 0–670–53257–6 67–1284

A seventeen-year-old author depicts the youth-gang world following Pony-Boy, an orphan "Greaser," in his search for meaning in the gang rumbles and in Johnny's part in manslaughter, his curious heroism, and, later, his death. (Gr 6–up)

Holland, Isabelle. *Of Love and Death and Other Journeys*. Philadelphia, Lippincott, 1975. 159 p. $6.95 ISBN 0–397–31566–X   74–30012

From a happy, easygoing life as an emigré to Italy, Meg is thrown into an emotionally charged situation, with her mother dying of cancer and the father she has never known suddenly appearing. An incisive portrait of a young girl's growth. (Gr 8–up)

Holm, Anne S. *North to Freedom*. Tanslated from the Danish by L. W. Kingsland. New York, Harcourt, Brace & World, 1965. 190 p. $5.95 ISBN 0–15–257550–2   65–12612

The haunting odyssey of a young escapee from a central European concentration camp and his search for faith and identity as he struggles to reach Denmark. (Gr 6–up)

Hunt, Irene. *Across Five Aprils*. Chicago, Follett, 1964. 223 p. $4.95 ISBN 0–695–80100–7 (lib. ed. $4.98 ISBN 0–695–40100–9)   64–17209

A moving story, based on family records, of the impact of the Civil War on an Illinois family—with two sons and a cousin fighting for the Union, one son for the South, and young Jethro shouldering the burdens of the farm. (Gr 5–7)

———. *The Soul Brothers and Sister Lou*. New York, Scribner, 1968. 241 p. $8.95 ISBN 0–684–12661–3   68–29365

In this story of Harlem teenagers, Louretta Hawkins discovers what hatred is when young Jethro dies in gunplay. (Gr 7–9)

Jones, Adrienne. *The Hawks of Chelney*. Drawings by Stephen Gammell. New York, Harper & Row,

1978. 245 p. $7.95 ISBN 0–06–023057–6 (lib. ed. $7.89 ISBN 0–06–023058–4)   77–11855

A timeless seacoast setting, of rough cliffs and nesting birds, contributes to an almost mythological sense of conflict when villagers turn against a boy who loves the hawks. (Gr 8–up)

Jones, Diana Wynne. *Dogsbody.* New York, Greenwillow Books, 1977. 242 p. $7.25 ISBN 0–688–80074–2 (lib. ed. $6.96 ISBN 0–688–84074–4)   76–28715

A high-flown fantasy introduces the Dog Star Sirius (convicted of murder) and his heavenly peers to some very real characters, human and canine, when Sirius is sentenced to an earthly dog's life. (Gr 5–8)

Kerr, Judith. *The Other Way Round.* New York, Coward, McCann & Geoghegan, 1975. 256 p. $7.95 ISBN 0–698–20335–6   75–4254

In an absorbing sequel to *When Hitler Stole Pink Rabbit,* Anna, now a teenager, spends the war years working in London and developing her talents as an artist while her brother Max, a university student, is at first interned and then allowed to serve in the RAF. (Gr 7–up)

Kerr, M. E. *Dinky Hocker Shoots Smack.* New York, Harper & Row, 1972. 198 p. $6.95 ISBN 0–06–023150–5   72–80366

Dinky's problem is that under a flip facade dwells a fat, unhappy teenager crying for the attention of a busy, do-gooder mother. A fresh, funny look at contemporary girls by an understanding author. (Gr 7–9)

Lee, Mildred. *Fog.* New York, Seabury Press, 1972. 250 p. $5.95 ISBN 0–8164–3092–6   72–81259

In a realistic high school story set in a small town, Luke is sobered by his father's death and the loss of his girl friend. (Gr 7–9)

——. *The Skating Rink.* New York, Seabury Press, 1969. 126 p. $6.50 ISBN 0–8164–3063–2 69–13443

A boy, closed within himself as a result of a childhood tragedy, finds release through his part in the opening of a neighborhood skating rink. (Gr 6–8)

LeGuin, Ursula K. *Very Far Away from Anywhere Else.* New York, Atheneum, 1976. 89 p. $6.95 ISBN 0–689–30525–7   76–4472

In this short but resonant novel of precollege youth, Owen, an intellectual, and Natalie, a serious musician, wrestle with personal integrity as they consider their priorities. (Gr 8–up)

——. *A Wizard of Earthsea.* Berkeley, Calif., Parnassus Press, 1968. 205 p. $7.50 ISBN 0–87466–057–2 (lib. ed. $7.11 ISBN 0–87466–032–7)   68–21992

Young Sparrowhawk, having used his power arrogantly during his apprenticeship to the Master Wizard of Earthsea, must undertake a quest to face the Nameless Thing called up by his meddling. Maps and drawings by Ruth Robbins. Sequels, *The Tombs of Atuan* ($7.95. Atheneum, New York. ISBN 0–689–20680–1) and *The Farthest Shore* ($8.95 ISBN 0–689–30054–9). (Gr 6–9)

L'Engle, Madeleine. *A Swiftly Tilting Planet.* New York, Farrar, Straus & Giroux, 1978. 278 p. $7.95 ISBN 0–374–37362–0   78–9648

In this sequel to *A Wrinkle in Time* ($6.95 ISBN 0–374–38613–7), Charles Wallace Murry, now fifteen, sets out in a world threatened by nuclear holocaust to match wits with the evil Echthroi. (Gr 6–8)

Lester, Julius. *Long Journey Home: Stories from Black History.* New York, Dial Press, 1972. 147 p. $5.95 ISBN 0–8037–4953–8 (paper $0.95. Dell. ISBN 0–440–94954–8)   75–181791

Six pieces of historical fiction sensitively portraying the black experience in America. (Gr 7–up)

Levoy, Myron. *Alan and Naomi.* New York, Harper & Row, 1977. 192 p. $6.95 ISBN 0–06–023799–6 (lib. ed. $6.79 ISBN 0–06–023800–3)   76–41522

Alan, a very ordinary junior high school student, befriends twelve-year-old Naomi who is so traumatized by her father's death at the hands of the Nazis that she cannot speak. (Gr 6–8)

Lipsyte, Robert. *The Contender.* New York, Harper & Row, 1967. 182 p. $5.95 ISBN 0–06–023919–0 (lib. ed. $5.79 ISBN 0–06–023920–4)   67–3590

A boy in Harlem finds through boxing a way out of the dead-end of drop-out and ghetto crime, in a novel of tense action and strong characterization, written with gripping vitality. (Gr 7–up)

——. *One Fat Summer.* New York, Harper & Row, 1977. 152 p. (An Ursula Nordstrom book) $6.95 ISBN 0–06–023895–X (lib. ed. $6.79 ISBN 0–06–023896–6)   76–49746

An overweight adolescent's humorous approach to the harsh realities of a crucial summer help build his self-esteem. (Gr 6–9)

Lively, Penelope. *The House in Norham Gardens.* New York, Dutton, 1974. 154 p. $6.95 ISBN 0–525–32315–5   74–7891

A carved shield brought from New Guinea years ago by Clare's grandfather causes this imaginative fourteen-year-old girl disturbing dreams which transport her back into the past. Superb characterizations of Clare, the elderly aunts with whom she lives, and a friendly Oxford student from Uganda. (Gr 6–8)

Lowry, Lois. *A Summer to Die*. Illustrated by Jenni Oliver. Boston, Houghton Mifflin, 1977. 154 p. $6.95 ISBN 0-395-25338-1   77-83

When Meg's beautiful and popular sister, whom Meg always envied, falls victim to leukemia, a touching relationship develops as the close-knit family copes with grief. (Gr 5-7)

McCaffrey, Ann. *Dragonsong*. New York, Atheneum, 1976. 202 p. map. $7.95 ISBN 0-689-30507-9   75-30530

Forbidden by her stern father to make the music she loves, Menolly runs away from Half-Circle Sea Hold on the planet Pern, takes shelter with fire lizards, and finds a new life opening up for her. Followed by *Dragonsinger* (ISBN 0-689-30570-2). (Gr 6-8)

McIlwraith, Maureen M. H. M. *A Sound of Chariots*, by Mollie Hunter. New York, Harper & Row, 1972. 242 p. $6.89 ISBN 0-06-022669-2   72-76523

Bridie, nearly devastated by the death of the father she idolized and subsequently aware of the impermanence of life, struggles to get the education she craves, to fulfill a dream of writing. A powerful, sensitive novel of a young girl's growing. (Gr 6-up)

McKinley, Robin. *Beauty; a Retelling of the Story of Beauty & the Beast*. New York, Harper & Row, 1978. 247 p. $7.95 ISBN 0-06-024149-7 (lib. ed. $7.49 ISBN 0-06-024150-0)   77-25636

An engrossing expansion of the traditional tale in which Beauty recounts her romantic story. (Gr 7-up)

Mathis, Sharon B. *Teacup Full of Roses*. New York, Viking Press, 1972. 125 p. $5.95 ISBN 0-670-69434-7   74-162675

A haunting picture of the inner-city drug problem shown within a family which sees the youngest of its three teenage sons killed because of the eldest's addiction. (Gr 6-8)

Mayne, William. *Earthfasts*. New York, Dutton, 1967. 154 p. $7.95 ISBN 0-525-29008-7   67-84033

Local legend and a time-space dislocation are intricately interwoven in an absorbing story in which two English boys witness an eighteenth-century drummer boy's emergence from the earth, and suffer cataclysmic sequences. (Gr 6-8)

Morey, Walter. *Kävik the Wolf Dog*. Illustrated by Peter Parnall. New York, Dutton, 1968. 192 p. $6.95 ISBN 0-525-33093-3 (paper $1.95 ISBN 0-525-45018-1)   68-24727

A champion sled dog, after an almost fatal plane crash, makes a valiant escape alone across the Arctic wastes, back to his real friends. (Gr 5-8)

Moser, Don. *A Heart to the Hawks*. New York, Atheneum, 1975. 208 p. (A Margaret K. McElderry book) $6.95 ISBN 0-689-50024-6   74-18190

Fourteen-year-old Mike's passion for natural history causes him to fight a land developer's destruction of his woodland haven, first with persuasion and then with violence. A story of the 1940s that perceptively and humorously reveals Mike's emotions about his pet hawk and neighboring Angeline. (Gr 7-up)

Murray, Michele. *The Crystal Nights; a Novel*. New York, Seabury Press, 1973. 310 p. $7.95 ISBN 0-8164-3098-5   72-93807

Stagestruck Elly's problems and desires are sympathetically portrayed: work in the high school drama group; yearning to move from farm to a town; and facing up to family crowding by Nazi-escaped relatives and a girl cousin used to luxuries. (Gr 7-9)

Myers, Walter D. *Fast Sam, Cool Clyde, and Stuff*. New York, Viking Press, 1975. 190 p. $6.95 ISBN 0-670-30874-9   74-32383

A humorous recounting by Stuff, a newcomer, of experiences of the 116th Street Good People—Harlem teenagers who share loneliness and friendship, good and bad times. Also set in Harlem is *It Ain't All for Nothin'* ($8.95 ISBN 0-670-40301-6). (Gr 7-up)

Nöstlinger, Christine. *Fly Away Home*. Translated from the German by Anthea Bell. New York, Watts, 1975. 135 p. $5.88 ISBN 0-531-01096-1 75-16255

Christel is the thoroughly engaging heroine of an episodic story of deprivations in occupied Vienna at the close of World War II. (Gr 6-7)

O'Brien, Robert C. *Z for Zachariah*. New York, Atheneum, 1975. 249 p. $8.95 ISBN 0-689-30442-0 (paper $1.25. Dell. ISBN 0-440-99901-4)   74-76736

Seemingly the only survivor of the holocaust of a war, fifteen-year-old Ann ingeniously keeps alive in a valley singularly unaffected by radiation and is relieved to see a man in a plastic safe-suit—until she comes to know him as a tyrant from whom she must escape. (Gr 8-up)

O'Dell, Scott. *The Black Pearl*. Illustrated by Milton Johnson. Boston, Houghton Mifflin, 1967. 140 p. $5.95 ISBN 0-395-06961-0   67-23311

A haunting, legendlike novel of Mexican Pearl divers, especially of young Ramon who finds a fabulous pearl in the cave of the Manta Diablo. (Gr 7-up)

———. *The King's Fifth*. Decorations and maps by Samuel Bryant. Boston, Houghton Mifflin, 1966. 264 p. $5.95 ISBN 0-395-06963-7 (paper $1.50. Dell. ISBN 0-440-44538-8)   66-10726

An exciting story unfolds as young Estéban de Sandoval, cartographer with General Alarcón off New Spain in 1539, tells how he joined a captain of Coronado's army on an expedition to the Seven Cities. (Gr 7–9)

————. *Sing Down the Moon*. Boston, Houghton Mifflin, 1970. 137 p. $3.95 ISBN 0–395–10919–1 (paper $0.95. Dell. ISBN 0–440–47975–4)
71–98513
With quiet dignity a young Navaho girl recounts the tragic story of her people's long march into captivity. (Gr 5–8)

Orgel, Doris. *The Devil in Vienna*. New York, Dial Press, 1978. 246 p. $7.95 ISBN 0–8037–1920–5
78–51319
The friendship between a Jewish girl and the daughter of a Nazi officer survives the Anschluss of 1938 in occupied Vienna. (Gr 6–8)

Paterson, Katherine. *The Master Puppeteer*. Illustrated by Haru Wells. New York, Crowell, 1976. 179 p. $6.95 ISBN 0–690–00913–5   75–8614
Eighteenth-century Japan, with famine, violence, and the patterned world of the puppet theater, frames a powerful story of friendship and loyalty, as young Jiro, an apprentice to the Bunraku puppet troop, unwittingly becomes embroiled in the affairs of a Robin Hood-like brigand. Haru Wells's black-and-white drawings heighten the strength of the story. 1977 National Book Award.
Two other novels set in early Japan are *The Sign of the Chrysanthemum* ($7.95 ISBN 0–690–73625–8) and *Of Nightingales That Weep* (ISBN 0–690–00485–0). (Gr 6–8)

Paton Walsh, Jill. *Fireweed*. New York, Farrar, Straus & Giroux, 1970. 133 p. (An Ariel book) $3.95 ISBN 0–374–32310–0   73–109554
Tender, poignant, and memorable is this story of a boy and girl who in war-ravaged London find temporary refuge together from Hitler's bombs. (Gr 6–up)

————. *Goldengrove*. New York, Farrar, Straus & Giroux, 1972. 130 p. $4.50 ISBN 0–374–32696–7
72–81484
The agonies of growing up are depicted in a moving, poetic account of Madge's traumatic experiences in a golden September when she put childhood behind her. (Gr 6–8)

————. *Unleaving*. New York, Farrar, Straus & Giroux, 1976. 145 p. $5.95 ISBN 0–374–38042–2
76–8857
The events of two summers are enmeshed as Madge of *Goldengrove* looks back on herself in her late teens,

meeting Patrick, who will become her husband, and witnessing the death of his retarded young sister. (Gr 7–up)

Peck, Robert N. *A Day No Pigs Would Die*. New York, Knopf, 1972. 150 p. $6.95 ISBN 0–394–48235–2   72–259
A spare telling captures the flavor of Vermont farm life, Shaker traditions, warm family life, and the agonies of growing up, from the point of view of nearly thirteen-year-old Rob who must face up to the sacrifice of his pet pig and, shortly after, the death of his father. (Gr 7–up)

Petry, Ann L. *Tituba of Salem Village*. New York, Thomas Y. Crowell, 1964. 254 p. $8.95 ISBN 0–690–82677–X   64–20691
Of mature interest, this is the biographical story of a Negro slave from Barbados who in Salem, Massachusetts, was tried for witchcraft in 1692. A strong picture of mounting mass hysteria. (Gr 8–up)

Peyton, K. M., *pseud. Flambards*. Illustrated by Victor G. Ambrus. Cleveland, World Pub. Co., 1968. 206 p. $4.91. Collins, New York. ISBN 0–529–00507–7   68–3561
A strong young novel that tells of violent conflicts on a horse-mad English estate where orphaned Christina's problems deepen in romance. Sequels include *The Edge of the Cloud* ($4.86 ISBN 0–529–00712–6). (Gr 6–9)

————. *Pennington's Last Term*. Illustrated by the author. New York, Crowell, 1971. 216 p. $6.95 ISBN 0–690–61271–0   75–139099
A British school story, fast and compelling. Penn hates the world, defies authority, and plays the piano "like an angel." He tops his 196-pound hulk with shoulder-length hair, aimlessly muddles most encounters, and seems headed for reform school to the strains of a Bach cantata but finally licks the establishment. Followed by *The Beethoven Medal* (ISBN 0–690–12846–0). (Gr 6–9)

Pope, Elizabeth M. *The Perilous Gard*. Illustrated by Richard Cuffari. Boston, Houghton Mifflin, 1974. 280 p. $5.95 ISBN 0–395–18512–2   73–21648
A well-wrought, suspensefully told fantasy in which imprisoned Kate finds herself struggling for a young man's life against the power of the Queen of the Faery Folk. (Gr 5–up)

Preussler, Otfried. *The Satanic Mill*. Translated by Anthea Bell. New York, Macmillan, 1973. 250 p. $5.95 ISBN 0–02–775170–8 (paper $1.95 ISBN 0–02–044770–1)
72–90992

A West German prize-winning story of black magic perpetrated in medieval times at a mill which holds would-be apprentices in thrall to a demonic master. (Gr 6–8)

Raskin, Ellen. *Figgs & Phantoms*. New York, Dutton, 1974. 152 p. $7.50 ISBN 0–525–29680–8 73–17309
Fat, unattractive Mona Lisa Figg, saddled with an eccentric set of relatives, comes to accept the death of a dearly loved uncle. A poignant tale enriched by brilliant word play and inventiveness. (Gr 5–8)

————. *The Westing Game*. New York, Dutton, 1978. 185 p. $7.95 ISBN 0–525–42320–6 77–18866
In a swiftly paced mystery, the handpicked tenants of Sunset Towers are launched on a peculiar treasure hunt to find a murderer and win a fortune. A brilliant and very funny story—the winner of the 1979 Newberry Medal. (Gr 6–8)

Richards, Adrienne. *Pistol*. Boston, Little, Brown, 1969. 245 p. $5.95 ISBN 0–316–74320–8 69–17753
A richly detailed story of a boy in Montana cow country during the 1930s, who refuses to be suppressed by the failures of his family but makes his own way in the tough world of the wranglers. (Gr 7–up)

Richter, Hans P. *I Was There*. Translated by Edite Kroll. New York, Holt, Rinehart & Winston, 1972. 206 p. $5.95 ISBN 0–03–088372–5 72–75681
The author describes in memorable fashion what happened to him and two of his friends from the time they joined Hitler's Youth Movement at the age of eight through their days on the western front when they had nothing left but despair. (Gr 6–8)

Roberts, Willo D. *The View from the Cherry Tree*. New York, Atheneum, 1975. 181 p. $7.95 ISBN 0–689–30483–8 75–6759
A compelling murder mystery set against the background confusion of wedding preparations. No one except the unidentified murderer will believe that Rob has witnessed a murder, but the terrifying situation is lightened by his ingenuity and the independent behavior of S.O.B., his pestiferous cat. (Gr 5–9)

Roth, Arthur J. *The Iceberg Hermit*. New York, Four Winds Press, 1974. 201 p. $6.95 ISBN 0–590–07301–X (paper $1.25 ISBN 0–590–01582–6) 74–7435
Shipwrecked in 1757 on an iceberg in the Arctic seas, seventeen-year-old Allan undertakes a seemingly hopeless struggle for survival, his loneliness relieved by the companionship of an orphaned polar bear. (Gr 6–8)

Stolz, Mary S. *The Edge of Next Year*. New York, Harper & Row, 1974. 195 p. (An Ursula Nordstrom book) $6.79 ISBN 0–06–025858–6 74–3587
A realistic picture of how fourteen-year-old Orin manages his household after an automobile accident claims his mother and his father drowns his sorrow in alcohol. (Gr 6–8)

Suhl, Yuri. *Uncle Misha's Partisans*. New York, Four Winds Press, 1973. 211 p. $6.95 ISBN 0–590–07295–1 73–76459
A gripping story of how orphaned Motele, in World War II Ukraine, uses his violin playing to serve a partisan band in an assignment against the Nazis. (Gr 6–8)

Sutcliff, Rosemary. *Blood Feud*. New York, Dutton, 1977. 144 p. $6.95 ISBN 0–525–26730–1 76–58502
The British prizewinning writer makes vivid the long trail of adventure taken by Jestyn Englishman with his Viking captor on an avenging quest from Britain to Byzantium. (Gr 6–8)

————. *The Witch's Brat*. Illustrated by Richard Lebenson. New York, Walck, 1970. 144 p. $6.95 ISBN 0–8098–3095–7 73–119575
In a moving story set in twelfth-century England, a crippled lad finds both sanctuary and purpose in the monastery at Winchester. (Gr 5–8)

Thiele, Colin. *Blue Fin*. Pictures by Roger Haldane. New York, Harper & Row, 1974. 243 p. $6.79 ISBN 0–06–026105–6 (paper $1.50 ISBN 0–06–440077–8) 73–14328
A prizewinning Australian story in which gangling Luke, a teenager reluctantly admitted to the crew of his father's tuna-fishing boat, becomes a hero after grueling experiences. Also, *Fight against Albatross Two* (ISBN 0–06–026099–8). (Gr 5–8)

Thrasher, Crystal. *The Dark Didn't Catch Me*. New York, Atheneum, 1975. 182 p. (A Margaret K. McElderry book) $7.95 ISBN 0–689–50025–4 74–18193
In Indiana during the Great Depression, Seeley rises above family deprivations, personal discomfitures, and neighborhood tragedies, maintaining her spirits in a private hideaway where she can read and write. (Gr 5–7)

Townsend, John R. *The Intruder*. Illustrated by Graham Humphreys. Philadelphia, Lippincott, 1970. 176 p. $7.95 ISBN 0–397–31126–5 79–101903
A suspenseful account of Arnold Haithwaite's dilemma and peril when a stranger, in the guise of a relative, takes control of the boy's grandfather. (Gr 6–9)

————. *The Summer People*. Philadelphia, Lippincott, 1972. 223 p. $7.95 ISBN 0–397–31421–3
72–3270
A picture of boy-girl relationships in 1939 which relates to those of youth today. (Gr 7–up)

Westall, Robert. *The Machine Gunners*. New York, Greenwillow Books/Morrow, 1976. 186 p. $7.25 ISBN 0–688–80055–6 (lib. ed. $6.96 ISBN 0–688–84055–8)
76–13630
Chas, a teenager and the possessor of a machine gun found in a downed German plane, has but one desire—to use it against the enemy. A gripping tale, the 1976 Carnegie Medal winner. (Gr 6–9)

Wilkinson, Brenda S. *Ludell and Willie*. New York, Harper & Row, 1977. 181 p. $5.95 ISBN 0–06–026487–X (lib. ed. $5.79 ISBN 0–06–026488–8)
76–18402
In this sequel to *Ludell* the spunky heroine, now a senior in high school, is in love with Willie, the boy next door. Their romance flourishes despite frustrations due to a strict and ailing grandmother. Preceded by *Ludell* (ISBN 0–06–026491–8; lib. ed. ISBN 0–06–026492–6). (Gr 5–9)

Woodford, Peggy. *Please Don't Go*. New York, Dutton, 1973. 187 p. $6.95 ISBN 0–525–37140–0
72–89840
In an evocative story, an English teenage girl recounts two summers spent at a French seaside resort, the first dominated by her infatuation with an older man, the second by her tragic first love. (Gr 6–up)

Yep, Laurence. *Child of the Owl*. New York, Harper & Row, 1977. 217 p. $5.95 ISBN 0–06–026739–9 (lib. ed. $5.79 ISBN 0–06–026743–7) 76–24314
A haunting story, contemporary in feeling, of life in San Francisco's Chinatown over a decade ago. (Gr 6–up)

————. *Dragonwings*. New York, Harper & Row, 1975. 248 p. $6.95 ISBN 0–06–026737–2 (lib. ed. $6.79 ISBN 0–06–026738–0) 74–2625
A sensitive perception of oriental tradition permeates this credible historical fiction (with an element of fantasizing) in which Moon Shadow and his gentle father Windrider, an inventive genius, observe life among the Tang people and white "demons" in San Francisco of the early 1900s. (Gr 6–up)

Folklore

Aardema, Verna. *Why Mosquitoes Buzz in People's Ears, a West African Tale.* Pictures by Leo and Diane Dillon. New York, Dial Press, 1975. [32] p. $7.95 ISBN 0–8037–6089–2 (lib. ed. $7.45 ISBN 0–8037–6087–6; paper $2.50 ISBN 0–8037–6088–4) 74–2886

A repetitive tale—source not given—explains why mosquitoes buzz in people's ears. Stylized full-color illustrations suggest West African art. The 1976 Caldecott Medal winner. (Gr 2–4)

Alegria, Ricardo E. *The Three Wishes; a Collection of Puerto Rican Folktales.* Selected and adapted by Ricardo E. Alegria. Translated by Elizabeth Culbert. Illustrated by Lorenzo Homar. New York, Harcourt, Brace & World, 1969. 128 p. $6.75 ISBN 0–15–28687–2 69–13770

A collection of tales, selected by the director of the Puerto Rican Institute of Culture, revealing the blend of Indian, Spanish, and African cultures. (Gr 4–6)

Alger, Leclaire. *Twelve Great Black Cats, and Other Eerie Tales,* by Sorche Nic Leodhas. New York, Dutton, 1971. 173 p. $6.95 ISBN 0–525–41575–0 73–135855

A vigorous, fresh selection of Scottish ghost stories suitable for telling and for reading aloud. Vera Bock's illustrations bring out the eeriness and, at times, the humor in the text. (Gr 4–7)

Bang, Molly G. *Wiley and the Hairy Man.* Adapted from an American Folk Tale. New York, Macmillan, 1976. 64 p. (Ready-to-read) $7.95 ISBN 0–02–708370–5 75–38581

A brief retelling of an Alabama folktale about the boy Wiley who has heard that "the Hairy Man will get you if you don't watch out." The author's expressive black-and-white drawings illustrate the text. (Gr 2–3)

Barth, Edna. *Cupid and Psyche, a Love Story.* Retold. Pictures by Ati Forberg. New York, Seabury Press, 1976. 64 p. (A Clarion book) $6.95 ISBN 0–8164–3174–4 76–8821

A lucid retelling of the myth about the Greek god of love, who succumbed to the beauty of the mortal maiden Psyche. Handsomely illustrated. (Gr 4–6)

———. *Witches, Pumpkins, and Grinning Ghosts; the Story of Halloween Symbols.* Illustrated by Ursula Arndt. New York, Seabury Press, 1972. 95 p. $6.95 ISBN 0–8164–3087–X 72–75705

Explains the origins of and relates stories associated with familiar Halloween symbols. (Gr 3–6)

Bason, Lillian. *Those Foolish Molboes!* Illustrated by Margot Tomes. New York, Coward, McCann & Geoghegan, 1977. 47 p. (A Break-of-day book) $4.98 ISBN 0–698–20397–6 76–42459

Three easy-to-read and lively stories about Danish fisherfolk who are both clever and foolish. Told in the pattern of universal noodlehead tales and illustrated with humor. (Gr 2–3)

Belpré, Pura. *Perez y Martina; un cuento Folklórico Puertorriqueño.* Illustrated by Carlos Sánchez. New York, Frederick Warne Co., 1966. 64 p. Rev. ed. $5.95 ISBN 0–7232–6017–6 66–95610

The droll Puerto Rican folktale about the mouse and the cockroach has its original bright picture-book format for this new printing in Spanish. (Gr 2–4)

Bernstein, Margery, *and* Janet Kobrin. *The First Morning, an African Myth.* Retold. Illustrated by Enid Warner Romanek. New York, Scribner, 1976. [48] p. $5.95 ISBN 0–684–14533–2   75–27705
Dramatic black-and-white illustrations lend power to this easy-to-read story based on a creation myth of the Sukuma people. (K–Gr 3)

Bryan, Ashley. *The Ox of the Wonderful Horns, and Other African Folktales.* Retold and illustrated by Ashley Bryan. New York, Atheneum, 1971. 42 p. $6.95 ISBN 0–689–20690–9   75–154749
Bryan's striking African-style drawings impart the flavor of these five appealing, humorous, and easy-to-read folktales. (Gr 2–5)

Chafetz, Henry. *Thunderbird, and Other Stories.* Illustrated by Ronni Solbert. New York, Pantheon, 1964. 41 p. $5.99 ISBN 0–394–91747–2   64–18317
Red-and-black illustrations in the style of Indian sand paintings, on brown paper, and a sparse, unembellished storyteller's style appropriate to American Indian legend combine to make a distinctive book. (Gr 3–5)

Colwell, Eileen H. *Round About and Long Ago; Tales from the English Counties.* Illustrated with lino-cuts by Anthony Colbert. Boston, Houghton Mifflin, 1974. 124 p. $4.95 ISBN 0–395–18515–7 73–21962
Twenty-eight short tales impeccably retold by an English storyteller who keeps the crispness and full humor of old folktales while also providing color and background. (Gr 3–5)

Courlander, Harold. *The Piece of Fire and Other Haitian Tales.* Illustrated by Beth and Joe Krush. New York, Harcourt, Brace & World, 1964. 128 p. $4.95 ISBN 0–15–261610–1   64–12507
These twenty-six tales of sly trickery among animals and people include some from this folklorist's *Uncle Bouqui of Haiti* (now out of print). (Gr 4–7)

————, *comp. Olode the Hunter, and Other Tales from Nigeria*, by Harold Courlander with Ezekiel A. Eshugbayi. Illustrated by Enrico Arno. New York, Harcourt, Brace & World, 1968. 153 p. $4.50 ISBN 0–15–257826–9   68–13370
Creation myths and tales of the trickster hero, Ijapa the tortoise, are relayed authentically in good storytelling style. (Gr 4–6)

Curtis, Edward S. *The Girl Who Married a Ghost and Other Tales from the North American Indian.* Edited by John Bierhorst. New York, Four Winds Press, 1978. 115 p. $9.95 ISBN 0–590–07505–5   77–21515
An authoritative selection of nine tales, with pictures superbly well produced in sepia from the many taken by Curtis, the famous photographer of Indian life. (Gr 5–up)

D'Aulaire, Ingri. *D'Aulaires' Trolls.* Garden City, N.Y., Doubleday, 1972. 62 p. $5.95 ISBN 0–385–08255–X (lib. ed. $6.90 ISBN 0–385–01275–6)   76–158897
Descriptions and stories of many types of Norwegian trolls—mountain, water, and forest trolls; one- to twelve-headed species; keepers of cats, horses, and cocks—all vigorously depicted in full-color stone lithographs characteristic of the artists Ingri and Edgar Parin D'Aulaire. (Gr 3–6)

————, *and* Edgar P. d'Aulaire. *Norse Gods and Giants.* Garden City, N.Y., Doubleday, 1967. 154 p. $8.95 ISBN 0–385–04908–0 (lib. ed. $9.90 ISBN 0–385–04908–0)   67–19109
A lavishly illustrated presentation of Norse myths, with clear identification of the gods and other distinctive mythological figures. (Gr 4–6)

De Regniers, Beatrice S. *Little Sister and the Month Brothers.* Retold. Pictures by Margot Tomes. New York, Seabury Press, 1976. [48] p. (A Clarion book) $8.00 ISBN 0–8164–3147–7   75–4594
In a direct retelling of the old Slavic tale, the author describes a little girl who is befriended by the twelve Month Brothers when her cruel stepmother sends her out into the snow to gather violets and strawberries. (K–Gr 3)

Farmer, Penelope. *Daedalus and Icarus.* Illustrated by Chris Connor. New York, Harcourt Brace Jovanovich, 1971. [47] p. $4.95 ISBN 0–15–221212–4   71–96318
Relayed in simple prose and colorful paintings the myth follows Daedalus from his imprisonment in the Minoan labyrinth to the fatal flight with homemade wings and the loss of Icarus. (Gr 3–6)

Faulkner, William J. *The Days When the Animals Talked; Black American Folktales and How They Came to Be.* Illustrations by Troy Howell. Chicago, Follett Pub. Co., 1977. 190 p. $7.95 ISBN 0–695–80755–2 (lib. ed. $7.98 ISBN 0–695–40755–4)   76–50315
Eleven stories heard from a former slave, demonstrating the spirit of his people in enduring the injus-

tices and cruelty of plantation slave days, precede some two dozen Brer Rabbit tales, retold in standard English. (Gr 5–up)

Fuja, Abayomi, *comp. Fourteen Hundred Cowries, and Other African Tales*. With an introduction by Anne Pellowski. Illustrated by Ademola Olugebefola. New York, Lothrop, Lee & Shepard, 1971. 256 p. $6.48 ISBN 0–688–51240–2   79–142811
From the Yoruba of West Africa come these thirty-one authentic tales designed to entertain and to explain the ways of men and beasts. The artist's use of traditional African motifs in his striking black-and-white drawings enhances the text. (Gr 3–6)

Ginsburg, Mirra. *How the Sun Was Brought Back to the Sky*. Adapted from a Slovenian folk tale. Pictures by José Aruego and Ariane Dewey. New York, Macmillan, 1975. [32] p. $6.95 ISBN 0–02–735750–3   74–19060
In a pleasingly adapted cumulatve tale, chick and entourage coax the sun out of his house and help him to shine again. The large pictures have fresh bright colors and humorous details. (K–Gr 2)

Godden, Rumer. *The Old Woman Who Lived in a Vinegar Bottle*. New York, Viking Press, 1972. [48] p. $4.95 ISBN 0–670–52318–6   77–168563
In this expanded version of "The Fisherman and His Wife," it is an old woman and her cat who take advantage of the fish's grateful gift-giving. Mairi Hedderwick's watercolor pictures are refreshing. (Gr 1–4)

Grimm, Jakob L. K. *King Thrushbeard; a Story of the Brothers Grimm*. With pictures by Felix Hoffmann. New York, Harcourt, Brace & World, 1970. [32] p. $5.95 ISBN 0–15–242940–9   74–128390
Hoffmann's elegant art embellishes this story of a king who gave his hateful daughter to the first beggar to come through the castle gates. (K–Gr 3)

————, *and* Wilhelm K. Grimm. *About Wise Men and Simpletons; Twelve Tales from Grimm*. Translated by Elizabeth Shub. New York, Macmillan, 1971. 118 p. $5.95 ISBN 0–02–737290–1   79–146628
Nonny Hogrogian's soft etchings subtly convey the atmosphere of a dozen favorite German folktales, in a fresh, close translation. (Gr 3–6)

————. *King Grisly-Beard, a Tale from the Brothers Grimm*. Translated by Edgar Taylor. Pictures by Maurice Sendak. New York, Farrar, Straus & Giroux, 1973. [24] p. $3.95 ISBN 0–374–34133–8 (lib. ed. $2.95 ISBN 0–374–34134–6)   73–77911

The ancient tale of the over-proud princess gains new life in a pictorial framework which pantomimes the action, showing the princess and her suitor in a series of color frames with balloon-speech words. (K–Gr 4)

————. *Snow White*. Freely translated from the German by Paul Heins. Illustrated by Trina Schart Hyman. Boston, Little, Brown, 1974. 48 p. (An Atlantic Monthly Press book) $6.95 ISBN 0–316–35450–3   73–13585
A favorite tale freshly translated and complemented with large full-color paintings which sometimes suggest Arthur Rackham. (Gr 1–3)

————. *Snow-White and the Seven Dwarfs*. A tale from the Brothers Grimm translated by Randall Jarrell. Pictures by Nancy Ekholm Burkert. New York, Farrar, Straus & Giroux, 1972. [32] p. $7.95 ISBN 0–374–37099–0   72–81489
Double-spread paintings create a medieval aura for a beloved folktale. (K–Gr 4)

————. *Wanda Gág's Jorinda and Joringel*. Illustrated by Margot Tomes. New York, Coward, McCann & Geoghegan, 1978. [32] p. $6.95 ISBN 0–698–20440–9   77–26680
Earthy tones of brown, green, and tan enliven Tomes's illustrations for the familiar Gág translation of this German folktale about a maiden changed by sorcery into a nightingale. (Gr 2–3)

Guirma, Frederic. *Princess of the Full Moon*. Translated by John Garrett. New York, Macmillan, 1970. [32] p. $4.95 ISBN 0–02–737710–5   76–89587
An African tale of a beautiful princess, wicked transformations, and other deeds of magic, accompanied by spirited line-and-wash drawings in bright colors. (Gr 1–3)

————. *Tales of Mogho; African Stories from Upper Volta*. New York, Macmillan, 1971. 113 p. $4.95 ISBN 0–02–737690–7   78–146625
African tales of people and animals, magic and trickery—all pictured graphically in an attractive volume. (Gr 4–6)

Haviland, Virginia, *comp. The Fairy Tale Treasury*. Illustrated by Raymond Briggs. New York, Coward, McCann & Geoghegan, 1972. 192 p. $8.49 ISBN 0–698–30438–1   72–76706
Vigorous and humorous are the full-color and black-and-white illustrations which interpret a well-balanced selection of familiar and less familiar nursery tales. (PreS–Gr 3)

————. *Favorite Fairy Tales Told in Japan*. Retold by Virginia Haviland. Illustrated by George Suyeoka. Boston, Little, Brown, 1967. 89 p. $6.95 ISBN 0–316–35091–5   67–3846

A collection of six tales retold for younger readers in a style that preserves the rich flavor of folk literature. Other welcome additions to the Favorite Fairy Tale series include volumes for Denmark, Greece, and India. (Gr 2–4)

Hieatt, Constance B. *The Sword and the Grail*. Illustrated by David Palladini. New York, Crowell, 1972. 82 p. $6.95 ISBN 0–690–79873–3   78–139097

A fresh retelling of the Perceval story which portrays Perceval as a likable but rather bumbling youth. Stylized black-and-white drawings add to the total attractiveness of this version which draws on the early tellings of Chrestien de Troyes and Wolfram von Eschenbach. (Gr 5–8)

Highwater, Jamake. *Anpao; an American Indian Odyssey*. Pictures by Fritz Scholder. Philadelphia, Lippincott, 1977. 256 p. $8.95 ISBN 0–397–31750–6   77–9264

Woven into the well-known legend of Scarface (Anpao) are myths of North American Indians, the whole related in a clear, rhythmic, storytelling prose. Anpao journeys to his father, the Sun, to have his scar removed and receive permission to marry the beautiful Ko-ko-mik-e-is. (Gr 7–up)

Hodges, Margaret. *The Fire Bringer; a Paiute Indian Legend*. Retold by Margaret Hodges. Illustrated by Peter Parnall. Boston, Little, Brown, 1972. 31 p. $5.95 ISBN 0–316–36783–4   70–182247

A handsome visual interpretation complements this storyteller's skillful retelling of how Coyote brought fire to man. (Gr 2–4)

Hogrogian, Nonny. *The Contest*. Adapted from an Armenian folktale. New York, Greenwillow Books/Morrow, 1976. [32] p. $7.95 ISBN 0–688–80042–4 (lib. ed. $7.63 ISBN 0–688–84042–6)   75–40389

Two thieves who find themselves engaged to the same girl determine by contest who is cleverest and most deserving of her. The adapter-artist's large, full-color illustrations reflect the story's humor, with Oriental rug border designs adding a special flavor to the background. (K–Gr 3)

Homerus. *Demeter and Persephone; Homeric Hymn Number Two*. Translated and adapted by Penelope Proddow. Illustrated by Barbara Cooney. Garden City, N.Y., Doubleday, 1972. [48] p. $5.95 ISBN 0–385–06726–7   76–155852

A rhythmic free-verse translation of one of the most beautiful Greek myths, as sung by Homer. Full-color scenes suggesting much of Greek motif serve as backdrops for activities on earth and in Hades. (Gr 3–6)

Houston, James A. *Kiviok's Magic Journey; an Eskimo Legend*. Written and illustrated by James Houston. New York, Atheneum, 1973. [40] p. (A Margaret K. McElderry book) $5.25 ISBN 0–689–30419–6   73–75435

The Eskimo hero Kiviok, of whom many tales are told, appears here in a poignant story of how he wins and loses his beautiful wife and makes a hundred-mile trek in search of her. (Gr 3–5)

Htin Aung, U, and Helen G. Trager. *A Kingdom Lost for a Drop of Honey, and Other Burmese Folktales*, by Maung Htin Aung and Helen G. Trager. Illustrations by Pau Oo Thet. New York, Parents' Magazine Press, 1968. 96 p. $5.95 ISBN 0–8193–0219–8 (lib. ed. $5.41 ISBN 0–8193–0220–1)   68–11653

Tales retold with liveliness and humor from Dr. Htin Aung's scholarly collections for adults. Attractively designed and illustrated. (Gr 4–6)

Jatakas. English. Selections. 1975. *Jataka Tales*. Edited by Nancy DeRoin. With original drawings by Ellen Lanyon. Boston, Houghton Mifflin, 1975. 82 p. $5.95 ISBN 0–395–20281–7   74–20981

Fables of India, in a welcome selection of thirty from the hundreds told by the Buddha, are freshly set forth with characteristic openings and rhyming morals appended. (Gr 3–6)

Jones, Hettie. *Longhouse Winter; Iroquois Transformation Tales*. Adapted by Hettie Jones. Illustrated by Nicholas Gaetano. New York, Holt, Rinehart and Winston, 1973. [41] p. $5.95 ISBN 0–03–089887–0   77–182786

The haunting, mystical quality of four brief legends, gracefully retold, is mirrored in intricate, geometric watercolor paintings which suggest Iroquois designs. (Gr 5–7)

Leach, Maria. *Riddle Me, Riddle Me, Ree*. Illustrated by William Wiesner. New York, Viking Press, 1970. 142 p. $4.95 ISBN 0–670–59762–7 (paper $1.50. Penguin. ISBN 0–14–030960–8)   74–106922

Familiar and unfamiliar riddles from around the world make this collection a boon for the enthusiast. (All ages)

————. *Whistle in the Graveyard: Folktales to Chill Your Bones*. Illustrated by Ken Rinciari. New York, Viking Press, 1974. 128 p. $6.95 ISBN 0–670–76245–8   73–22255

Macabre anecdotes and bits of local legend, drawn from present folk tradition and well documented in scholarly notes. Expressive pen-and-ink sketches accent the spinetingling parade of shivery happenings. (Gr 4–7)

Lester, Julius. *The Knee-High Man, and Other Tales.* Pictures by Ralph Pinto. New York, Dial Press, 1972. 28 p. $5.95 ISBN 0–8037–4593–1 (lib. ed. $5.47 ISBN 0–8037–4607–5)   72–181785
A collection of lively black American folktales, chiefly about animals, presented attractively for young children. (K–Gr 4)

McHargue, Georgess. *The Impossible People; a History Natural and Unnatural of Beings Terrible and Wonderful.* Illustrated by Frank Bozzo. New York, Holt, Rinehart & Winston, 1972. 169 p. $6.95 ISBN 0–03–012541–3   75–150033
Examines the origins and evolution of various mythological beings such as giants, fairies, trolls, werewolves, and mermaids in European and American folklore. An entertaining, speculative examination. (Gr 5–up)

Manning-Sanders, Ruth. *A Book of Dragons.* Drawings by Robin Jacques. New York, Dutton, 1965. 128 p. $6.95 ISBN 0–525–26824–3   65–19578
Fourteen stories of dragons, from a wide range of folklore sources, reveal both familiar and unique characteristics. Smooth storytelling versions, attractively illustrated. (Gr 4–6)

———. *A Book of Ghosts and Goblins.* Illustrated by Robin Jacques. New York, Dutton, 1969. 126 p. $6.95 ISBN 0–525–26883–9   71–81719
Both scary and amusing are these twenty-one tales from various countries about supernatural beings. (Gr 3–6)

Marriott, Alice L., *comp. Winter-Telling Stories.* Illustrated by Richard Cuffari. New York, Crowell, 1969. 82 p. $5.50 ISBN 0–690–89636–0   73–78264
New illustrations in black and white decorate this reissue of the humorous Kiowa Indian tales about Saynday, who "got things started in the world." (Gr 3–6)

Martin, Frances G. M. *Raven-Who-Sets-Things-Right, Indian Tales of the Northwest Coast.* Pictures by Dorothy McEntee. New York, Harper & Row, 1975. 90 p. $5.50 ISBN 0–06–024071–7 (lib. ed. $5.79 ISBN 0–06–024072–5)   74–2631
Minor text alterations, a title change, the addition of an extensive introduction, and new illustrations constitute this new edition of the now out-of-print *Nine Tales of Raven.* (Gr 4–6)

Mehdevi, Anne S. *Persian Folk and Fairy Tales.* Illustrated by Paul E. Kennedy. New York, Knopf, 1965. 117 p. $5.99 ISBN 0–394–91496–1   65–11969
Vividly retold as heard from a Persian nurse, these tales of men and beasts reflect universal human foibles and have a typically Persian color and humor. Appropriately stylized line drawings. (Gr 4–6)

Mosel, Arlene. *The Funny Little Woman.* Retold. Pictures by Blair Lent. New York, Dutton, 1972. [40] p. $7.95 ISBN 0–525–30265–4 (paper $1.95 ISBN 0–525–45036–X)   75–179046
A folktale of old Japan, from Lafcadio Hearn's collection, tells of a runaway rice dumpling and an old woman who chases it into the lair of some three-eyed *oni,* wicked monsters who keep her captive as their cook. Lent's large color pictures make an attractive volume. (Gr 1–3)

Nye, Robert. *Taliesin.* Illustrated by Dorothy Maas. New York, Hill and Wang, 1967. 121 p. $3.95 ISBN 0–8090–9110–0   67–3518
A witty, poetic, and somewhat enlarged retelling of episodes from the legendary Welsh *Mabinogion:* about the magical creation of the young poet Taliesin and his humorous triumphs in contest. (Gr 5–up)

Ransome, Arthur. *The Fool of the World and the Flying Ship; a Russian Tale.* New York, Farrar, Straus & Giroux, 1968. [43] p. $6.95 ISBN 0–374–32442–5   68–54105
A favorite old tale with magical wonders captured in robust, vividly colored illustrations by Uri Shulevitz. (Gr 1–3)

San Souci, Robert. *The Legend of Scarface; a Blackfeet Indian Tale.* Adapted. Illustrated by Daniel San Souci. Garden City, N.Y., Doubleday, 1978. [40] p. $7.95 ISBN 0–385–13247–6 (lib. ed. $8.90 ISBN 0–385–13248–4)   77–15170
A faithful retelling of the famous legend about the young brave who travels to the land of the Sun to ask for the hand of his beloved. Distinguished full-page color art. (Gr 2–4)

Sarnoff, Jane, *and* Reynold Ruffins. *Take Warning! A Book of Superstitions.* New York, Scribner, 1978. 159 p. $8.95 ISBN 0–684–15550–8   77–26295
Superstitions, mainly humorous and of interest to children, arranged alphabetically by key word. Equally amusing are the bold, black-ink illustrations. (Gr 4–6)

Schwartz, Alvin, *comp. Cross Your Fingers, Spit in Your Hat; Superstitions and Other Beliefs.* Illustrated by Glen Rounds. Philadelphia, Lippincott, 1974. 161 p. $7.95 ISBN 0–397–31530–9 (paper $2.95 ISBN 0–397–31531–7)   73–21912

A fourth amusing collaboration of compiler and artist is this amply illustrated selection of superstitions, charms, and other American traditional beliefs. (Gr 4–7)

———. *A Twister of Twists, a Tangler of Tongues.* Illustrated by Glen Rounds. Philadelphia, Lippincott, 1977. 125 p. $6.95 ISBN 0–397–31387–X (paper $1.95 ISBN 0–397–31412–4) 72–1434
Tickling tongue-twisters turned on almost twenty topics from toads to travel, as told in times past and contemporary and in ten tongues; tempting pictures, too. (Gr 3–up)

Serwadda, W. Moses. *Songs and Stories from Uganda.* Transcribed and edited by Hewitt Pantaleoni. Illustrated by Leo and Diane Dillon. New York, Crowell, 1974. 80 p. $6.50 ISBN 0–690–75240–7 (lib. ed. $7.39 ISBN 0–690–75241–5) 72–7556
Thirteen songs with accompanying stories retold from Ugandan folklore. (Gr 3–6)

Singer, Isaac B. *Mazel and Shlimazel; or, The Milk of a Lioness.* Translated from the Yiddish by the author and Elizabeth Shub. New York, Farrar, Straus & Giroux, 1967. [48] p. $6.95 ISBN 0–374–34884–7 67–19887
Two spirits—good luck and bad luck—contest in a battle of wits affecting the romance between a peasant boy and a lovely princess. Margot Zemach's drawings in warm hues add humor, gusto, and Slavic flavor to this unusual folktale. (Gr 3–6)

———. *Zlateh the Goat, and Other Stories.* Pictures by Maurice Sendak. Translated from the Yiddish by the author and Elizabeth Shub. New York, Harper & Row, 1966. 90 p. $8.95 ISBN 0–06–025698–2 (lib. ed. $8.49 ISBN 0–06–025699–0) 66–10173
A master storyteller recreates tales spun in the Jewish ghettos of Eastern Europe. Their humor, mysticism, and a quiet acceptance of fate are perfectly interpreted in Sendak's fine-line sketches. (Gr 4–6)

The Squire's Bride; a Norwegian Folk Tale. Originally collected and told by P. C. Asbjornsen. Illustrated by Marcia Sewall. New York, Atheneum, 1975. [32] p. $6.95 ISBN 0–689–30463–3 74–19316
The farmer's daughter outwits a doddering country squire who wants to marry her by sending in her place a mare. (K–Gr 2)

Stalder, Valerie. *Even the Devil Is Afraid of a Shrew; a Folktale of Lapland.* Retold. Adapted by Ray Broekel. Reading, Mass. Addison-Wesley, 1972. [40] p. $6.95 ISBN 0–201–07188–6 70–177415

A subtle, humorous story which tells how a quiet man finally freed himself from a nagging wife. Illustrated in bright color by Richard Brown. (Gr 1–3)

Sutcliff, Rosemary. *The High Deeds· of Finn Mac Cool.* Retold. With drawings by Michael Charlton. New York, Dutton, 1967. 189 p. Paper $1.25. Penguin. ISBN 0–14–030380–4 67–3412
An exciting retelling of the exploits of Finn Mac Cool, Captain of the Fianna who guarded Ireland's shores in the ancient days. (Gr 5–7)

Tashjian, Virginia A., comp. *Juba This and Juba That; Story Hour Stretches for Large or Small Groups.* With illustrations by Victoria de Larrea. Boston, Little, Brown, 1969. 116 p. $6.95 ISBN 0–316–83230–8 69–10666
Chants, rhymes, finger plays, riddles, and songs— "fillers" to encourage child participation in the story hour. Humorous drawings. (K–Gr 5)

———. *Once There Was and Was Not.* Based on stories by H. Toumanian. Illustrated by Nonny Hogrogian. Boston, Little, Brown, 1966. 83 p. $4.95 ISBN 0–316–83225–1 66–11000
Armenian folktales retold with deftness and simplicity by an experienced storyteller. Delicately illustrated in color with just-right touches of folk art. (Gr 3–5)

———. *With a Deep Sea Smile; Story Hour Stretches for Large or Small Groups.* Illustrated by Rosemary Wells. Boston, Little, Brown, 1974. 132 p. $5.95 ISBN 0–316–83216–2 72–8874
The storyteller's second volume of chants, poems, finger plays, riddles, and songs for use with a group of children. (Gr 4–6)

Thompson, Vivian L. *Hawaiian Myths of Earth, Sea, and Sky.* Illustrated by Leonard Weisgard. New York, Holiday House, 1966. 83 p. $6.95 ISBN 0–8234–0042–5 66–2643
A skillful writer gives color, drama, and a sense of place to tales told by the Hawaiians to explain the natural wonders of their world. Pronouncing glossary. (Gr 4–6)

Towle, Faith M. *The Magic Cooking Pot; a Folktale of India.* Boston, Houghton Mifflin, 1975. 40 p. $6.95 ISBN 0–395–20273–6 74–20761
Handsomely reproduced batiks in rich colors highlight this Indian version of an old tale in which a magic pot serves up endless quantities of food. (K–Gr 1)

Toye, William. *The Loon's Necklace.* Retold. Pictures by Elizabeth Cleaver. New York, Toronto, Oxford University Press, 1977. [24] p. $5.95 ISBN 0–19–540278–2   77–82683
The prizewinning Canadian artist has done striking full-color collage paintings for this Tsimshian legend, made famous through a film released in 1950. (Gr 2–4)

Van Woerkom, Dorothy O. *Abu Ali: Three Tales of the Middle East.* Retold. Illustrated by Harold Berson. New York, Macmillan, 1976. 64 p. (Ready-to-read) $6.95 ISBN 0–02–791310–4   76–8401
Three wittily illustrated short stories about the wise fool Abu Ali are retold in simple language. (Gr 2–up)

——. *Meat Pies & Sausages: Three Tales of Fox and Wolf.* Retold. Illustrated by Joseph Low. New York, Greenwillow Books/Morrow, 1976. 56 p. (Greenwillow read-alone) $5.95 ISBN 0–688–80034–3 (lib. ed. $5.71 ISBN 0–688–84034–5)
75–33160
Three stories of trickery from Russian fable lore, about Fox and Wolf, Ivan and his broom-whipping wife, are amply illustrated in Low's free style. (Gr 1–3)

Vasilisa the Beautiful. Translated from the Russian by Thomas P. Whitney. Illustrated by Nonny Hogrogian. New York, Macmillan, 1970. [32] p. $4.95 ISBN 0–02–792540–4   73–102971
A favorite Afanasiev tale in which Cinderella-like Vasilisa escapes from the wicked witch Baba Yaga. Full-color drawings enhance the Russian atmosphere. (Gr 1–3)

Wiesner, William. *A Pocketful of Riddles.* New York, Dutton, 1966. 119 p. $5.50 ISBN 0–525–37206–7 (paper $1.50 ISBN 0–525–45032–7)   66–4593
Fun for two, and fun for a group—a collection of jolly riddles which the compiler has illustrated with spirited little drawings in a tiny volume. (Gr 3–6)

Williams, Jay. *The Wicked Tricks of Tyl Uilenspiegel.* Illustrated by Friso Henstra. New York, Four Winds Press, 1978. 51 p. $8.95 ISBN 0–590–07478–4
77–7884
Roguish Tyl and four of his pranks are presented in Williams's witty style, with colorful illustrations underscoring the humor, action, and setting. Inviting for either reading aloud or the child's own reading. (Gr 2–4)

Ziner, Feenie. *Cricket Boy; a Chinese Tale Retold.* Illustrated by Ed Young. Garden City, N.Y., Doubleday, 1977. [46] p. $6.95 ISBN 0–385–12506–2 (lib. ed. $7.90 ISBN 0–385–12507–0)   76–51999
The Chinese-American artist provides twenty-one authentically styled and colored paintings appropriate to this dignified retelling of an ancient fable about cricket fighting. (Gr 2–4)

——. *Tristan and Iseult.* New York, Dutton, 1971. 150 p. $6.95 ISBN 0–525–41565–3 (paper $1.50. Penguin. ISBN 0–14–030650–1)   77–157947
The omission here of the traditional love potion gives a more natural inevitability to this Arthurian romance reshaped in stark, poetic prose. (Gr 6–up)

Poetry, Plays, and Songs

Adoff, Arnold, *comp. Black Out Loud; an Anthology of Modern Poems by Black Americans.* New York, Macmillan, 1970. 86 p. $6.95 ISBN 0–02–700100–8
74–99117

Exciting poems by black poets speak of love, rage, sadness, victory, dreams, despair, and hope. Strong illustrations by Alvin Hollingsworth. (Gr 5–up)

————, *comp. I Am the Darker Brother; an Anthology of Modern Poems by Negro Americans.* Foreword by Charlemae Rollins. New York, Macmillan, 1968. 128 p. $7.95 ISBN 0–02–700080–X (paper $1.95 ISBN 0–02–041120–0)
68–12077

Thought-provoking poems express the Negro experience in America. Attractive fine-line drawings by Benny Andrews. (Gr 7–up)

Aiken, Conrad. *Cats and Bats and Things with Wings; Poems.* Drawings by Milton Glaser. New York, Atheneum, 1965. [32] p. $6.95 ISBN 0–689–30017–4
65–21724

Illustrations in many different styles and media depict the creatures celebrated in this poet's light-hearted play with words. (Gr 3–5)

Aiken, Joan. *Street; a Play.* Illustrated by Arvis Stewart. Music by John Sebastian Brown. New York, Viking Press, 1978. 79 p. $7.95 ISBN 0–670–67823–6
77–21736

A witty two-act play has as its central theme environmental problems, but with an interweaving of witchery and folk beliefs and a tender love story. (Gr 6–8)

————. *The Skin Spinners, Poems.* Drawings by Ken Rinciari. New York, Viking Press, 1976. 83 p. $6.95 ISBN 0–670–64950–3
75–29306

Music in rhythms and rhymes distinguish the poet's inspirations about People, Simple Things, Mysterious Things, Legends, and Ballads. (Gr 5–8)

An Arkful of Animals. Selected by William Cole. Illustrated by Lynn Munsinger. Boston, Houghton Mifflin, 1978. 88 p. $5.95 ISBN 0–395–27205–X
78–70041

Fifty-three short, humorous poems, chiefly by twentieth-century poets. Amusing sketches accompany them. (Gr 1–4)

Amelia Mixed the Mustard and Other Poems. Selected and illustrated by Evaline Ness. New York, Scribner, 1975. 47 p. $6.95 ISBN 0–684–14271–6 74–14077
Amelia, who put mustard in the custard, and Isabel, who "ate the bear up," are among the spunky girls whose deeds are described in vigorous verse. The three-color drawings are equally lighthearted. (Gr 2–5)

Armour, Richard. *A Dozen Dinosaurs.* New York, McGraw-Hill, 1967. 32 p. $5.95 ISBN 0–07–002226–7 (lib. ed. $6.95 ISBN 0–07–002227–5)
67–21593
With Paul Galdone's animated double-spreads, this master of light verse introduces the dinosaurs: "Give thought, then, to the dinosaurs,/Whom one no longer dreads./They used their teeth and used their claws /But didn't use their heads." (Gr 4–up)

Baron, Virginia O. *Sunset in a Spider Web: Sijo Poetry of Ancient Korea.* Adapted from translations by Chung Seuk Park. Illustrated by Minja Park Kim. New York, Holt, Rinehart & Winston, 1974. [79] p. $4.95 ISBN 0–03–012–071–3 73–14657
The artistry of long-ago writers who are still popular in Korea reveals universal emotions, simply expressed. (Gr 6–up)

Behn, Harry, *tr. Cricket Songs.* New York, Harcourt, Brace & World, 1964. 64 p. $4.95 ISBN 0–15–220890–9 64–11489
In this attractive small volume, Japanese prints illustrate a selection of haiku—illuminating gems of unrhymed nature poetry translated here by a well-known poet. (Gr 5–up)

Belloc, Hilaire. *Hilaire Belloc's the Yak, the Python, the Frog.* A picture book production by Steven Kellogg. New York, Parents' Magazine Press, 1975. [33] p. $5.95 ISBN 0–8193–0785–8 (lib. ed. $5.41 ISBN 0–8193–0786–6) 74–12441
Steven Kellogg's rollicking pictures enhance the ebullience of Belloc's nonsensical verses in praise of exotic pets. (Gr 1–4)

Bierhorst, John, *comp. In the Trail of the Wind; American Indian Poems and Ritual Orations.* New York, Farrar, Straus & Giroux, 1971. 201 p. $6.95 ISBN 0–374–33640–7 (paper $4.95 ISBN 0–374–50901–8) 71–144822
A dignified presentation of Indian poetry from tribes in South, Central, and North America—effectively arranged by theme and illustrated by old engravings. (Gr 6–up)

Bodecker, N. M. *Hurry, Hurry, Mary Dear! And Other Nonsense Poems.* New York, Atheneum, 1976. 118 p. (A Margaret K. McElderry book) $6.95 ISBN 0–689–50066–1 76–14841
Freewheeling rhymes, with Bodecker's nonsense—sometimes Lear-like—appear in both words and drawings. (K–Gr 3)

————. *Let's Marry Said the Cherry, and Other Nonsense Poems.* New York, Atheneum, 1974. 79 p. (A Margaret K. McElderry book) $5.95 ISBN 0–689–50004–1 (paper $1.95 ISBN 0–689–70434–8)
74–76271
The author-artist provides witty nonsense in both words and pictures and fun with sounds that makes this a delight for reading aloud. (Gr 4–6)

Bogan, Louise, *and* William Jay Smith, *eds. The Golden Journey; Poems for Young People.* Woodcuts by Fritz Kredel. Chicago, Reilly & Lee, 1965. 275 p. Paper $3.95. Contemporary Books. ISBN 0–8092–7963–0 65–21489
A rich and inviting feast of poetry, chosen with discernment by two poets—from simple rhymes to "supreme flights of the imagination." (Gr 5–up)

Brewton, Sara W., *and* John E. Brewton, *comps. America Forever New: A Book of Poems.* New York, Crowell, 1968. 270 p. $6.50 ISBN 0–690–06988–X
67–23663
An unhackneyed anthology reflecting the American scene from the days of Emily Dickinson to the present. (Gr 5–up)

————, *comps. Shrieks at Midnight; Macabre Poems, Eerie and Humorous.* New York, Crowell, 1969. 177 p. $6.95 ISBN 0–690–73518–9 69–11824
With Ellen Raskin's drawings, this collection of verses is a natural for Halloween and the campfire. (Gr 5–7)

————, *and* G. Meredith Blackburn, *comps. My Tang's Tungled and Other Ridiculous Situations, Humorous Poems.* Illustrated by Graham Booth. New York, Crowell, 1973. 111 p. $6.50 ISBN 0–690–57223–9 73–254
A collection of tongue twisters, limericks, and humorous verse—some old, some new—their hilarity magnified by Graham Booth's drawings. (All ages)

Bryan, Ashley, *comp. Walk Together Children: Black American Spirituals.* New York, Atheneum, 1974. 53 p. $7.95 ISBN 0–689–30131–6 73–84821
For biblical and other subjects in well-known spirituals, Bryan has supplied stark woodcut illustration, appropriate to themes of sadness, deprivation, and other injustices. (Gr 4–up)

Causley, Charles. *Figgie Hobbin.* Illustrated by Trina Schart Hyman. Introduction by Ethel L. Heins. New York, Walker, 1974. 48 p. $4.95 ISBN 0–8027–6131–3 (lib. ed. $4.85 ISBN 0–8027–6132–1)
72–87351
An artist's perfect capturing of mood adds much to this baker's dozen of fresh poems—both nonsense and lyrics—from an English poet of today. (Gr 1–4)

Childress, Alice. *Let's Hear It for the Queen.* Illustrated by Loring Eutemey. New York, Coward, McCann & Geoghegan, 1976. 48 p. $6.95 ISBN 0–698–20388–7
76–16075
Rose Ann, who can cast, costume, and set a drama "in her mind's eye," acts as Everyperson in this contemporary play based on the nursery rhyme "Queen of Hearts." Delightfully illustrated, fun to perform, the play serves splendidly as an introduction to the performing arts. (Gr 3–5)

Ciardi, John. *Fast and Slow; Poems for Advanced Children and Beginning Parents.* Illustrated by Becky Gaver. Boston, Houghton Mifflin, 1975. 67 p. $6.95 ISBN 0–395–20282–5 (paper $1.95 ISBN 0–395–26680–7)
74–22405
Line drawings add their own humor to a new collection of Ciardi's musings on the world, including "A Fog Full of Apes" and "A Fine Fat Fireman." (Gr 4–8)

Cole, William, *ed. Beastly Boys and Ghastly Girls.* Drawings by Tomi Ungerer. Cleveland, World Pub. Co., 1964. 124 p. $4.91. Collins, New York ISBN 0–529–03903–6
64–20962
A collection of fiendish rhymes by such humorists as Gellett Burgess, Hilaire Belloc, Shelley Silverstein, A. A. Milne, and Lewis Carroll, with impudent line drawings. (Gr 3–6)

———. *Oh, What Nonsense!* Poems. Drawings by Tomi Ungerer. New York, Viking Press, 1966. 60 p. $6.95 ISBN 0–670–52117–5 (paper $0.75. Penguin. ISBN 0–670–05025–3)
66–10249
A happy, fresh combination of nonsense verse, from Mother Goose to Ciardi, with equally comic illustrations. (Gr 3–6)

Crofut, Bill. *The Moon on the One Hand, Poetry in Song.* Music by William Crofut. Arrangements by Kenneth Cooper & Glenn Shattuck. Illustrations by Susie Crofut. New York, Atheneum, 1975. 80 p. (A Margaret K. McElderry book) $9.95 ISBN 0–689–50018–1
74–18179
A selection of animal and nature poems, by such well-known poets as E. E. Cummings, Robert Louis Stevenson, and Randall Jarrell, has been set to music. Gray wash drawings add to the attractiveness of the book. (All ages)

Davis, Ossie. *Escape to Freedom; a Play about Young Frederick Douglass.* New York, Viking Press, 1978. 89 p. $7.95 ISBN 0–670–29775–5
77–25346
An episodic portrayal of the childhood and young manhood of the slave-born leader who was to play an important role in the development of human rights. The playwright's production suggestions allow room for improvisation. (Gr 6–8)

De Forest, Charlotte B. *The Prancing Pony; Nursery Rhymes from Japan.* Adapted into English verse for children by Charlotte B. De Forest. With kusa-e illustrations by Keiko Hida. New York, Walker/ Weatherhill, 1968. 63 p. $4.50 ISBN 0–8348–2000–5
68–15968
Translated from an early collection of anonymous folk poetry, these lullabies and children's songs are distinctively illustrated with collage pictures that are three-dimensional in effect. (All ages)

Downie, Mary A., *and* Barbara Robertson, *comps. The Wind Has Wings; Poems from Canada.* Illustrated by Elizabeth Cleaver. New York, Walck, 1968. 95 p. Reprinted. $7.95. Toronto, Oxford Univ. Press. ISBN 0–19–540287–1
68–3541
Poetry of many kinds, from a variety of sources including French Canadian and Eskimo, illustrated with pictorial effects to suit the different moods. (Gr 5–up)

Dunning, Stephen, Edward Leuders, *and* Hugh Smith, *comps. Reflections on a Gift of Watermelon Pickle . . . and Other Modern Verse.* New York, Lothrop, Lee & Shepard, 1967. 144 p. $6.95 ISBN 0–688–41231–9 (lib. ed. $6.67 ISBN 0–688–51231–3)
67–29527
A fresh collection of modern poetry and verse, whose inviting variety of subject and unhackneyed images speak of today's world. Striking photographs are imaginatively matched to subject. (Gr 7–up)

———, *eds. Some Haystacks Don't Even Have Any Needle, and Other Complete Modern Poems.* Glenview, Ill., Scott, Foresman, 1969. 192 p. $8.95 ISBN 0–688–41445–1
75–5424
An unhackneyed, varied anthology which speaks to the teenage reader. Full-color reproductions of modern paintings and sculpture. (Gr 7–up)

Farber, Norma. *As I Was Crossing Boston Common.* Pictures by Arnold Lobel. New York, Dutton, 1975. [32] p. $6.95 ISBN 0–525–25960–0
75–6520
In easy rhyming lines a turtle comments on a parade of animals crossing Boston Common—all fantastic (from angwantibo to zibet) but zoologically true, as an appendix of definitions reveals. The humorous soft

gray drawings with a background of Beacon Hill create a lively ambience. (Gr 1–4)

Field, Edward, trans. *Eskimo Songs and Stories*. Collected by Knud Rasmussen on the Fifth Thule Expedition. Selected and translated by Edward Field. With illustrations by Kiakshuk and Pudlo. New York, Delacorte/Seymour Lawrence, 1973. 103 p. (A Merrloyd Lawrence book) $6.95 ISBN 0–440–02336–X   73–3263

Original Eskimo prints appropriately illustrate unrhymed poems based on traditional Netsilik folklore—stories and magic incantations (sometimes recast with modern expression)—collected by the famous part-Eskimo explorer across Arctic America in the 1920s. (Gr 5–up)

Garson, Eugenia, comp. and ed. *The Laura Ingalls Wilder Songbook; Favorite Songs from the Little House Books*. Arr. for piano and guitar by Herbert Haufrecht. New York, Harper & Row, 1968. 160 p. $7.95 ISBN 0–06–021933–5 (lib. ed. $7.49 ISBN 0–06–021934–3)   68–24327

A varied selection of songs carried west by the pioneers, as played on Pa's fiddle and sung by the family in the beloved "Little House" books. Includes piano music, with guitar chords indicated, and illustrations by Garth Williams, which like the song introductions relate each selection to a particular volume. (Gr 4–up)

Glazer, Tom. *Eye Winker, Tom Tinker, Chin Chopper: Fifty Musical Fingerplays*. Illustrated by Ron Himler. Garden City, N.Y., Doubleday, 1973. 89 p. $5.95 ISBN 0–385–08200–2 (lib. ed. $6.90 ISBN 0–385–09453–1; paper $1.95 ISBN 0–385–13344–8)   72–97497

Familiar fingerplays, some set to music for the first time, plus some delightful old songs with actions newly added. Intended as a stimulus to rhythmic play and improvisation. Guitar chords are provided, as well as simple notation for other instruments or a capella singing. (PreS–K)

Graham, Lorenz B. *David He No Fear*. Pictures by Ann Grifalconi. New York, Crowell, 1971. [47] p. $5.79 ISBN 0–690–23265–9   71–109898

The story of David and Goliath is graphically presented in picture-book format. A companion retelling, *A Road Down to the Sea*, presents the story of the Exodus, also in speech patterns and images of Africans newly acquainted with the English language. Each is handsomely illustrated. (All ages)

————. *Every Man Heart Lay Down*. Pictures by Colleen Browning. New York, Crowell, 1970. [47] p. $5.95 ISBN 0–690–27134–4   75–109899

The Nativity story as it was heard in Liberia and originally published in the author's *How God Fix Jonah*: "little poems . . . told here in the words and thought patterns of a modern African boy." (Gr 3–up)

The Great Song Book. Edited by Timothy John. Music edited by Peter Hankey. Illustrated by Tomi Ungerer. New York, Doubleday, 1978. 112 p. (The Benn Book Collection) $12.50 ISBN 0–385–13328–6   77–74707

The artist's lavish full-color pictures—by turn animated, amusing, and luminous—have a primary importance for this ample collection of some well-known and some less familiar songs. (All ages)

Hoberman, Mary Ann. *The Raucous Auk*. Illustrated by Joseph Low. New York, Viking Press, 1973. [48] p. $6.50 ISBN 0–670–58848–2   73–5140

For a picture book with large pages, poet and artist have collaborated successfully in evoking unusual aspects of such remarkable birds and animals as the "Raucous Auk," which "must squawk to talk./The squawk auks squawk to talk goes auk." (Gr 1–4)

Horder, Mervyn Horder, baron, arr. *On Christmas Day: First Carols to Play and Sing*. Illustrated by Margaret Gordon. New York, Macmillan, 1969. 32 p. $5.95 ISBN 0–02–744400–7   69–11103

Thirteen carols—five of them familiar and traditional, the others little known, from a number of lands—with choral arrangements and glowing illustration. (Gr 4–up)

Houston, James A., comp. *Songs of the Dream People: Chants and Images from the Indians and Eskimos of North America*. New York, Atheneum, 1972. 83 p. (A Margaret K. McElderry book) $5.95 ISBN 0–689–30306–8   72–77130

Short poems—often like haiku in spirit—are infused with the magic of words and ritual. Houston's own two-colored drawings of artifacts are nicely related. (All ages)

Hughes, Langston. *Don't You Turn Back*. Poems selected by Lee Bennett Hopkins. Illustrated by Ann Grifalconi. New York, Knopf, 1969. 83 p. $5.69 ISBN 0–394–90846–5   78–82549

Strong woodcuts in red and black give added distinction to this selection of Hughes's poems made by school children in Harlem. (All ages)

Jones, Hettie, comp. *The Trees Stand Shining; Poetry of the North American Indians*. Paintings by Robert Andrew Parker. New York, Dial Press, 1971. [32] p. $5.95 ISBN 0–8037–9083–X (lib. ed. $5.47 ISBN 0–8037–9084–8; paper $1.75 ISBN 0–8037–8933–5)   79–142452

Thirty-two short haiku-like poems from the oral tradition of fifteen North American tribes are richly illustrated with full-color paintings. (Gr 3–up)

Kapp, Paul. *Cock-a-Doodle-Doo, Cock-a-Doodle-Dandy!* Pictures by Anita Lobel. New York, Harper & Row, 1966. 70 p. $6.89 ISBN 0–06–022388–X
66–1035
A gay collection of traditional rhymes and well-known poems set to music with simple piano accompaniments and entertaining illustration. (PreS–G 4)

Key, Francis Scott. *The Star-Spangled Banner.* Illustrated by Peter Spier. Garden City, N.Y., Doubleday, 1973. [49] p. $7.95 ISBN 0–385–09458–2 (lib. ed. $8.90 ISBN 0–385–07746–7)
73–79712
An oversized, full-color picture book contains the artist's imaginative conception of the background and meanings of the U.S. national anthem. Endpapers show over a hundred official flags; appendixes provide a Baltimore map, music, and a reproduction of the original manuscript. (Gr 3–up)

Korty, Carol. *Plays from African Folktales, with Ideas for Acting, Dance, Costumes, and Music.* Illustrated by Sandra Cain. Music by Saka Acquaye and Afolabi Ajayi. New York, Scribner, 1975. 128 p. $6.95 ISBN 0–684–14199–X
74–24418
For a nonformal approach to production notes, four plays adapted from African folklore are creatively reinforced with selections on music, dance, scenery, props, and related topics. (Gr 3–up)

Langstaff, John M., *comp. Hi! Ho! The Rattlin' Bog, and Other Folk Songs for Group Singing.* With piano settings by John Edmunds [and others] With guitar chords suggested by Happy Traum. Illustrated by Robin Jacques. New York, Harcourt, Brace & World, 1969. 111 p. $5.50 ISBN 0–15–234400–4
75–76616
The concert artist and folksinger makes available folksongs he has shared with children. (Gr 4–up)

———. *Sweetly Sings the Donkey; Animal Rounds for Children to Sing or Play on Recorders.* Pictures by Nancy Winslow Parker. New York, Atheneum, 1976. 28 p. (A Margaret K. McElderry Book) $6.95 ISBN 0–689–50063–7
76–9530
A selection of simple rounds for voice, recorder, flute, etc., accompanied by humorous, poker-faced illustrations, provides easy musical experiences for all ages. By the same team, *Oh, A-Hunting We Will Go* ($7.95 ISBN 0–688–50007–6). (Gr 3–up)

Langstaff, Nancy, *and* John M. Langstaff, *comps. Jim Along, Josie; a Collection of Folk Songs and Singing*

Games for Young Children. Piano arrangements by Seymour Barab. Guitar chords by Happy Traum. Optional percussion accompaniment for children. Illustrated by Jan Pienkowski. New York, Harcourt Brace Jovanovich, 1970. 127 p. $7.50 ISBN 0–15–240250–0
79–115757
For home, school, and other fun—eighty-one traditional songs and singing games, attractively presented with new arrangements. (K–up)

Larrick, Nancy, *comp. Room for Me and a Mountain Lion; Poetry of Open Space.* New York, M. Evans, 1974. 191 p. $5.95 ISBN 0–87131–124–0 73–87710
An outstanding modern anthology, this will please especially those interested in nature and outdoor life. Sandscape and animal photographs. (Gr 7–9)

Lear, Edward. *The Scroobious Pip.* Completed by Ogden Nash. Illustrated by Nancy Ekholm Burkert. New York, Harper & Row, 1968. [24] p. $8.95 ISBN 0–06–023764–3 (lib. ed. $8.79 ISBN 0–06–023765–1)
68–10373
Imaginative, full-color illustrations introduce the indefinable Pip in this posthumously published nonsense rhyme. (K–Gr 4)

Livingston, Myra C. *Listen, Children, Listen; an Anthology of Poems for the Very Young.* New York, Harcourt Brace Jovanovich, 1972. 96 p. $5.50 ISBN 0–15–245570–1
70–167836
Trina Schart Hyman's appealing illustrations add charm to a felicitous selection of poems pleasing to the young child. (K–Gr 3)

———, *comp. What a Wonderful Bird the Frog Are; an Assortment of Humorous Poetry and Verse.* New York, Harcourt Brace Jovanovich, 1973. 192 p. $5.25 ISBN 0–15–295400–7
72–88171
A broad variety of poems from ancient times to the present, and from many lands around the world—chosen because they offer fun. (Gr 6–up)

Lobel, Arnold. *Gregory Griggs and Other Nursery Rhyme People.* New York, Greenwillow Books, 1978. 47 p. $7.95 ISBN 0–688–80128–5 (lib. ed. $7.63 ISBN 0–688–84128–7)
77–22209
Lighthearted drawings add delight to the artist's well-chosen collection of nursery rhymes, many of them little known. (PreS–Gr 1)

McCord, David T. W. *All Day Long; Fifty Rhymes of the Never Was and Always Is.* Drawings by Henry B. Kane. Boston, Little, Brown, 1966. 104 p. $4.95 ISBN 0–316–55508–8
66–17688
Gay rhymes and true poetry again from a poet who shares his great delight in words. The soft-pencil drawings are also important. (Gr 6–8)

————. *Every Time I Climb a Tree*. Boston, Little, Brown, 1967. [48] p. $5.95 ISBN 0–316–55514–2
67–25611
An irresistible collection of McCord's verses with youngest appeal, their verve and informality jauntily interpreted in Marc Simont's gay and witty paintings. (K–Gr 3)

McGinley, Phyllis. *Wonders and Surprises*. Philadelphia, Lippincott, 1968. 160 p. $3.95 ISBN 0–397–31053–6
67–19271
A discriminating and inviting anthology to introduce young people to the great poets of today. (Gr 6–up)

Mackay, David, *comp. A Flock of Words; an Anthology of Poetry for Children and Others*. Preface by Benjamin DeMott. Drawings by Margery Gill. New York, Harcourt, Brace & World, 1970. 328 p. $8.50 ISBN 0–15–228599–7
77–91070
An English anthologist's refreshing collection, ranging through countries and centuries to provide delight. (All ages)

Merriam, Eve. *It Doesn't Always Have to Rhyme*. Illustrated by Malcolm Spooner. New York, Atheneum, 1964. 85 p. $5.95 ISBN 0–689–20671–2
64–11893
Jolly poems about the fun of poetry and its endless possibilities, some expressing the poet's ideas about figures of speech. (Gr 4–6)

Moore, Lilian. *I Thought I Heard the City*. Collage by Mary Jane Dunton. New York, Atheneum, 1969. [40] p. $4.95 ISBN 0–689–20623–2
69–18964
A poet's observations of the city landscape (and some general phenomena) are expressed in fresh, sensitive imagery. Delicately colored illustrations. (Gr 3–5)

Morrison, Lillian. *The Sidewalk Racer and Other Poems of Sports and Motion*. New York, Lothrop, Lee & Shepard, 1977. 62 p. $6.25 ISBN 0–688–41805–8 (lib. ed. $6.00 ISBN 0–688–51805–2)
77–907
These poems for today's sports enthusiasts celebrates the poet's empathy with the exhilaration and rhythm of sports. Her subjects are such popular athletic activities as skateboard, biking, and stickball. Illustrated with evocative photographs. (Gr 6–8)

————, *comp. Sprints and Distances; Sports in Poetry and the Poetry in Sport*. Illustrated by Clare and John Ross. New York, Crowell, 1965. 211 p. $7.95 ISBN 0–690–76571–1
65–14906
The affinity of poetry for the action, rhythm, and beauty of sports is celebrated in this discriminating selection which includes both light verse and poetry ranging from the ancient Greek to the modern. (All ages)

Mother Goose. *Granfa' Grig Had a Pig and Other Rhymes without Reason*. Compiled and illustrated by Wallace Tripp. Boston, Little, Brown, 1976. 96 p. $7.95 ISBN 0–316–85282–1 (paper, $3.95 ISBN 0–316–85284–8)
76–25234
The bounce of these familiar and unfamiliar nursery rhymes is reflected in full-color, ebullient drawings. (PreS–Gr 2)

Of Quarks, Quasars, and Other Quirks; Quizzical Poems for the Supersonic Age. Collected by Sara and John E. Brewton and John Brewton Blackburn. Illustrated by Quentin Blake. New York, Crowell, 1977. 114 p. $6.95 ISBN 0–690–01286–1
76–54747
A space-age anthology which scrutinizes with irony and sophistication the world of science and its offerings. (Gr 7–up)

The Poetry Troupe; an Anthology of Poems to Read Aloud. Compiled by Isabel Wilner. New York, Scribner, 1977. 223 p. $8.95 ISBN 0–684–15198–7
77–9439
More than two hundred well-chosen poems that have proven to be favorites in the compiler's school library experience. (K–Gr 6)

A Poison Tree and Other Poems. New York, Scribner, 1977. 46 p. $7.95 ISBN 0–684–14904–4   76–57732
A slender anthology of chiefly modern poems, chosen by Mercer Mayer for their expression of emotion, has his luminous illustrations to capture their moods. (Gr 5–7)

Prelutsky, Jack. *It's Halloween*. Pictures by Marylin Hafner. New York, Greenwillow Books, 1977. 56 p. (Greenwillow read-alone books) $5.95 ISBN 0–688–80102–1 (lib. ed. $5.71 ISBN 0–688–84102–3)
77–2141
An easy-to-read baker's dozen of poems on familiar aspects of Halloween have light rhymes and rhythms and are humorously illustrated with alternating two- and three-color line-and-wash pictures. (Gr 1–3)

————. *Lazy Blackbird, and Other Verses*. Pictures by Janosch. New York, Macmillan, 1969. [24] p. $3.95 ISBN 0–02–775080–9
69–14273
The gay humor of these nonsense verses is captured in exuberant, boldly colored illustrations. (K–Gr 3)

———. *The Queen of Eene; Poems.* Pictures by Victoria Chess. New York, Greenwillow Books, 1978. 32 p. $6.95 ISBN 0–688–80144–7 (lib. ed. $6.43 ISBN 0–688–84144–9)   77–17311
Ludicrous characters are the subjects of rollicking rhymes which have illustrations of equal verve. Also from this free-flying poet is *The Mean Old Mean Hyena,* a nonsense story in verse, illustrated with appropriate gusto by Arnold Lobel (ISBN 0–688–80163–3; lib. ed. ISBN 0–688–84163–5). (Gr 1–4)

———. *Nightmares; Poems to Trouble Your Sleep.* Illustrated by Arnold Lobel. New York, Greenwillow Books/Morrow, 1976. 38 p. $7.25 ISBN 0–688–80053–X (lib. ed. $6.96 ISBN 0–688–84053–1)   76–4820
Ghoulish drawings and words with rhythm and alliteration create nightmarish creatures for young monster lovers. (Gr 2–5)

Prieto, Mariana B. de. *Play It in Spanish; Spanish Games and Folk Songs for Children.* New York, Day, 1973. 43 p. $7.49 ISBN 0–381–99726–X   79–140474
Folk motifs illustrate an attractive collection. For each game or song there is background information, a free English translation, and, where appropriate, lyrics and melody with piano and guitar accompaniment. (PreS–Gr 4)

Rounds about Rounds. Collected and edited by Jane Yolen. Musical arrangements by Barbara Green; illustrated by Gail Gibbons. New York, Watts, 1977. 120 p. $7.90 ISBN 0–531–00125–3   77–7919
More than a hundred "follow-the-leader" game songs, a popular early form of part singing. Melody lines have piano accompaniments to aid in teaching the songs. (Gr 3–7)

Smith, John, *comp. My Kind of Verse.* Decorations by Uri Shulevitz. New York, Macmillan, 1968. 235 p. $5.95 ISBN 0–02–785940–1   68–20609
Poetry for many age levels, in many forms and from several centuries, including poems not often found in collections. (Gr 4–up)

Straight on Till Morning; Poems of the Imaginary World. Selected by Helen Hill, Agnes Perkins, and Althea Helbig. Illustrated by Ted Lewin. New York, Crowell, 1977. 150 p. $8.95 ISBN 0–690–01303–5   76–55414
Some hundred modern poems celebrating the child's world of the imagination—from Emily Dickinson, Edna St. Vincent Millay, and Robert Frost to John Ciardi and Robert Graves. Attractively printed and illustrated. (Gr 5–7)

Thayer, Ernest L. *Casey at the Bat; a Ballad of the Republic, Sung in the Year 1888.* Illustrated by Wallace Tripp. New York, Coward, McCann & Geoghegan, 1978. [32] p. $7.95 ISBN 0–698–20457–3   77–21199
Wallace Tripp's witty animal drawings bring an extra dimension of humor to this baseball classic. (Gr 1– up)

Updike, John. *A Child's Calendar.* Illustrated by Nancy E. Burkert. New York, Knopf, 1965. [32] p. $4.99 ISBN 0–394–91059–1   65–21555
Changing seasonal moods and child responses are suggested with fresh imagery in poems for each month of the year. The artist's clear line drawings touched with red or blue define the calendar changes with equally sharp, evocative expression. (Gr 3–6)

Wilbur, Richard. *Opposites.* New York, Harcourt Brace Jovanovich, 1973. 39 p. $4.95 ISBN 0–15–258720–9   72–88175
The poet himself has illustrated, with cartoonlike sketches, his brief amusing rhymes which form a kind of word game in suggesting "opposites." (Gr 7–9)

Wilder, Alec. *Lullabies and Night Songs.* Pictures by Maurice Sendak. Edited by William Engvick. New York, Harper & Row, 1965. 77 p. $15.00 ISBN 0–06–021820–7 (lib. ed. $12.89 ISBN 0–06–021821–5)   65–22880/M
With full-color illustrations on large pages the artist has given strong visual interest to forty-eight traditional songs, nursery rhymes, and poems newly set to music. Piano music, words, and melody line are all hand lettered in a distinctive volume. (PreS–up)

Winn, Marie, *ed. The Fireside Book of Children's Songs.* Musical arrangements by Allan Miller. Illustrations by John Alcorn. New York, Simon and Schuster, 1966. 192 p. $9.95 ISBN 0–671–25820–6   65–17108/M
Bold illustrations in pink, black, orange, and yellow add fun to this varied collection of songs grouped in sections entitled "Good Morning and Good Night," "Birds and Beasts," "Nursery Songs," "Silly Songs," and "Singing Games and Rounds." (PreS–up)

———, *ed. What Shall We Do and Allee Galloo! Play Songs and Singing Games for Young Children.* Illustrated by Karla Kuskin. Musical arrangements by Allan Miller. New York, Harper & Row, 1970. 87 p. $5.79 ISBN 0–06–026537–X   72–85039
Forty-seven play games and songs, both familiar and less known, have large-print music and lyrics (piano and guitar accompaniment) and instructions for group participation. (PreS–Gr 1)

Worth, Valerie. *Small Poems*. Pictures by Natalie Babbitt. New York, Farrar, Straus and Giroux, 1972. 41 p. $4.95 ISBN 0–374–37072–9   72–81488

Brief poems in varied forms and apt imagistic expression call attention to qualities of such animals, natural phenomena, and objects as "Sun," "Pig," "Hollyhocks," "Pebbles," "Coins," and "Jewels." The line drawings for each capture exactly the essence of the poems. (All ages)

Yankee Doodle (*Song*) *Yankee Doodle*, by Richard Schackburg. Woodcuts by Ed Emberley. Notes by Barbara Emberley. Englewood Cliffs, N.J., Prentice-Hall, 1965. [33] p. Paper $1.50 ISBN 0–13–971379–6   65–15000

Dashing woodcut figures march across these pages, capturing the martial spirit of the old song. (All ages)

Yurchenko, Henrietta, *comp. Fiesta of Folk Songs from Spain and Latin America*. Illustrated by Jules Maidoff. New York, Putnam, 1967. 88 p. $5.97 ISBN 0–399–60165–1   67–1545

A gaily illustrated collection of thirty-seven songs: about animals and nature, singing games and dances, songs about people, and songs for Christmas. Each has a lively introduction, clear musical notation, and both English and Spanish words. (Gr 2–6)

Arts and Hobbies

Adkins, Jan. *Toolchest; a Primer of Woodcraft.* New York, Walker, 1973. 48 p. $5.95 ISBN 0–8027–6153–4 (lib. ed. $6.83 ISBN 0–8027–6154–2)
72–81374

The author's meticulous drawings introduce measuring, cutting, and shaping tools used in hand woodworking and also common woods and their qualities. (Gr 5–up)

Allport, Alan J. *Model Theaters, and How to Make Them.* New York, Scribner, 1978. 96 p. $7.95 ISBN 0–684–15723–3
77–93901

Innumerable creative possibilities for amateur circus, opera, and play productions are suggested by the directions, sometimes technical, given here for matchbox and pop-up theaters as well as for stages complete with orchestra pit, proscenium, and movable wings. (Gr 5–up)

Amon, Aline. *Talking Hands; Indian Sign Language.* Written and illustrated by Aline Amon. Garden City, N.Y., Doubleday, 1968. 80 p. $4.95 ISBN 0–385–08891–4 (lib. ed. $5.90 ISBN 0–385–09425–6)
68–10123

Children will want to try their hand at sign language after reading this inviting guide with its simple explanations and attractive, clear diagrams. (Gr 3–6)

Antonacci, Robert J., *and* Anthony J. Puglisi. *Soccer for Young Champions.* Illustrated by Patti Boyd. New York, McGraw-Hill, 1978. 183 p. (Young champion series) $7.95 ISBN 0–07–002147–3
77–27565

An authoritative and comprehensive guide, with rules for boys and girls of differing ages, covers skills and drills useful for self-instruction and coaching. Detailed drawings of maneuvers. (Gr 4–6)

Barth, Edna. *Hearts, Cupids, and Red Roses; the Story of the Valentine Symbols.* Illustrated by Ursula Arndt. New York, Seabury Press, 1974. [64] p. $6.95 ISBN 0–8164–3111–6
73–7128

The history of Valentine's Day and the little known stories behind its symbols—cards, paper lace, and goodies. (Gr 3–5)

————. *Shamrocks, Harps, and Shillelaghs: the Story of the St. Patrick's Day Symbols.* Illustrated by Ursula Arndt. New York, Seabury Press, 1977. 95 p. (A Clarion book) $7.95 ISBN 0–8164–3195–7
77–369

Irish history, lore, and legend are part of a wealth of information provided about Patrick the real missionary, St. Patrick's Day, and its celebration. Includes lists of stories for St. Patrick's Day and sources. (Gr 3–7)

Batterberry, Ariane R., *and* Michael Batterberry. *The Pantheon Story of American Art for Young People.* Introduction by Tom Armstrong. New York, Pantheon Books, 1976. [159] p. $14.95 ISBN 0–394–82842–9
75–22249

A good introduction for gallery visitors, this inviting survey begins with the art of the Indians and first settlers and carries the reader up to the 1960s. (Gr 5–up)

Baylor, Byrd. *They Put on Masks*. Illustrated by Jerry Ingram. New York, Scribner, 1974. 46 p. $6.95 ISBN 0–684–13767–4   73–19557
A poetic text conveys the significance to Indians and Eskimos of the masks they make from wood, skin, bones, and other natural materials, for use in prayers and dances. (Gr 3–5)

————. *When Clay Sings*. Illustrated by Tom Bahti. New York, Scribner, 1972. [32] p. $6.95 ISBN 0–684–12807–1   70–180758
The Southwest Indian's way of life in the past is suggested in a simple text accompanied by pleasing designs, in earthy colors, taken from pottery fragments. (Gr 3–up)

Berger, Melvin, *and* J. B. Handelsman. *The Funny Side of Science*. New York, Crowell, 1973. [48] p. $6.95 ISBN 0–690–32088–4   71–187944
An amusing, illustrated collection of riddles, jokes, brief stories, and cartoons, each dealing with some aspect of science. (Gr 4–up)

Blake, Quentin, *and* John Yeoman, *comps. The Improbable Book of Records*. Illustrated by Quentin Blake. New York, Atheneum, 1976. [32] p. $6.95 ISBN 0–689–30535–4   76–4466
Blake's hilarious full-color illustrations heighten this riotous takeoff on the *Guinness Book of World Records* (Gr 4–up)

Charlip, Remy, Mary Beth, *and* George Ancona. *Handtalk; an ABC of Finger Spelling & Sign Language*. New York, Parents' Magazine Press, 1974. [48] p. $5.95 ISBN 0–8193–0705–X (lib. ed. $5.41 ISBN 0–8193–0706–8)   73–10199
A challenging introduction to finger spelling and sign language for the deaf, with expressive faces and hands, and body language captured in color photographs. (Gr 2–up)

Chase, Alice E. *Looking at Art*. New York, Crowell, 1966. 119 p. $8.95 ISBN 0–690–50869–7 66–11947
Through comparisons of similar subjects painted by many different hands, the author helps us see the development of perspective, brushwork, patterns, focus, and abstraction, from the earliest Assyrian art to Chagall and Leger. (Gr 7–9)

Collier, James L. *Inside Jazz*. New York, Four Winds Press, 1973. 176 p. $6.95 ISBN 0–590–07282–X   73–76455
An enthusiastic, knowledgeable introduction to the history, style, and "greats" of jazz. Also, *The Great Jazz Artists* ($7.95 ISBN 0–590–07493–8). (Gr 7–9)

Comins, Jeremy. *Eskimo Crafts and Their Cultural Backgrounds*. New York, Lothrop, Lee & Shepard, 1975. 125 p. $6.00 ISBN 0–688–51705–6   75–9573
This how-to book is built on awareness of Eskimo cultural and artistic contributions and generously illustrated with black-and-white photographs of Eskimo artifacts as well as ample sketches · and step-by-step directions for reproducing from readily available materials sculpture, scrimshaw, stencils, and ookpiks (owl-like furry dolls). (Gr 4–up)

Cutler, Katherine N. *From Petals to Pinecones: A Nature Art and Craft Book*. Illustrated by Giulio Maestro. New York, Lothrop, Lee & Shepard, 1969. 128 p. $6.96 ISBN 0–688–51594–0 (paper $2.95 ISBN 0–688–45003–2)   79–81753
Explicit drawings illustrate ways in which materials in nature can be used to create gifts, decorations, and indoor gardens. (Gr 4–6)

D'Amato, Janet, *and* Alex D'Amato. *Colonial Crafts for You to Make*. New York, Messner, 1975. 64 p. $7.29 ISBN 0–671–32706–2   74–19005
Clear diagrams and scaled drawings accompany detailed instructions for making a number of items important to the daily life of colonial Americans. (Gr 5–8)

————. *Indian Crafts*. New York, Lion Press, 1968. 72 p. $5.95 ISBN 0–87460–004–9 ($5.49 ISBN 0–87460–088–X)   68–19688
Explicit directions for a variety of original Indian crafts including instructions for miniature and full-size models of homes and artifacts using inexpensive, readily available materials. (Gr 3–6)

DePree, Mildred. *A Child's World of Stamps: Stories, Poems, Fun, and Facts from Many Lands*. New York, Parents' Magazine Press, 1973. 126 p. $5.95 ISBN 0–8193–0661–4 (lib. ed. $5.41 ISBN 0–8193–0662–2)   72–10178
A colorful and readable introduction to stamps of the world, arranged by country, emphasizes subjects appeals to children: kites, fish, puffins, and the like. (All ages)

Dietz, Elizabeth W., *and* Michael B. Olatunji. *Musical Instruments of Africa; Their Nature, Use, and Place in the Life of a Deeply Musical People*. Illustrated by Richard M. Powers. New York, J. Day, 1965. 115 p. $9.95 ISBN 0–381–97013–2
65–13733/M
For young people interested in making their own music—and even their own instruments—this fully illustrated study shows how native African instruments are made and used. Includes two songs with words and melody and a long-playing record of African music recorded in Africa by Colin M. Turnbull. (Gr 6–up)

Fisher, Leonard E. *The Weavers*. New York, Watts, 1966. 45 p. $4.90 ISBN 0–531–01037–6　66–1058
In this volume of the artist's picture-story series about colonial craftsmen, intricacies of weaving and pattern-drafting are carefully explained. Also published in 1966 are his *The Cabinetmakers* (ISBN 0–531–01026–0) and *The Tanners* (ISBN 0–531–01038–4). (Gr 5–8)

Foster, Laura L. *Keeping the Plants You Pick*. Illustrated by the author. New York, Crowell, 1970. 149 p. $8.50 ISBN 0–690–47140–8　74–101926
A botanical artist documents her suggestions for preserving ferns, flowers, and leaves to make decorative arrangements, pictures, and gifts. (Gr 5–up)

Gardner, Martin. *Perplexing Puzzles and Tantalizing Teasers*. Illustrated by Laszlo Kubinyi. New York, Simon & Schuster, 1969. 95 p. Paper $0.95. Pocket Books. ISBN 0–671–29327–3　69–16871
Riddles, palindromes, noodles, tricky questions, and other puzzles for fun and stimulus. (Gr 3–up)

Gilbreath, Alice T. *Candles for Beginners to Make*. Illustrated by Jenni Oliver. New York, Morrow, 1975. 64 p. $6.25 ISBN 0–688–22010–X (lib. ed. $6.00 ISBN 0–688–32010–4)　74–14968
Directions for making a wide variety of candles stress safety rules and include instructions for chopping, melting, pouring, and coloring wax. (Gr 4–6)

Glubok, Shirley. *The Art of Ancient Peru*. Designed by Gerard Nook. Special photography by Alfred H. Tamarin. New York, Harper & Row, 1966. 41 p. $7.89 ISBN 0–06–022044–9　66–18651
Reproductions of early Peruvian arts and crafts on every page and a text that relates them to ancient life contribute effectively to an understanding of pre-Columbian civilization. (Gr 4–8)

————. *The Art of China*. Designed by Gerard Nook. New York, Macmillan, 1973. 48 p. $6.95 ISBN 0–02–736170–5　72–81059
Four thousand years of Chinese civilization are presented in a brief survey which includes samples of architecture, porcelain, pottery, silk fabrics, figurines, silk screen paintings, paintings on paper, and scrolls. Also, *The Art of Japan* ($5.95 ISBN 0–02–736080–6). (Gr 4–up)

————. *The Art of the Eskimo*. New York, Harper & Row, 1964. 48 p. $7.89 ISBN 0–06–022056–2　64–16637
Handsome bookmaking displays photographs of driftwood masks, ivory and stone carvings of animals, and the hunt. A feeling for Eskimo culture is simply conveyed in brief explanations. (Gr 4–up)

————. *The Art of the Plains Indians*. Designed by Gerard Nook. Special photography by Alfred Tamarin. New York, Macmillan, 1975. 48 p. $7.95 ISBN 0–02–73630–0　75–14064
Customs, traditions, and ceremonies of the Plains Indians are interpreted here through·their art: beadwork and leatherwork, dolls, headdresses, pipes, and other items of particular interest to children. Also, *The Art of the Southwest Indians* ($7.95 ISBN 0–02–736120–9). (Gr 4–up)

————. *The Art of the Spanish in the United States and Puerto Rico*. Designed by Gerard Nook. Photographs by Alfred Tamarin. New York, Macmillan, 1972. 48 p. $7.95 ISBN 0–02–736130–6　75–185218
Including St. Augustine, the Southwest, and Puerto Rico, the art historian's brief text with pictures on every page interprets the heritage from three centuries of Spanish domination in colonial America. (Gr 5–8)

Greenfeld, Howard. *Passover*. Illustrated by Elaine Grove. Designed by Bea Feitler. New York, Holt, Rinehart & Winston, 1978. 32 p. $5.95 ISBN 0–03–039921–1　77–13910
A clear explanation of the meaning today and the historical significance of the Jewish holiday of Passover with emphasis on customs connected with the Seder, the traditional service conducted at home. (Gr 3–5)

Helfman, Elizabeth S. *Signs and Symbols around the World*. New York, Lothrop, Lee & Shepard, 1967. 192 p. $6.97 ISBN 0–688–51249–6　67–22596
An unusual and fascinating survey of "picture-writing," from prehistory to contemporary sign-writing, with many illustrations conveying the communicative power of graphic signs. (All ages)

————. *Signs and Symbols of the Sun*. New York, Seabury Press, 1974. 192 p. $8.95 ISBN 0–8164–3122–1　73–20121
An explanation of the major role played by the sun in the mythology, arts, and religions of various world cultures—past and present. Decorated with drawings of sun symbols and illustrated with photographs of artifacts and art objects. (Gr 6–8)

Hirsh, Marilyn. *The Hanukkah Story*. New York, Bonim Books, 1977. [32] p. $7.95 ISBN 0–88482–756–9　77–22183
An account of the struggle of Judah Maccabee and his small army against the overwhelming might of the Syrians and how this event gave rise to the celebration of Hanukkah. Illustrated with color by the author. (Gr 2–5)

Hoople, Cheryl G. *The Heritage Sampler: A Book of Colonial Arts & Crafts.* Pictures and diagrams by Richard Cuffari. New York, Dial Press, 1975. 132 p. $6.95 ISBN 0–8037–5414–0 (lib. ed. $6.49 ISBN 0–8037–5430–2) 75–9203
A lively introduction to the skills and crafts of colonial America with detailed directions that allow children today to try their hand at them. (Gr 5–up)

Horwitz, Elinor L. *Mountain People, Mountain Crafts.* Photographs by Joshua Horwitz and Anthony Horwitz. Philadelphia, Lippincott, 1974. 143 p. $6.95 ISBN 0–397–31498–1 (paper $3.95 ISBN 0–397–31499–X) 73–19665
A survey of crafts and folk culture which is also a picture of the Appalachian way of life, fully illustrated with photographs. (Gr 7–up)

Johnson, Hannah L. *Let's Make Jam.* Photographs by Daniel Dorn, Jr. New York, Lothrop, Lee & Shepard, 1975. [39] p. $6.25 ISBN 0–688–41682–9 (lib. ed. $6.00 ISBN 0–688–51682–3) 74–20806
Black-and-white photographs accompany clear step-by-step instructions for preparing strawberry jam the natural way, from picking the fruit to bottling the preserves. (Gr 2–5)

Krementz, Jill. *A Very Young Gymnast.* New York, Knopf [distributed by Random House], 1978. [128] p. $8.95 ISBN 0–394–50080–6 78–5502
In the pattern of her earlier books (about a dancer and a rider) the author describes in photographs the training and triumphs of ten-year-old Torrance. Also, *A Very Young Rider* ($8.95 ISBN 0–394–41092–0). (Gr 3–6)

Macaulay, David. *Castle.* Boston, Houghton Mifflin, 1977. [80] p. $9.95 ISBN 0–395–25784–0 77–7159
Another in the artist-historian's brilliant series of works on the process of building a complex structure. Invents a composite example of a Welsh castle of the late thirteenth century and in large detailed drawings shows how it took six years to create what became a successful war machine. (All ages)

———. *Cathedral: The Story of Its Construction.* Boston, Houghton Mifflin, 1973. 77 p. $9.95 ISBN 0–395–17513–5 73–6634
The thirteenth-century Gothic cathedral of Chutreaux (imaginary) took eighty-six years to build, from the hiring of the architects to the grand opening. Construction is shown in the author's meticulously detailed, step-by-step drawings of craftsmen at work. A 1974 Caldecott Medal Honor Book. (Gr 4–up)

———. *City: a Story of Roman Planning and Construction.* Boston, Houghton Mifflin, 1974. 112 p. $9.95 ISBN 0–395–194–92–X 74–4280

An architect presents another distinctive book of drawings to show how an imaginary Roman city, designed for the people who lived in it, was built from 26 B.C. to A.D. 100. (Gr 7–up)

Maginley, C. J. *Models of America's Past and How to Make Them.* Illustrated by Elisabeth D. McKee. New York, Harcourt, Brace & World, 1969. 144 p. $6.25 ISBN 0–15–255051–8 69–17116
Step-by-step directions for making, from inexpensive materials, a variety of models of pioneer houses, barns, vehicles, furniture, a covered bridge, a district school, and a meetinghouse. (Gr 6–9)

Marks, Mickey K. *Op-Tricks; Creating Kinetic Art.* Kinetics by Edith Alberts. Photographs by David Rosenfeld. Philadelphia, Lippincott, 1972. [40] p. $5.95 ISBN 0–397–31539–2 79–38550
A clear introductory guide to the mechanics of kinetic art, with concise directions for straight-line drawings, plexiglass constructions, and simple sculpture in motion. Intended as a guide to creative adaptation of techniques and materials. (Gr 5–up)

Meyer, Carolyn. *The Bread Book: All about Bread and How to Make It.* Illustrated by Trina Schart Hyman. New York, Harcourt Brace Jovanovich, 1971. 96 p. $6.95 ISBN 0–15–212040–8 76–140780
As satisfying as a good loaf itself, this book touches on bread in history and religion and suggests simple recipes, with crisp drawings lightening every page. (Gr 3–6)

———. *Christmas Crafts: Things to Make the 24 Days before Christmas.* Pictures by Anita Lobel. New York, Harper & Row, 1974. 136 p. $5.95 ISBN 0–06–024197–7 (lib. ed. $5.79 ISBN 0–06–024198–5) 74–2608
Explanations of traditions associated with seasonal crafts and recipes precede the detailed directions for each project suggested. (Gr 4–up)

Miller, Irene P., *and* Winifred Lubell. *The Stitchery Book; Embroidery for Beginners.* Garden City, N.Y., Doubleday, 1965. 96 p. $4.95 ISBN 0–385–05550–1 65–16370
Many color and black-and-white photographs of museum pieces and other finished embroidery plus Mrs. Lubell's clear diagrams illustrate a text containing historical background as well as hints for creative stitchery.

Fun with Crewel Embroidery by Erica Wilson (Scribner $5.95 ISBN 0–684–12894–2), a briefer book with fewer pictures (one in color), suitable for younger beginners as well as older, offers a variety of designs and directions for the basic stitches. (Gr 7–up)

Moore, Janet G. *The Many Ways of Seeing; an Introduction to the Pleasures of Art*. Cleveland, World Pub. Co., 1969. 141 p. $9.95. Collins, New York, ISBN 0–529–00954–4 (lib. ed. $9.91 ISBN 0–529–04017–4)   67–23348

A museum lecturer's introduction to great paintings from Giotto to Picasso. Over eighty black-and-white illustrations and thirty-two pages in color. (Gr 6–up)

Myller, Rolf. *Symbols & Their Meaning*. New York, Atheneum, 1978. [95] p. $9.95 ISBN 0–689–30638–5   77–17015

The uses of many kinds of symbols for quick and simple communication are handled clearly in text and pictures. (Gr 4–7)

Naylor, Penelope. *Black Images: the Art of West Africa*. With photographs by Lisa Little. Garden City, N.Y., Doubleday, 1973. 95 p. $6.95 ISBN 0–385–07462–X   72–92233

Striking photographs, many of them accompanied by evocative poems, present a dramatic view of West African art—masks, figures, and ritual objects. (Gr 5–up)

Paine, Roberta M. *Looking at Architecture*. New York, Lothrop, Lee & Shepard, 1974. 127 p. $6.96 ISBN 0–688–51553–3   73–17718

In this introduction to architecture large photographs illustrate "shapes, forms, materials and techniques." Includes biographical notes, map, and reading list, as well as a glossary and an index. (Gr 4–7)

Parish, Peggy. *Costumes to Make*. Illustrated by Lynn Sweat. New York, Macmillan, 1970. 111 p. $6.95 ISBN 0–02–769950–1   75–102969

Detailed instructions for making costumes representative of historical periods, foreign countries, holidays, and storybook characters. (Gr 3–up)

––––––. *Let's Be Early Settlers with Daniel Boone*. New York, Harper & Row, 1967. 96 p. $5.79 ISBN 0–06–024648–0   67–3110

An imaginative how-to-do-it book for young would-be pioneers, with clear instructions and diagrams for projects in building, sewing, and model-making to re-create the life of settlers in the days of Daniel Boone. Humorous illustrations by Arnold Lobel. (Gr 1–4)

––––––. *Let's Celebrate; Holiday Decorations You Can Make*. Illustrated by Lynn Sweat. New York, Greenwillow Books/Morrow, 1976. 56 p. (Greenwillow read-alone) $5.95 ISBN 0–688–80050–5 (lib. ed. $5.71 ISBN 0–688–84050–7)   76–2726

A clearly illustrated first-reading book offers beginners instruction on how to enliven Christmas and other holidays. (Gr 1–3)

Paul, Aileen. *Kids Gardening; a First Indoor Gardening Book for Children*. Illustrated by Arthur Hawkins. Garden City, N.Y., Doubleday, 1972. 96 p. $4.95 ISBN 0–385–02492–4   73–177239

Succinct directions are accompanied by clear diagrams and informal, attractive drawings. After preliminary general advice, successive chapters treat specific kinds of plants. (Gr 3–6)

Perl, Lila. *Slumps, Grunts, and Snickerdoodles; What Colonial America Ate and Why*. Drawings by Richard Cuffari. New York, Seabury Press, 1975. 128 p. (A Clarion book) $7.95 ISBN 0–8164–3152–3   75–4894

Within discussion of the diets and cookery of the American colonists, thirteen colonial recipes are given including succotash, snickerdoodles, and spoon bread. (Gr 4–8)

Pettit, Florence H. *Christmas All around the House; Traditional Decoraitons You Can Make*. Drawings by Wendy Watson. New York, Crowell, 1976. 226 p. $9.95 ISBN 0–690–01013–3   75–37876

Clear instructions, detailed drawings, and simple patterns show the reader how to make Christmas decorations—many from other countries—from inexpensive, easily found materials. (Gr 5–up)

Pflug, Betsy. *Boxed-In Doll Houses*. Philadelphia, Lippincott, 1971. 48 p. $5.95 ISBN 0–397–31348–9   71–137219

Well-illustrated ideas, simple enough for small children to carry out, for making doll houses and furnishings out of cardboard boxes, paper, plastic, and other easily available materials. (Gr 3–5)

––––––. *Funny Bags*. Princeton, N.J., Van Nostrand, 1968. 40 p. Reprint $6.95. Lippincott, Phila. ISBN 0–397–31549–X   73–21723

From a Halloween mask to puppets, party decorations, and gift wrapping, the basis for this craft work is the paper bag. Simple step-by-step directions, each illustrated. (Gr 3–6)

Pinkwater, Jill. *The Natural Snack Cookbook; 151 Good Things to Eat*. New York, Four Winds Press, 1975. 258 p. $9.95 ISBN 0–590–07374–5 75–11717

A lighthearted introduction to healthful foods with recipes for cakes, breads, sandwiches, puddings, and candies made with natural ingredients. (Gr 5–up)

Price, Christine. *Dancing Masks of Africa*. New York, Scribner, 1975. [47] p. $6.95 ISBN 0–684–14332–1   75–4028

Striking linocuts in red, black, and mustard depict a varied selection of ceremonial masks indigenous to West African countries. An accompanying, rhythmic text describes their use. Also, *The Mystery of Masks* ($7.95 ISBN 0–684–15653–9) and *Talking Drums of Africa* ($5.95 ISBN 0–684–13492–6). (Gr 4–up)

————. *Made in West Africa*. New York, Dutton, 1975. 150 p. $9.95 ISBN 0–525–34400–4   74–4202
A lucid introduction to the role that art—carving, pottery, masks, sculpture, jewelry, and textiles—plays in the life of West Africa, lavishly illustrated with excellent photographs by the author. (Gr 5–up)

Punch and Judy. *Punch & Judy; a Play for Puppets.* Illustrated by Ed Emberley. Boston, Little, Brown, 1965. 27 p. $4.95 ISBN 0–316–23584–9 65–10793
This presents "a short history of Mr. Punch," the cast of traditional characters, and a series of brief playlets, with many suitably boisterous illustrations. (Gr 3–6)

————. *Festivals for You to Celebrate.* Philadelphia, Lippincott, 1969. 192 p. $7.95 ISBN 0–397–31071–4   69–12005
Suggestions for celebrating twenty-nine holidays of various lands and seasons include a wide range of craft work, foods, and activities, illustrated with clear diagrams for adult and child to follow together.
Another festivals book is this author's *Jewish Holidays, Facts, Activities, and Crafts* ($8.95 ISBN 0–397–31076–5), with historical background for each celebration and many suggestions for party decorations, games, and recipes. (Gr 4–up)

————. *Holiday Cards for You to Make.* Philadelphia, Lippincott, 1967. 64 p. $7.95 ISBN 0–397–31574–0   67–10375
With clear, colored illustration this rich compilation of suggestions for all the seasons provides instruction for working with linoleum-print, silk screen, collage, stencil, pressed-flower, and other techniques. (Gr 5–up)

Roche, Patricia K. *Dollhouse Magic; How to Make and Find Simple Dollhouse Furniture.* Photographs by John Knott; drawings by Richard Cuffari. New York, Dial Press, 1977. 58 p. $7.95 ISBN 0–8037–2122–6 ($7.45 ISBN 0–8037–2123–4)   76–42932
For child alone as well as for child-adult companionship, many fresh ideas for creating a dollhouse full of furniture. Ingenious ways of setting up rooms on stairs, on bookshelves, or in boxes. (Gr 2–up)

Rockwell, Anne F. *Games (and How to Play Them).* Pictures by Anne Rockwell. New York, Crowell, 1973. 43 p. $9.95 ISBN 0–690–32159–7 (lib. ed. $9.79 ISBN 0–690–32160–0)   72–10936

Forty-three parlor and outdoor games, clearly explained, are made more intriguing by imaginative picture-book illustration in full color which depicts animals as players. (K–up)

Ross, Laura. *Hand Puppets; How to Make and Use Them.* New York, Lothrop, Lee & Shepard, 1969. 192 p. $6.96 ISBN 0–688–51615–7 (paper $2.95 ISBN 0–688–45015–6)   73–82100
Materials, sources, and detailed instructions for making paper-bag puppets for *Rumpelstiltskin*, rod puppets for a shadow play of *Peter and the Wolf*, and papier-mâché puppets for *Punch and Judy*. (Gr 4–6)

————. *Mask-Making with Pantomime and Stories from American History.* Drawings by Frank Ross, Jr. New York, Lothrop, Lee & Shepard, 1975. 112 p. $6.00 ISBN 0–688–51721–8   75–11960
Advice to the beginner on mask construction (materials needed and special cautions such as leaving nose holes for breathing!) and on the use of masks plus mime to interpret a story. Details are given for four plays: *Pocahontas and John Smith, The Boston Tea Party, Harriet Tubman,* and *The Discovery of the North Pole.* (Gr 3–6)

Rubenstone, Jessie. *Knitting for Beginners.* Photographs by Edward Stevenson. Philadelphia, Lippincott, 1973. 64 p. $5.95 ISBN 0–397–31473–6 (paper $2.95 ISBN 0–397–31474–4)   72–6755
Clear instructions and photographs make this an ideal beginning book for young knitters. Includes simple, useful projects. (Gr 3–6)

Sarnoff, Jane, *and* Reynold Ruffins. *The Chess Book.* Consultant: Bruce Pandolfini. New York, Scribner, 1973. 39 p. $6.95 ISBN 0–684–13494–2 73–1385
Large color illustrations and a lucid text together diagram for the interested novice a sample chess game, its moves and elementary strategy. (Gr 4–6)

————. *The Code & Cipher Book.* New York, Scribner, 1975. 37 p. $6.95 ISBN 0–684–14246–5   74–24419
A lighthearted look at codes and ciphers, breezily illustrated in cartoon style. (Gr 3–6)

————. *A Great Bicycle Book.* Rudy "The Bicycle Man." Veselsky, technical consultant. New York, Scribner, 1973. 31 p. New ed. $6.95 ISBN 0–684–14580–4 (paper $2.95 ISBN 0–684–14615–0)   75–33507
For the young bicycle rider, a simple guide to buying, maintaining, repairing, and understanding a bicycle. (Gr 3–up)

————. *The Monster Riddle Book*. New York, Scribner, 1975. [32] p. $6.95 ISBN 0–684–14395–X
75–4465
Ghosts, vampires, witches, werewolves, and other monsters get merry treatment in this singular book with full-color fiendish illustrations. (All ages)

Sattler, Helen R. *Recipes for Art and Craft Materials.* Written and illustrated by Helen Roney Sattler. New York, Lothrop, Lee & Shepard, 1973. 128 p. $6.00 ISBN 0–688–51557–6   73–4950
A wide variety of inexpensive recipes for basic craft materials, including modeling compounds, paints, and pastes. (Gr 3–up)

Scheffer, Victor B. *The Seeing Eye.* Words and photographs by Victor B. Scheffer. New York, Scribner, 1971. 47 p. $5.95 ISBN 0–684–92311–4 70–140773
Striking color photographs and brief text stimulate awareness of form, color, and texture in nature, and dramatically illustrate the interrelationships of design, mathematics, and nature study. (Gr 5–up)

Schnurnberger, Lynn E. *Kings, Queens, Knights, & Jesters; Making Medieval Costumes.* In association with the Metropolitan Museum of Art. Drawings by Alan Robert Showe; photographs by Barbara Brooks and Pamela Hort. New York, Harper & Row, 1978. 113 p. $6.95 ISBN 0–06–025241–3 (lib. ed. $6.79 ISBN 0–06–025242–1)   77–25682
Explicit directions for using three basic pattern pieces—the circle, the *T*, and the tunic—help the young producer to fashion costumes for plays and pageants. (Gr 5–up)

Scott, Henry Joseph, *and* Lenore Scott. *Egyptian Hieroglyphs for Everyone; an Introduction to the Writing of Ancient Egypt.* New York, Funk & Wagnalls, 1969. 95 p. $8.95 ISBN 0–308–80223–3
68–13080
This fascinating introduction treats the grammar, pronunciation, and writing of words and sentences. Included are a basic vocabulary list and charts of pictographs showing how they can be combined to form phrases. (Gr 6–up)

Sobol, Harriet L. *Pete's House.* Photographs by Patricia Agre. New York, Macmillan, 1978. 58 p. $7.95 ISBN 0–02–785980–0   77–12564
A photographic essay records the work of a crew building young Pete's house: masons, carpenters, plumbers, electricians, roofers, and others. (Gr 5–8)

Streatfeild, Noel. *Young Person's Guide to Ballet.* Drawings by Georgette Bordier. New York, Warne, 1975. 120 p. $7.95 ISBN 0–7232–1814–5 74–81666

Dance-minded children will enjoy the historical and technical information given for a modern ballet school as well as the fictional narrative about two children training to be dancers. Illustrated with both drawings and photographs. (Gr 5–up)

Thomson, Peggy. *Museum People; Collectors and Keepers at the Smithsonian.* Illustrations by Joseph Low. Englewood Cliffs, N.J., Prentice-Hall, 1977. 305 p. $8.95 ISBN 0–13–606889–8   77–3175
Neither a guidebook nor a reference tool but a fascinating "people book" in which the journalist-author presents unique collectors, conservators, and exhibitors who serve the many museums and the zoo which make up the Smithsonian Institution. (Gr 7–up)

Warren, Fred. *The Music of Africa; an Introduction.* By Fred Warren with Lee Warren. Illustrated with photographs and line drawings by Penelope Naylor. Englewood Cliffs, N.J., Prentice-Hall, 1970. 87 p. $5.95 ISBN 0–13–608224–6   73–125329
Brief but substantial is this discussion of music in African life and the Western debt to contemporary African music, including a description of elements that make it unique as well as universal, and the musical instruments associated with it. (Gr 6–9)

Weisgard, Leonard. *The Plymouth Thanksgiving.* Garden City, N.Y., Doubleday, 1967. [64] p. $5.95 ISBN 0–385–07312–7 (lib. ed. $6.90 ISBN 0–385–08297)   67–15379
Dramatic illustration and brief text based on William Bradford's diary convey the struggle of the Pilgrims' first year in the new world. (Gr 1–4)

Weiss, Harvey. *Ceramics from Clay to Kiln.* Illustrated by the author. New York, Young Scott Books, 1964. 63 p. $6.95. Addison-Wesley, Reading, Mass. ISBN 0–201–09153–4   64–13583
Another of this sculptor-art teacher's clearly illustrated, step-by-step craft books, this interprets and explains basic techniques of using clay in slab, coil, and sculpture processes. (Gr 5–up)

————. *Collage and Construction.* New York, Young Scott Books, 1970. 62 p. (Beginning artists library) $6.95. Addison-Wesley, Reading, Mass. ISBN 0–201–09163–1   76–98115
A practical discussion of methods and materials for flat-surface collages and three-dimensional constructions. Illustrated with diagrams and with photographs of contemporary examples. (Gr 5–8)

————. *How to Make Your Own Books.* New York, Crowell, 1974. 71 p. $7.95 ISBN 0–690–00400–1
73–17267

A booklover's suggestions of kinds of books to make (diaries, scrapbooks, and others) with explicit directions for their construction. (Gr 5–up)

————. *How to Run a Railroad; Everything You Need to Know about Model Trains.* New York, Crowell, 1977. 127 p. $8.50 ISBN 0–690–01304–3
76–18128
The selection, assembling, construction, and operation of model railroad equipment, with clearly captioned diagrams and photographs indicating realistic and imaginative layouts. (Gr 5–8)

————. *Lens and Shutter; an Introduction to Photography.* Reading, Mass., Young Scott Books, 1971. 120 p. (The Beginning artist's library) $6.95. Addison-Wesley. ISBN 0–201–09240–9   79–115913
Helpful, photographic examples illustrate principles of photography, kinds of cameras and film, and techniques for getting artistic results. (Gr 7–up)

————. *Model Airplanes and How to Build Them.* New York, Crowell, 1975. 90 p. $7.50 ISBN 0–690–00594–6
74–19451
Diagrams, drawings, and photographs supplement clear step-by-step instructions for the hobbyist to make a wide variety of airplanes and helicopters out of wood and cardboard and power them by simple methods. (Gr 5–8)

————. *Paint, Brush and Palette.* New York, William R. Scott, 1966. 64 p. $6.95. Addison-Wesley, Reading, Mass. ISBN 0–201–09303–0   66–11410
Experiments with colors, shapes, textures, and kinds of paints, to open the eyes of a beginning painter who, after studying color relationships for himself, will look at great art with more critical perception. (Gr 7–up)

Willson, Robina B. *The Voice of Music.* Foreword by Yehudi Menuhin. Illustrated by Jeroo Roy. New York, Atheneum, 1977. 224 p. (A Margaret K. McElderry book) $7.95 ISBN 0–689–50096–3 77–3225
A highly readable introduction to classical, folk, and popular music. The voice, familiar and less well-known instruments, and individual composers are given brief attention. List of musical terms and a discography. (Gr 6–9)

Wolff, Diane. *Chinese Writing, an Introduction.* Calligraphy by Jeanette Chien. Photographs by Laura DeCoppet [and others]. New York, Holt, Rinehart & Winston, 1975. 46 p. $5.95 ISBN 0–03–013006–9   74–20579
A brief introduction about the country, its languages, and calligraphy precedes a description of basic characters—ancient and modern—and their brush strokes. (Gr 5–up)

Wolff, Robert J. *Seeing Red.* New York, Scribner, 1968. [32] p. $5.95 ISBN 0–684–12826–8 67–24052
An artist-teacher has made a stunningly simple introduction to color, clear enough for the very youngest. Its sequels, *Feeling Blue* and *Seeing Yellow*, show equally distinguished bookmaking. (K–Gr 2)

Wolters, Richard A. *Kid's Dog; a Training Book.* Garden City, N.Y., Doubleday, 1978. 128 p. $5.95 ISBN 0–385–11550–4 (lib. ed. $6.90 ISBN 0–385–11551–2)   76–23803
Useful instructions for selecting and training a puppy are illustrated with engaging black-and-white photographs. (Gr 6–8)

Yolen, Jane H. *Ring Out! A Book of Bells.* Drawings by Richard Cuffari. New York, Seabury Press, 1974. 128 p. $6.95 ISBN 0–8164–3127–2   74–4043
The making and uses of bells throughout history: in everyday and religious life, in town and country, in war and peace, and for music. Poems are interpolated. (Gr 5–up)

————. *World on a String; the Story of Kites.* Cleveland, World Pub. Co., 1969. 143 p. Reprint $5.95. Collins, New York. ISBN 0–529–00392–9 (lib. ed. $5.91 ISBN 0–529–00394–5)   68–26976
A splendid profusion of photographs amplifies interest in kites: scientific and military uses, importance as religious symbols, and fun for sport. (Gr 5–up)

Biography

Adoff, Arnold. *Malcolm X.* Illustrated by John Wilson. New York, Crowell, 1970. 41 p. (Crowell biographies) $6.95 ISBN 0–690–51413–1 (paper $1.95 ISBN 0–690–51415–8)   70–94787
The life of the young man who infused into American thought during the 1960s a knowledge of the beauty, dignity, and pride in being black. (Gr 3–5)

Alexander, Rae P., *comp. Young and Black in America.* Introductory notes by Julius Lester. New York, Random House, 1970. 139 p. $3.95 ISBN 0–394–80482–1 (lib. ed. $4.99 ISBN 0–394–90482–6)   70–117005
Autobiographical selections for eight men and women—from Frederick Douglass to a soldier of today. (Gr 6–up)

Atkinson, Linda. *Mother Jones, the Most Dangerous Woman in America.* New York, Crown, 1978. 246 p. $7.95 ISBN 0–517–53201–8   77–15863
Irish-born Mary Harris Jones, after losing her husband and four children in 1867, devoted the rest of her long life to the struggle of coal miners for economic justice. (Gr 6–8)

Burnett, Constance B. *Happily Ever After; a Portrait of Frances Hodgson Burnett.* New York, Vanguard Press, 1965. 160 p. $5.95 ISBN 0–8149–0283–9   65–17370
An engaging portrait of the Victorian novelist remembered today as the author of *The Secret Garden* and *Sara Crewe.* (Gr 7–9)

Coit, Margaret L. *Andrew Jackson.* Illustrated by Milton Johnson. Boston, Houghton Mifflin, 1965. 154 p. $3.50 ISBN 0–395–06698–0   65–14924
An able historian deals with the human intensity of a complex and controversial man and with the historic events and political issues of his long life. (Gr 6–up)

Collins, Michael. *Flying to the Moon and Other Strange Places.* New York, Farrar, Straus & Giroux, 1976. 159 p. $6.95 ISBN 0–374–32412–3 76–25496
An astronaut's discussion of his early career and training for space flight, his trips into space, including the first lunar landing, and projection of future possibilities for life and flight in space, is illustrated with photographs and diagrams. (Gr 5–8)

Coolidge, Olivia E. *Gandhi.* Boston, Houghton Mifflin, 1971. 278 p. $5.95 ISBN 0–395–12573–1 71–262645
A moving portrayal of the man whose long life was spent in a total effort to improve conditions for the people of India and whose philosophy of *satyagraha*—resistence by nonviolence—was to have meaning for other countries as well. (Gr 8–up)

—. *Tom Paine, Revolutionary.* New York, Scribner, 1969. 213 p. $10.00 ISBN 0–684–15152–9
69–17064

A thoroughly researched, vivid portrait of a man first hailed as a hero of the American Revolution and then rejected by those who had admired him. (Gr 7–up)

Crawford, Deborah. *Four Women in a Violent Time.* New York, Crown Publishers, 1970. 191 p. $6.95 ISBN 0–517–50313–1
74–127519

A lively presentation of four women who played historic roles in the seventeenth-century colonies: Anne Hutchinson and Mary Dyer protested religious intolerance; broad-minded Lady Deborah Moody built a town; and Penelope Stout survived scalping, severe wounds, and Indian captivity to leave over five hundred descendants when she died at 110 years of age. (Gr 6–8)

Dickinson, Alice. *Charles Darwin and Natural Selection.* New York, Watts, 1964. 212 p. $5.90 ISBN 0–531–00865–7
64–11921

Drawn considerably from Darwin's own writings, including *The Voyage of the Beagle*, the details of controversy and slow acceptance of his theories make exciting reading. (Gr 7–up)

Dobrin, Arnold. *I Am a Stranger on the Earth; the Story of Vincent Van Gogh.* New York, Warne, 1975. 95 p. $7.95 ISBN 0–7232–6121–0   75–8105

The lonely, self-tormented artist whose only happiness lay in painting is perceptively treated in this biography illustrated with color and black-and-white reproductions of his influential paintings and drawings. (Gr 6–9)

Douglass, Frederick. *Life and Times of Frederick Douglass.* Adapted by Barbara Ritchie. New York, Crowell, 1966. 210 p. $6.95 ISBN 0–690–50088–2
66–10063

Douglass's autobiography reveals the nineteenth-century hardships and cruelties endured by blacks in both the South and the North. A valuable original document adapted for young people. (Gr 7–up)

Edwards, Anne. *The Great Houdini.* Illustrated by Joseph Ciardiello. New York, Putnam, 1977. 62 p. (A See and read book) $4.29 ISBN 0–399–61020–0
76–8472

A beginner's biography of the man reputed to be the greatest magician and escape artist of all time. (Gr 2–4)

Epstein, Samuel, *and* Beryl Epstein. *Dr. Beaumont and the Man with the Hole in His Stomach.* Illustrated by Joseph Scrofani. New York, Coward,

McCann & Geoghegan, 1978. 57 p. $4.99 ISBN 0–698–30680–5
77–8236

An army doctor who saw service in the War of 1812, William Beaumont found an opportunity to make a name for himself with a patient whose severe wound provided him with a laboratory for a nearly lifelong study of the stomach. (Gr 5–7)

Faber, Doris. *Oh, Lizzie! The Life of Elizabeth Cady Stanton.* New York, Lothrop, Lee & Shepard, 1972. 159 p. $6.48 ISBN 0–688–51405–7 (paper $0.75. Pocket Books. ISBN 0–671–29617–5)   79–177322

A lively personality stands forth in the nineteenth-century pioneer in the women's rights movement. (Gr 5–8)

Facklam, Margery. *Wild Animals, Gentle Women.* Illustrated with line drawings by Paul Facklam and with photographs. New York, Harcourt Brace Jovanovich, 1978. 139 p. $5.95 ISBN 0–15–296987–X
77–88961

Engrossing portraits of eleven women who have collected animals or watched their behavior in the wild. Includes such well-known persons as Jane Goodall. (Gr 5–8)

Fecher, Constance. *The Last Elizabethan; a Portrait of Sir Walter Raleigh.* New York, Farrar, Straus & Giroux, 1972. 241 p. $5.50 ISBN 0–374–34361–6
74–178882

Courtier, sea captain, poet, explorer, historian, and amateur scientist, Sir Walter Raleigh, Renaissance man, emerges as an admirable human tragically caught in the interplay of political intrigue at the courts of Queen Elizabeth and her successor, King James I of England. Illustrated with photographs. (Gr 7–9)

Fisher, Aileen L. *Jeanne d'Arc.* Illustrated by Ati Forberg. New York, Crowell, 1970. 52 p. $5.79 ISBN 0–690–45828–2
74–81950

A simple direct text, an open format, and muted illustrations make this a fine introduction to the story of Joan of Arc. (Gr 3–5)

Fritz, Jean. *And Then What Happened, Paul Revere?* Pictures by Margot Tomes. New York, Coward, McCann & Geoghegan, 1973. 45 p. $5.95 ISBN 0–698–20274–0
73–77423

Facts and a touch of legend are attractively blended in this engaging portrait of Paul Revere, one of America's bustlers: silversmith, maker of artificial teeth, businessman, and ardent patriot. Margot Tomes's pictures capture Revere's indefatigable energy. Other titles in a similar vein are: *Can't You Make Them Behave, King George?* (ISBN 0–698–20315–1);

What's the Big Idea, Ben Franklin? (ISBN 0–698–20365–8); *Where Was Patrick Henry on the 29th of May?* (ISBN 0–698–20307–0); *Why Don't You Get a Horse, Sam Adams?* (ISBN 0–698–20292–9); and *Will You Sign Here, John Hancock?* (ISBN 0–698–20308–9). (Gr 1–4)

-- *where do you think you're going, Christopher Columbus)*

Greenfield, Eloise. *Mary McLeod Bethune.* Illustrated by Jerry Pinkney. New York, Crowell, 1977. 32 p. (Crowell biographies) $6.95 ISBN 0–690–01129–6   76–11522

A simply written biography recounts the life of the great black educator, from her childhood in North Carolina to the founding of her famous school. Attractively illustrated in soft-pencil line. (Gr 2–4)

Hamilton, Virginia. *Paul Robeson: The Life and Times of a Free Black Man.* New York, Harper & Row, 1974. 217 p. $6.95 ISBN 0–06–022188–7 (lib. ed. $6.79 IBSN 0–06–022189–5)   72–82892

A moving portrait of the courageous, lonely man who experienced enormous fame and then oblivion. Illustrated with photographs. (Gr 8–up)

————. *W. E. B. Du Bois; a Biography.* New York, Crowell, 1972. 218 p. $6.95 ISBN 0–690–87256–9   70–175106

A competently documented portrait of this black leader-author-sociologist's successes and failures in attempts to attain equality for his people in America. (Gr 6–up)

Harnan, Terry. *African Rhythm—American Dance; a Biography of Katherine Dunham.* New York, Knopf, 1974. 213 p. $5.99 ISBN 0–394–92644–7   73–15113

The engrossing story of the gifted dancer, choreographer, and anthropologist who combined her talents to create an authentic and influential modern dance style based on African and Caribbean sources. Photographs. (Gr 5–8)

Haskins, James. *Barbara Jordan.* New York, Dial Press, 1977. 215 p. $7.95 ISBN 0–8037–0452–6   77–71522

Emphasizes the political career of the first black woman to become a Texas state senator and the first to represent a southern state in the House of Representatives. Illustrated with photographs. (Gr 6–up)

Hautzig, Esther R. *The Endless Steppe; Growing Up in Siberia.* New York, Crowell, 1968. 243 p. $7.95 ISBN 0–690–26371–6 (paper $1.25. Scholastic Book Service. ISBN 0–590–04445–1)   68–13582

The author tells of her adolescent years in Siberian exile, which she endured with an indomitable will to live and to extract good from the cruelest circumstances. (Gr 6–up)

Hodges, Margaret. *Hopkins of the Mayflower; Portrait of a Dissenter.* New York, Farrar, Straus and Giroux, 1972. 274 p. $5.95 ISBN 0–374–33324–6   72–81485

Capturing the period and the temper of the times (Elizabeth I and James I), this remarkable book weaves the story of a believer in freedom for all and self-determination for man, the individual who was not only instrumental in the settling of Jamestown but was also a passenger on the Mayflower and a settler of Plymouth Plantation. (Gr 6–8)

————. *Lady Queen Anne; a Biography of Queen Anne of England.* New York, Farrar, Straus & Giroux, 1969. 275 p. $4.95 ISBN 0–374–34290–3   69–14978

Adroitly used quotations from original sources bring authenticity, life, and color to a well-constructed biography of the last of the Stuarts. (Gr 6–8)

Hoobler, Dorothy, *and* Thomas Hoobler. *Photographing History; the Career of Mathew Brady.* New York, Putnam, 1977. 143 p. $8.95 ISBN 0–399–20602–7   77–3009

There is a sizable slice of American history in this account of the photographer of famous men and women who left his studio at the zenith of his career to travel with Union troops photographing the Civil War. Lavishly illustrated with Brady's photographs. (Gr 7–9)

Iverson, Genie. *Louis Armstrong.* Illustrated by Kevin Brooks. New York, Crowell, 1976. 38 p. $5.79 ISBN 0–690–01127–X   76–4975

An easy-to-read biography describes the life of the famous trumpeter, from his childhood in New Orleans to the time when he became known as "Ambassador Satch" and "King of Jazz." (Gr 3–5)

Jacobs, David. *Beethoven.* By the editors of Horizon Magazine. Consultant: Elliot Forbes. New York, American Heritage Pub. Co.; book trade and institutional distribution by Harper & Row, 1970. 152 p. (A Horizon Caravel book) $5.95 ISBN 0–06–022796–6 (lib. ed. $6.89 ISBN 0–06–022797–4)   70–98624

Reproductions of paintings and sketches, together with photographs of some of the musician's possessions, enhance this lively account of the composer's life. (Gr 6–8)

J
920
Johnston, Johanna. *A Special Bravery.* New York, Dodd, Mead, 1967. 94 p. $4.50 ISBN 0–396–06728–X (paper $0.95 ISBN 0–396–06302–0) 67–3141
Moving stories highlight the accomplishments of fifteen outstanding American Negroes from revolutionary times to the present, including James Forten, Benjamin Banneker, Matthew Henson, Martin Luther King, Jr., and others of today. Illustrated with lively, full-page ink sketches by Ann Grifalconi. (Gr 3–5)

J
B
Jordan, June. *Fannie Lou Hamer.* Illustrated by Albert Williams. New York, Crowell, 1973. 39 p. (A Crowell biography) $5.95 ISBN 0–690–28893–X (lib. ed. $5.79 ISBN 0–690–28894–8; paper $1.45 ISBN 0–690–00634–9) 70–184982
A meaty, if brief, biography accents Mrs. Hamer's activities for Mississippi voter registration and the establishment of the Freedom Farm Cooperative. (Gr 3–5)

J
B
Koehn
Koehn, Ilse. *Mischling, Second Degree; My Childhood in Nazi Germany.* With a foreword by Harrison E. Salisbury. New York, Greenwillow Books, 1977. 240 p. $7.95 ISBN 0–688–80110–2 (lib. ed. $7.63 ISBN 0–688–84110–4) 77–6189
Because having one Jewish grandparent gives Ilse a precarious position in Hitler's Germany, her loving parents divorce to protect her. A moving narrative based on the author's personal experience of growing up in Berlin and in a Nazi youth camp in Czechoslovakia. (Gr 6–8)

J
970.1
Kroeber, Theodora. *Ishi, Last of His Tribe.* Drawings by Ruth Robbins. Berkeley, Calif., Parnassus Press, 1964. 211 p. $7.50 ISBN 0–87466–049–1 (lib. ed. $7.11 ISBN 0–87466–018–1) 64–19401
A poetic and significant interpretation of the Yahi Indian way of life. Ishi, who in childhood survived his tribe's massacre by California goldseekers and alone in adulthood took the road he believed led to death, became the protégé of an anthropologist. Drawings evoke the symbolism of the Yahi world. (Gr 6–up)

J
B
Land, Barbara. *Evolution of a Scientist; The Two Worlds of Theodosius Dobzhansky.* Illustrated with photographs. New York, Crowell, 1973. 262 p. $4.50 ISBN 0–690–27214–6 72–83788
Taped interviews with the brilliant Russian emigré cohere into a readable, provocative account of an influential thinker, his life in academia, and the infant years of the science of genetics. (Gr 6–up)

J
796.83
ALI
Lipsyte, Robert. *Free to Be Muhammad Ali.* New York, Harper & Row, 1978. 124 p. (An Ursula Nordstrom book) $5.95 ISBN 0–06–023901–8 (lib. ed. $5.79 ISBN 0–06–023902–6) 77–25640
A realistic, balanced, and sensitive look at the childhood and turbulent adult life of this colorful heavyweight champion who admits that some of the "legendary facts" of his life are just that. (Gr 6–up)

J
B
Longsworth, Polly. *I, Charlotte Forten, Black and Free.* New York, Crowell, 1970. 248 p. $6.95 ISBN 0–690–42869–3 79–109901
An absorbing biography developed from the journal kept by Charlotte—from 1854 when she was a schoolgirl in Salem, Mass., to 1864 when she taught newly emancipated slaves at Port Royal, S.C., as part of a government social experiment. (Gr 6–9)

J
B
Lord, Athena V. *Pilot for Spaceship Earth; R. Buckminster Fuller, Architect, Inventor, and Poet.* New York, Macmillan, 1978. 168 p. $7.95 ISBN 0–02–761420–4 77–12629
An account of how Bucky Fuller, expelled from Harvard University for "lack of interest," goes on to invent the geodesic dome and the Dymaxion Car. (Gr 6–8)

J
B
Meltzer, Milton. *Langston Hughes.* New York, Crowell, 1968. 281 p. $6.95 ISBN 0–690–48525–5 68–21952
A life of the great black poet, who understood his people and expressed their cause with eloquence. (Gr 7–9)

O
————. *Tongue of Flame; the Life of Lydia Maria Child.* New York, Crowell, 1965. 210 p. $4.95 ISBN 0–690–82961–2 (paper $0.95. Dell. ISBN 0–440–97814–9) 65–14903
A sharply revealing picture of the "lady writer" in antislavery circles of Boston and New York who pioneered in antislavery publishing and also, earlier, wrote for children. (Gr 7–up)

E
Monjo, E. N. *Poor Richard in France.* Pictures by Brinton Turkle. New York, Holt, Rinehart and Winston, 1973. 58 p. $4.95 ISBN 0–03–088598–1 (paper $0.95. Dell. ISBN 0–440–46110–3) 72–76582
With lively wit, seven-year-old Benny Franklin Bache reports on a trip to Paris with his famous grandfather. The "fictional memoir" is enhanced by jaunty two-color drawings in soft crayon and chalk. (Gr 1–5)

J
B
Moore, Carman. *Somebody's Angel Child; the Story of Bessie Smith.* New York, Crowell, 1970. 121 p. (Women of America) Paper $0.95. Dell. ISBN 0–440–97778–9 77–94797
A revealing life story of the black singer whose name has become synonymous with the blues. Included are

some of her compositions, lyrics of some of her famous songs, and a selected discography. Illustrated with photographs. (Gr 5–7)

Oritz, Victoria. *Sojourner Truth, a Self-Made Woman.* Philadelphia. Lippincott, 1974. 157 p. $7.95 ISBN 0-397-31504-X   73-22290
A vigorous story as well as a commentary on the times of a remarkable woman who was born into slavery, gained her freedom, fought as an ardent abolitionist, and then turned her intelligence and talents to the fight for women's suffrage. Illustrated with photographs. (Gr 5–9)

Powers, Elizabeth. *The Journal of Madame Royale.* New York, Walker, 1976. 150 p. $7.50 ISBN 0-8027-6251-4 (lib. ed. $7.39 ISBN 0-8027-6252-2)   75-43990
A simply presented, first-person account of the French Revolution, based on the journal of Marie Antoinette's daughter. (Gr 6–9)

Scott, John Anthony. *Fanny Kemble's America.* Illustrated with photographs. New York, Crowell, 1973. 146 p. (Women of America) $6.95 ISBN 0-690-28911-1   72-7557
An illuminating biography of the English Shakespearean actress emphasizes her years in America as the wife of plantation owner Pierce Butler, her strong antislavery beliefs, and her authorship of *Journal of a Residence on a Georgian Plantation in 1838-1839.* Documents the plight of nineteenth-century women as well as black history. (Gr 6–8)

———. *Woman against Slavery; the Story of Harriet Beecher Stowe.* Illustrated with photographs. New York, Crowell, 1978. 169 p. (Woman of America) $7.95 ISBN 0-690-00701-9 (lib. ed. $7.89 ISBN 0-690-03844-5)   77-5310
A well-documented, often moving account of the author whose life story projects a feminist as well as an antislavery protest. (Gr 7–9)

Starkey, Marion L. *The Visionary Girls; Witchcraft in Salem Village.* Boston, Little, Brown, 1973. 176 p. $5.95 ISBN 0-316-81087-8   72-13940
An engrossing fictionalized reconstruction of the Salem witch trials, attributed by this author to the hysteria of several young girls who were led by twelve-year-old Ann Putnam. (Gr 5–8)

Sterling, Dorothy, *and* Benjamin Quarles. *Lift Every Voice; the Lives of Booker T. Washington, W. E. B. Du Bois, Mary Church Terrell, and James Weldon Johnson.* Illustrated by Ernest Crichlow. Garden City, N.Y., Doubleday, 1965. 116 p. $4.95 ISBN 0-385-03651-5 (paper $2.50 ISBN 0-385-04192-6)   65-17237

Four great Negroes who strove to open doors for their people—through education, writing, organization, and participation in political affairs. (Gr 7–9)

Stern, Philip V. *Edgar Allan Poe, Visitor from the Night of Time.* New York, Crowell, 1973. 172 p. $6.95 ISBN 0-690-25554-3   72-83786
Thwarted by desperate poverty and personal tragedy during most of his life, Poe struggled to make a name through his poetry, suspenseful tales, and other writings. A sympathetic and forceful presentation. (Gr 7–up)

Veglahn, Nancy. *Coils, Magnets, and Rings; Michael Faraday's World.* Illustrated by Christopher Spollen. New York, Coward, McCann & Geoghegan, 1976. 64 p. $5.95 ISBN 0-698-20384-4
          76-14385
Against a backdrop of nineteenth-century England, an engaging portrait emerges of the man who discovered electromagnetism, made other scientific breakthroughs, and still had time to enjoy life and people. Attractive illustrations capture the spirit of the man and the period. (Gr 4–6)

Warner, Lucille S. *From Slave to Abolitionist: The Life of William Wells Brown.* Adapted. Illustrated by Tom Feelings. New York, Dial Press, 1976. 135 p. $6.95 ISBN 0-8037-2743-7   76-2288
A fictionalized first-person treatment traces the career of a slave, who when freed devoted his life to the abolitionist movement. This attractively produced volume is based on Brown's journal and other works, which are quoted freely. (Gr 6–9)

Walker, Alice. *Langston Hughes, American Poet.* Illustrated by Don Miller. New York, Crowell, 1974. 33 p. (A Crowell biography) $6.95 ISBN 0-690-00218-1   73-9565
An easy-to-read biography emphasizing the subject's life as a young man before his first book of poems was published.
James Weldon Johnson by Ophelia Settle Egypt ($5.95 ISBN 0-690-00214-9) and *Roberto Clemente* by Kenneth Rudeen ($5.95 ISBN 0-690-00322-6) are two additional titles in this publisher's series. (Gr 2–4)

Wibberley, Leonard. *Man of Liberty; a Life of Thomas Jefferson.* New York, Farrar, Straus & Giroux, 1968. 404 p. $6.95 ISBN 0-374-34752-2
          68-24599
Originally published as four separate volumes, 1963-1966.
Contents: Young Man from the Piedmont, A Dawn in the Trees, The Gales of Spring, and Time of the Harvest. (Gr 7–9)

Wilder, Laura Ingalls. *West from Home: Letters of Laura Ingalls Wilder, San Francisco, 1915.* Edited by Roger Lea MacBride. Historical setting by Margaret Patterson Doss. New York, Harper & Row, 1974. 168 p. $6.95 ISBN 0–06–024110–1 (lib. ed. $6.79 ISBN 0–06–024111–X; paper $1.95 ISBN 0–06–440081–6) 73–14342

A delightful collection of letters written by Mrs. Wilder to her husband during her visit to their daughter and to the Panama-Pacific Exposition. (Gr 6–up)

Wilson, Ellen J. C. *American Painter in Paris; a Life of Mary Cassatt.* New York, Farrar, Straus & Giroux, 1971. 205 p. (An Ariel book) $4.95 ISBN 0–374–30270–7 70–149223

A biography of the nineteenth-century Pennsylvania woman who won fame as an artist and a place in the art circles of Paris, where she came to know Degas and others. (Gr 6–9)

History, People, and Places

Almedingen, Martha E. *Land of Muscovy; the History of Early Russia.* Illustrated by Michael Charlton. New York, Farrar, Straus & Giroux, 1972. 147 p. $4.95 ISBN 0–374–34310–1   72–79864

The romance and vigor of early Russia are conveyed in an informal history replete with vignettes of such important personages as Ivan IV and including the legend of a woodcutter's rescue of czar-elect Michael Romanov from Polish soldiers. (Gr 6–8)

Bacon, Margaret H. *Rebellion at Christiana.* New York, Crown, 1975. 216 p. $5.95 ISBN 0–517–51576–8   74–77272

Centering on the 1866 account by William Parke, an escaped slave who organized other slaves, the author vividly describes events surrounding the unsuccessful attempt in 1851 of a Maryland slaveowner to reclaim four slaves who had fled to Pennsylvania. (Gr 6–8)

Baldwin, Gordon C. *The Apache Indians; Raiders of the Southwest.* New York, Four Winds Press, 1978. 221 p. $9.95 ISBN 0–590–07321–4 77–21439

Well-documented, this generously illustrated volume describes the Apache life-style. (Gr 7–9)

Barker, Albert. *From Settlement to City.* New York, Messner, 1978. 64 p. $6.97 ISBN 0–671–32865–4   78–12896

Period photographs lend authentic flavor to this study of a hypothetical midwestern city from its beginning as a stopping-off place for covered wagons to today. (Gr 4–8)

Baumann, Hans. *Lion Gate and Labyrinth.* Translated by Stella Humphries. New York, Pantheon Books, 1967. 182 p. $6.39 ISBN 0–394–91881–9   67–4156

The prehistory of ancient Greek civilizations, as well as events described in mythology which archaeology proves actually to have occurred, are revealed in this account of the work of Heinrich Schliemann and Arthur Evans. Illustrated with handsome color plates. (Gr 6–8)

Bealer, Alex W. *Only the Names Remain; the Cherokees and the Trail of Tears.* Illustrated by William Sauts Bock. Boston, Little, Brown, 1972. 88 p. $5.95 ISBN 0–316–08520–0   71–169008

An honest picture of the tragic exile of the Cherokee Nation in 1839 told from the Indian point of view. Fully illustrated. (Gr 4–6)

Bergman Sucksdorff, Astrid. *Tooni, the Elephant Boy.* New York, Harcourt Brace Jovanovich, 1971. [48] p. $5.95 ISBN 0–15–289426–8   73–137762

Color photographs document Indian village life in Assam with clear and positive pictures of family life, school, and jungle scenes. (Gr 3-up)

Bernheim, Marc, *and* Evelyne Bernheim. *African Success Story: The Ivory Coast.* New York, Harcourt, Brace & World, 1970. 96 p. $6.95 ISBN 0–15–201650–3   72–84772

A profusely illustrated study explains how and why this African nation has succeeded since its independence from France in 1960 and also describes life there today. (Gr 6–8)

———. *The Drums Speak; the Story of Kofi, a Boy of West Africa.* New York, Harcourt Brace Jovanovich, 1972. [48] p. $6.50 ISBN 0–15–224233–3
70–137761

A picture-book volume with a minimal, generalized text is distinctive with its large, technically excellent, and appealing color photographs which depict two weeks' activities of a village boy on the Ghana-Ivory Coast border. (Gr 3–6)

Branley, Franklyn M. *The Mystery of Stonehenge.* Illustrated by Victor G. Ambrus. New York, Crowell, 1969. 51 p. $6.95 ISBN 0–690–57046–5
69–11823

A brief summary of theories about the hows and whys of the massive pillars placed at Stonehenge, with many drawings and labeled diagrams. (Gr 4–6)

Campbell, Elizabeth A. *Jamestown: The Beginning.* Illustrated by William Sauts Bock. Boston, Little, Brown, 1974. 86 p. $5.95 ISBN 0–316–12599–7
73–14652

A simply written, accurate account of the first permanent English colony in America. Attractively illustrated. (Gr 3–4)

Carpenter, Francis R. *The Old China Trade; Americans in Canton, 1784–1843.* Illustrated by Demi Hitz. New York, Coward, McCann & Geoghegan, 1976. 152 p. $7.95 ISBN 0–698–20358–5
75–30985

Amply illustrated with black-and-white drawings, this engrossing account brims with details of the China trade in silk, porcelain, tea, silver, ginseng fur, and opium. (Gr 5–8)

Slightly more advanced and equally compelling is Alfred Tamarin and Shirley Glubok's *Voyaging to Cathay; Americans in the China Trade* ($10.00. Viking Press. ISBN 0–670–74857–9). (Gr 7–up)

Cheng, Hou-Tien. *The Chinese New Year.* New York, Holt, Rinehart & Winston, 1976. [32] p. $5.50 ISBN 0–03–017511–9   76–8229

A brief text, illustrated handsomely with traditional scissor-cut silhouettes, describes preparations for and celebration of this festive month-long holiday period. (Gr 4–up)

Cohen, Robert C. *The Color of Man.* New York, Random House, 1968. 109 p. $4.95 ISBN 0–394–81039–2 (lib. ed. $6.99 ISBN 0–394–91039–7)

The superb photography of Ken Heyman enriches this introduction to the biological and chemical bases for difference in skin color. (Gr 7–9)

Colorado, Antonio. *First Book of Puerto Rico.* New York, Watts, 1965. 74 p. Rev. ed. $4.90 ISBN 0–531–01292–1   77–17520

A brief but informative discussion of the geography, history, and way of life of this island commonwealth, well illustrated by photographs and maps. (Gr 6–8)

Corbett, Scott. *Bridges.* Illustrated by Richard Rosenblum. New York, Four Winds Press, 1978. 122 p. $6.95 ISBN 0–590–07464–4   77–13871

An anecdotal history of the art of bridge building—arches, suspension spans, trusses—is illustrated with clear fine-line drawings. (Gr 4–6)

Coy, Harold. *Chicano Roots Go Deep.* Foreword by José Vazquez-Amaral. New York, Dodd, Mead, 1975. 210 p. $5.95 ISBN 0–396–07186–4
75–11434

By tracing Chicano roots back to the dawn of history, this book provides a readable introduction to this large minority group. A flavorful, informal account, using many Spanish terms (translated), describes the heritage of one particular family. (Gr 7–up)

Davis, Burke. *Runaway Balloon; the Last Flight of Confederate Air Force One.* Drawings by Salvatore Murdocca. New York, Coward, McCann & Geoghegan, 1976. 45 p. $5.95 ISBN 0–698–20372–0
75–29060

A short, humorous embellishment of a historical incident concerns a hapless Confederate "volunteer," whose ascent in a colorful patchwork observation balloon ended with his being captured, naked and unrecognized, by another branch of his own army. (Gr 3–5)

De Pauw, Linda G. *Founding Mothers; Women in America in the Revolutionary Era.* Wood engravings by Michael McCurdy. Boston, Houghton Mifflin, 1975. 228 p. $6.95 ISBN 0–395–21896–9
75–17031

This exploration of a little-examined part of American history describes the lives of "the hidden heroines of the Revoluitonary generation"—the women on farms and plantations, in cities and forests, and in businesses and armies. (Gr 7–up)

Deggan, Alfred L. *The Romans*. Illustrated by Richard M. Powers. Cleveland, World Pub. Co., 1964. 125 p. $5.91. Collins, New York. ISBN 0–529–03764–5   64–13513
The story of Rome, from legendary beginning to conquests and ultimate fall, with a summary chapter on Roman contributions to civilization. In the *Major Cultures of the World* series. (Gr 7–up)

Earle, Alice M. *Home and Child Life in Colonial Days*. Edited by Shirley Glubok. Special photography by Alfred Tamarin. New York, Macmillan, 1969. 357 p. $7.95 ISBN 0–02–733250–0
                    69–11295
The flavor of everyday life in Colonial America is conveyed in a skillfully edited, well-illustrated consolidation and abridgment of Alice Earl's *Home Life in Colonial Days* (1898) and *Child Life in Colonial Days* (1899). (Gr 6–up)

Eiseman, Alberta. *Mañana Is Now; the Spanish-Speaking in the United States*. Illustrated with photographs. New York, Atheneum, 1973. 184 p. $6.95 ISBN 0–689–30100–6   72–86933
A review of the history, problems, and goals of Cubans, Chicanos, Puerto Ricans, and other Hispanos in the United States. (Gr 5–9)

Faber, Doris. *The Perfect Life: the Shakers in America*. New York, Farrar, Straus & Giroux, 1974. 215 p. illus. $6.95 ISBN 0–374–35819–2
                    73–90968
A well-researched, entertainingly written history of the Shaker movement in America which reaches up to the few surviving colonies today in New England. (Gr 7–9)

Glubok, Shirley. *Discovering Tut-ankh-Amen's Tomb*. Designed by Gerard Nook. New York, Macmillan, 1968. 143 p. $12.95 ISBN 0–02–736030–X (paper $5.95 ISBN 0–02–043320–4)   68–12069
Profusely illustrated with reproductions of photographs taken on the site, this abridgment of the three volumes by Howard Carter and A. C. Mace conveys a sense of the excitement of discovery and the meticulous care with which the archaeologists worked. (Gr 7–9)

———. *Knights in Armor*. Designed by Gerard Nook. New York, Harper & Row, 1969. 48 p. $7.89 ISBN 0–06–022038–4   69–10208
Descriptions of armor surviving as museum pieces and works of art depict the history and customs of the era of knighthood and chivalry. (Gr 4–8)

Goble, Paul, *and* Dorothy Goble. *Brave Eagle's Account of the Fetterman Fight, 21 December, 1866*. Illustrated by Paul Goble. New York, Pantheon Books, 1972. 58 p. $4.95 ISBN 0–394–82314–1 (lib. ed. $5.99 ISBN 0–394–92314–6)   79–153978
Keeping the spirit of published Indian accounts, this picture-history counteracts the much-repeated image of savage Sioux attacks against Western forts. The tragic results of the white man's failure to understand that "one does not sell the lands which the Great Spirit gave" are movingly conveyed in vivid narrative and panoramic illustrations. (Gr 5–up)

Gurko, Miriam. *The Ladies of Seneca Falls; the Birth of the Woman's Rights Movement*. New York, Macmillan, 1974. 328 p. illus. $7.95 ISBN 0–02–737770–9   73–6049
A broad overview of the early feminist movement brings vividly to life the struggles of such great leaders as Elizabeth Cady Stanton and Susan B. Anthony, as well as those of lesser known personalities. (Gr 7–9)

Haley, Gail E. *Jack Jouett's Ride*. Written and illustrated by Gail E. Haley. New York, Viking Press, 1973. [31] p. $5.95 ISBN 0–670–40466–7 (paper $1.75. Penguin. ISBN 0–670–05102–0)   73–5137
Vibrantly colored linoleum cuts and balladlike verse relate a lesser known event in American history —when a hero galloped forty miles through the darkness to Charlottesville, Va., to warn southern revolutionaries of the coming of King George's men. (K–Gr 3)

Hay, John. *Ancient China*. Illustrated with photographs and maps and with drawings by Rosemonde Nairac and Pippa Brand. New York, Walck, 1974. 128 p. (A Walck archaeology) Paper $4.95 ISBN 0–8098–3808–7   73–15528
Archaeological finds from 1920 to the late 1960s are the basis for an engrossing text and its superb illustrations of life in China from 6,000 B.C. to A.D. 90. (Gr 7–9)

Hodges, C. Walter. *Shakespeare's Theatre*. Illustrated by the author. New York, Coward-McCann, 1964. 103 p. $7.50 ISBN 0–698–20127–2   64–13679
Informally presented history of the theater from pagan and early religious acting to the period of Shakespeare and the Globe. Chiefly important for the full-color paintings on almost every page. (Gr 6–up)

Horwitz, Elinor L. *The Bird, the Banner, and Uncle Sam; Images of America in Folk and Popular Art*. J. Roderick Moore, consultant. Philadelphia, Lippincott, 1976. 167 p. $8.95 ISBN 0–397–31690–9 (paper $5.95 ISBN 0–397–31691–7)   76–16492

An engrossing, fully illustrated account of the beginnings and uses in folk art and advertising of patriotic American symbols, including the eagle, the flag, "Miss Liberty," and Uncle Sam. (Gr 5–up)

Jenness, Aylette. *Along the Niger River: An African Way of Life*. New York, Crowell, 1974. 135 p. $8.95 ISBN 0–690–00514–8   73–20061
Many human-interest photographs by the author help to describe life in the town of Yelwa, Nigeria, and its surrounding countryside, where western technology has been adapted to the traditional culture in beneficial ways. (Gr 5–up)

———. *Dwellers of the Tundra; Life in an Alaskan Eskimo Village*. With photographs by Jonathan Jenness. New York, Crowell-Collier Press, 1970. 112 p. $7.95. Macmillan. ISBN 0–02–747720–7   74–93716
Photographs and text are fused into a warm and sensitive documentary which reveals the loneliness and deprivation of daily life throughout the seasons. (Gr 5–8)

Karen, Ruth. *Kingdom of the Sun; the Inca, Empire Builders of the Americas*. New York, Four Winds Press, 1975. 272 p. $9.95 ISBN 0–590–17288–3   75–9886
In a volume handsomely illustrated with photographs of Cuzco, Machu Picchu, and other Inca cities, the author provides a straightforward history of daily life, customs, art, and architecture and adds two fictional chapters about a young prince and a "chosen girl." (Gr 7–9)

Katz, William L. *Black People Who Made the Old West*. Illustrated with photographs. New York, Crowell, 1977. 181 p. $7.95 ISBN 0–690–01253–5   76–7051
Easily read sketches of thirty-five black people—explorers, traders, settlers, prospectors, cowpokes, and lawmen—who contributed to the founding and expansion of the western frontiers. (Gr 5–7)

Kurelek, William. *Lumberjack*. Boston, Houghton Mifflin, 1974. 48 p. $6.95 ISBN 0–395–19922–0   74–9377
The author-artist's memories of his spells of working in Canadian lumber camps inspired these realistic paintings of the lumberjack's life outdoors and indoors and their accompanying brief though detailed text. (Gr 5–up)

Lasker, Joe. *Merry Ever After; the Story of Two Medieval Weddings*. New York, Viking Press, 1976. 48 p. $7.95 ISBN 0–670–47257–3   75–22017
Many aspects of medieval social life and customs are revealed in fiction about contrasting betrothals and weddings—one of nobility, one of peasantry. A brief text serves as captions for paintings, which in their decorative quality and glowing color consciously echo medieval and early Renaissance art. (Gr 3–6)

Leacroft, Helen, *and* Richard Leacroft. *The Buildings of Ancient Greece*. New York, Young Scott Books, 1966. 40 p. $6.95. Addison-Wesley, Reading, Mass. ISBN 0–201–09143–7   66–12056
Detailed drawings and colored pictures document interiors and exteriors of homes and public buildings throughout the history of ancient Greece. Also, *The Buildings of Ancient Rome* (ISBN 0–201–09145–3) and *The Buildings of Ancient Mesopotamia* (ISBN 0–201–09447–9). (Gr 4–8)

Lester, Julius. *To Be a Slave*. Illustrated by Tom Feelings. New York, Dial Press, 1968. 160 p. $5.95 ISBN 0–8037–8955–6   68–28738
A text constructed largely from the memories of ex-slaves, drawn together chronologically with an editor's meaningful commentary. Excellent firsthand historical material, much of it not published before, beautifully illustrated by an artist well acquainted with Africa. (Gr 7–up)

Loeper, John J. *The Golden Dragon; by Clipper Ship around the Horn*. Illustrated with old prints and paintings. New York, Atheneum, 1978. 61 p. $5.95 ISBN 0–689–30658–X   78–5085
A graphic introduction to sailing ships, in the true-to-life story of a ten-year-old's experiences aboard a clipper ship sailing from New York to San Francisco in 1850. (Gr 4–6)

Lomask, Milton. *The First American Revolution*. New York, Farrar, Straus & Giroux, 1974. 280 p. illus. $7.95 ISBN 0–374–32337–2   73–90972
A thoroughly researched and objective account of the Revolution points out both the usual, familiar aspects of the war and also the lack of unity prevailing in a large segment of the population. Discussion of possible origins of the conflict adds dimension. (Gr 6–9)

Macaulay, David. *Pyramid*. Boston, Houghton Mifflin, 1975. 80 p. $8.95 ISBN 0–395–21407–6   75–9964
With the meticulous detail of text and pen-and-ink drawings shown earlier in his *Cathedral* and *City*, the artist demonstrates the significance of a great pyramid of Egypt and the engineering methods used to build it. (Gr 5–up)

Meltzer, Milton. *Never to Forget; the Jews of the Holocaust*. New York, Harper & Row, 1976. 217 p. $6.95 ISBN–0–06–024174–8 (lib. ed. $7.49 ISBN–0–06–024175–6)   75–25409

First-person accounts of concentration camps, other atrocities, and resistance movements heighten the impact of an admittedly emotional book. (Gr 6–8)

————. *Slavery; From the Rise of Western Civilization to the Renaissance.* New York, Cowles Book Co., 1971. 255 p. $6.95. Contemporary Books. ISBN-0-8092-8518-5   70-104364
A study, emphasizing ancient times, concerns everyday life, ways of achieving freedom, and notable slaves and slave revolts. Illustrated with reproductions of ancient and medieval works of art. (Gr 6–up)

————. *Taking Root; Jewish Immigrants in America.* New York, Farrar, Straus & Giroux, 1976. 262 p. $7.95 ISBN 0-374-37369-8   76-18169
The author's balanced account, based on firsthand sources, tells of the immigration and Americanization of East European Jews who settled in New York's lower East Side around the turn of the century. Illustrated with photographs. (Gr 7–9)

————, ed. *In Their Own Words, a History of the American Negro, 1619–1865.* New York, Thomas Y. Crowell, 1964. 195 p. $6.95 ISBN 0-690-44691-8   64-22541
The first of three volumes of documents by and about Negroes. This spans the years that led to the Civil War; the following two cover 1865–1916 and 1916–1966. Each piece is briefly introduced, includes pictures, and has sources given. (Gr 6–up)

Meyer, Carolyn. *Eskimos; Growing Up in a Changing Culture.* With research assistance from Bernadine Larsen. Photographs by John McDonald. New York, Atheneum, 1977. 215 p. (A Margaret K. McElderry book) $7.95 ISBN 0-689-50078-5   77-9472
A combination of third-person narrative and editorial comment conveys the essence of life for a typical family in a hypothetical village and evokes an understanding of the problems of those whose society and folkways are affected by the intrusion of "civilization." (Gr 7–up)

Musgrove, Margaret. *Ashanti to Zulu; African Traditions.* Pictures by Leo and Diane Dillon. New York, Dial Press, 1976. [32] p. $8.95 ISBN 0-8037-0357-0 (lib. ed. $8.44 ISBN 0-8037-0358-9)   76-6610
Richly detailed paintings in glowing color distinguish this ABC of customs and traditions of a number of African peoples. (Gr 2–6)

Native American Testimony: An Anthology of Indian and White Relations; First Encounter to Dispossession. Edited by Peter Nabokov. New York, Crowell, 1978. 242 p. $8.95 ISBN 0-690-01313-2 (lib. ed. $8.79 ISBN 0-690-03840-2)   77-11558

Moving first-person accounts of the often tragic Native American experience. Liberally illustrated with photographs. (Gr 8–up)

Naylor, Phyllis R. *An Amish Family.* Illustrated by George Armstrong. Chicago, J. P. O'Hara, 1975. 181 p. Reprint. $5.95. Lamplight Pub., New York. ISBN 0-87955-209-3 (lib. ed. $5.97 ISBN 0-87955-809-1)   73-16813
In a factual report highlighting both strengths and weaknesses of the circumscribed life of the Amish people, the author centers on the Stolzfus family of Lancaster County, Pennsylvania. (Gr 5–up)

Perkins, Carol M., *and* Marlin Perkins. *"I Saw You from Afar"; a Visit to the Bushmen of the Kalahari Desert.* New York, Atheneum, 1965. 56 p. $6.95 ISBN 0-689-30011-5   65-10479
The director of the St. Louis Zoo and his wife describe the life and customs of Bushmen whom they came to know and admire in South Africa. Many beautiful photographs. (Gr 4–6)

Pitseolak, Peter. *Peter Pitseolak's Escape from Death.* Introduced and edited by Dorothy Eber. New York, Delacorte Press/S. Lawrence, 1978. [47] p. (A Merloyd Lawrence book) $7.95 ISBN 0-440-06894-0 (lib. ed. $7.45 ISBN 0-440-06896-7)   77-83236
An account of the Eskimo author-illustrator's near tragedy while walrus hunting in Arctic waters, told in spare prose and embellished with brilliant paintings. (Gr 1–4)

Rounds, Glen. *The Prairie Schooners.* New York, Holiday House, 1968. 95 p. $6.95 ISBN 0-8234-0088-3   68-31936
The author's spirited illustrations show how covered wagon companies were outfitted, made their way over the Oregon Trail, and contributed to the opening up of the West. *The Treeless Plains* (ISBN 0-8234-0122-7) offers further colorful social history of the period. (Gr 4–7)

Sanderlin, George W. *A Hoop to the Barrel: The Making of the American Constitution.* New York, Coward, McCann & Geoghegan, 1974. 222 p. $6.19 ISBN 0-698-30511-6   74-94139
A lucid account of the writing of the Constitution presents the men behind it and their conflicting philosophies (including the question of slavery). Well-chosen quotations from many sources give immediacy to the commentary. Numerous portraits. (Gr 6–9)

Sandler, Martin. *The Way We Lived; a Photographic Record of Work in Vanished America.* Boston, Little, Brown, 1977. 120 p. $7.95 ISBN 0-316-77020-5   77-10810

Social history emerges from workers' accounts and particularly from the large collection here of pre-twentieth-century photographs of men and women in many occupations, some of which are now virtually obsolete, like the chimneysweep, ice cutter, and lighthouse keeper. (Gr 9–12)

Sasek, Miroslav. *This Is Washington, D.C.* New York, Macmillan, 1969. 60 p. $4.95 ISBN 0–02–77840–9
69–13394
With his bright watercolor scenes and lighthearted observations, the artist presents, as to a visitor, official Washington and its treasures. (Gr 3–up)

Seeger, Elizabeth. *Eastern Religions.* Illustrated with photographs. New York, Crowell, 1973. 213 p. $7.95 ISBN 0–690–25342–7
73–10206
An admirably lucid presentation of Hinduism, Buddhism, Shintoism, and the religions of China. (Gr 7–up)

Simon, Nancy, *and* Evelyn Wolfson. *American Indian Habitats; How to Make Dwellings and Shelters with Natural Materials.* Drawing and diagrams by Nancy Poydar [and with photographs] New York, McKay, 1978. $7.95 ISBN 0–679–205004
78–4416
An attractively illustrated and well-documented description of construction methods and natural materials used in eight Native American cultural areas to build a wikiup, tipi, wigwam, and other dwellings. (Gr 6–8)

Sung, Betty L. *An Album of Chinese Americans.* New York, Watts, 1977. 65 p. $5.90 ISBN 0–531–00366–3
76–45185
Chiefly in pictures, this surveys the life of Chinese Americans, including both past history and present customs and problems. (Gr 4–8)

Tamarin, Alfred H. *We Have Not Vanished: Eastern Indians of the United States.* Chicago, Follett, 1974. 160 p. $5.97 ISBN 0–695–40332–X
73–90052

Eastern American Indians are introduced state by state in a survey that considers origins, cultures, and languages. Illustrated with photographs. (Gr 5–8)

Tunis, Edwin. *The Young United States, 1783–1830.* Cleveland, World Pub. Co., 1969. 159 p. Reprint. $9.95. Crowell, New York. ISBN 0–690–01065–6
71–82783
Edwin Tunis's detailed, soft-pencil drawings enhance his portrait of the United States during "a time of change and growth; a time of learning democracy; a time of new ways of living, thinking and doing."
Other titles depicting life in early United States history are *Colonial Craftsmen and the Beginnings of American Industry* (ISBN 0–690–01062–1); *Shaw's Fortune: The Picture Story of a Colonial Plantation* (ISBN 0–690–01066–4); and *The Tavern at the Ferry* (ISBN 0–690–00099–5). (Gr 4–up)

Uden, Grant. *A Dictionary of Chivalry.* Illustrated by Pauline Baynes. New York, Crowell, 1969. 352 p. $16.95 ISBN 0–690–23815–0
67–10477
Lavish illustrations enrich this introduction to the world of the knight. The 1969 winner of England's Kate Greenaway Medal. (Gr 5–up)

Weisgard, Leonard. *The Plymouth Thanksgiving.* Garden City, N.Y., Doubleday, 1967. [64] p. $5.95 ISBN 0–385–07312–7
67–15379
Dramatic illustration and brief text based on William Bradford's diary convey the struggle of the Pilgrim's first year in the new world. (Gr 1–4)

Williams, Selma R. *Kings, Commoners, and Colonists; Puritan Politics in Old New England, 1603–1660.* New York, Atheneum, 1974. 266 p. $7.95 ISBN 0–689–30150–2
73–84840
Based on research in primary sources, this is a lively study of conflicts during the reigns of James I and his successors and their influences on Puritan colonial institutions for self-government. Handsomely illustrated with reproductions of contemporary portraits, maps, and coins. (Gr 8–up)

Nature and Science

Aliki. *Corn Is Maize; the Gift of the Indians.* New York, Crowell, 1976. 33 p. (Let's-read-and-find-out science books) $5.79 ISBN 0–690–00975–5

75–6928

A handsomely illustrated text shows how corn was discovered and used by the Indians and became an important food throughout the world. (Gr 2–3)

———. *Fossils Tell of Long Ago.* New York, Crowell, 1972. 33 p. (Let's-read-and-find-out science books) $5.79 ISBN 0–690–31379–9   78–170999

An explanation for beginning readers of how fossils are formed and what they tell us about the past, with enjoyable illustrations of the fascinating facts. Also, *The Long Lost Coelacanth: And Other Living Fossils* ($5.95 ISBN 0–690–50478–0). (Gr 2–4)

Amon, Aline. *Reading, Writing, Chattering Chimps.* New York, Atheneum, 1975. 118 p. $7.95 ISBN 0–689–30472–2   75–9524

Chimpanzees taught to communicate with sign language, plastic symbols, and computers are well illustrated with drawings by the author. Emphasis is given also to the nature of language. (Gr 4–8)

Angrist, Stanley W. *Closing the Loop; the Story of Feedback.* Drawings by Enrico Arno. New York, Crowell, 1973. 85 p. $5.95 ISBN 0–690–19644–X

73–3

This introduction to feedback—"the property of being able to adjust future conduct by past performance"—covers the history of feedback, familiar systems, and automation. (Gr 6–up)

Arthur, Lee, Elizabeth James, *and* Judith B. Taylor. *Sportsmath: How It Works.* New York, Lothrop, Lee & Shepard, 1975. 96 p. $6.00 ISBN 0–688–51712–9   75–17714

How to calculate statistics in football, baseball, basketball, and tennis is explained here in a lively and practical manner. (Gr 5–7)

Asimov, Isaac. *Mars, the Red Planet.* New York, Lothrop, Lee & Shepard, 1977. 222 p. $8.25 ISBN 0–688–41812–0 (lib. ed. $7.92 ISBN 0–688–51812–5)

77–24151

A study of Mars from earliest discoveries concerning its distance, size, and satellites to recent data gathered during the Viking probes. Illustrated with diagrams and photographs. (Gr 7–up) For somewhat younger readers, Asimov's *How Did We Find Out about Outer Space?* ($5.85. Walker. ISBN 0–8027–6284–0) puts the technology of space flight in a historical framework. (Gr 5–7)

————. *Quick and Easy Math.* Boston, Houghton Mifflin, 1964. 180 p. $6.95 ISBN 0–395–06573–9
64–12276
Shortcuts to quick answers in arithmetic, following basic mathematical principles. (Gr 7–up)

Atwood, Ann. *The Wild Young Desert.* New York, Scribner, 1970. [32] p. $5.95 ISBN 0–684–12625–7
73–106536
In the evocative style of the earlier photographic *New Moon Cove*, this pictures the brilliant colors of the desert and details the factors which make its environment: water and its absence, the shaping wind, and unique life forms. (Gr 4–up)

Aylesworth, Thomas G., *comp. Mysteries from the Past; Stories of Scientific Detection from Nature and Science Magazine.* Garden City, N.Y., Published for the American Museum of Natural History [by] the Natural History Press, 1971. 114 p. $4.95 ISBN 0–385–06798–4
71–116184
Some of these nine archaeological puzzles, such as Stonehenge, have explanations, while others, like the tablet writings on Easter Island, the Piri Re'is map, and the great Mayan temples, remain mysteries. Photographs and diagrams encourage the reader in armchair detection. (Gr 6–8)

Baylor, Byrd. *Before You Came This Way.* New York, Dutton, 1969. [32] p. $6.50 ISBN 0–525–26312–8
74–81709
Serving as an introduction to the ancient Indians of the Southwest this gently poetic text is accompanied by artist Tom Bahti's interpretation of the early cave paintings. (Gr 3–6)

Bees and Honey. By Oxford Scientific Films. Photographs by David Thompson. New York, Putnam, 1977. [28] p. $5.95 ISBN 0–399–20589–6 76–45849
Based on award-winning British films, this and a companion, *The Butterfly Cycle* (ISBN 0–399–20590–X), have, respectively, full-color magnifications of activities inside the hive and time-lapse photographs of an individual butterfly's cycle. Single sentences serve as captions for easy reading; a detailed text offers more information for older readers. (Gr 3–6)

Berger, Melvin. *Energy from the Sun.* Illustrated by Giulio Maestro. New York, Crowell, 1976. 32 p. (Let's-read-and-find-out science books) $5.79 ISBN 0–690–01056–7
75–33310

The principle that all of the earth's energy is ultimately solar is made clear for youngest readers of science and is complemented by drawings in color and black-and-white. (Gr 2–4)

————. *Enzymes in Action.* New York, Crowell, 1971. 151 p. $5.95 ISBN 0–690–26735–5   76–132291
A highly readable text about enzymes: what they are and how various interesting ones are used—in foods, liquors, drugs, etc. Illustrated with diagrams. (Gr 7–9)

————. *Quasars, Pulsars, and Black Holes in Space.* New York, Putnam, 1977. 57 p. $5.29 ISBN 0–399–61051–0
76–50057
Theories about three recently discovered phenomena are discussed in a quietly impressive text with well-chosen black-and-white photographs. (Gr 4–6)

————, *and* Gilda Berger. *The New Food Book: Nutrition, Diet, Consumer Tips, and Foods of the Future.* Illustrated by Byron Barton. New York, Crowell, 1978. 150 p. $6.95 ISBN 0–690–01295–0 (lib. ed. $6.79 ISBN 0–690–03841–0)   77–7976
Important aspects of food are dealt with in readable fashion: nutrients, preservatives and additives, problems of widespread starvation, and new sources of food. (Gr 6–8)

Berloquin, Pierre. *100 Games of Logic.* Drawings by Denis Dugas. New York, Scribner, 1977. 145 p. $7.95 ISBN 0–684–14860–9   76–49947
Original puzzles of varying difficulty, including number progressions, logical story problems, sequential pictures out of order, and subtle, shared patterns in letter diagrams and pictures. Translated from the French. (Gr 7–up)

Brady, Irene. *A Mouse Named Mus.* Written and illustrated by Irene Brady. Boston, Houghton Mifflin, 1972. 93 p. $4.95 ISBN 0–395–13151–0 (lib. ed. $4.23 ISBN 0–395–13723–3)   74–161651
Scientifically accurate story of the adventures of a boy's pet, a *Mus muscularis* who escapes and lives for a time in the woods in a natural habitat. Enhancing sketches depict many inhabitants of the woods encountered by Mus. (Gr 3–5)

Branley, Franklyn M. *A Book of Stars for You.* Illustrated by Leonard Kessler. New York, Crowell, 1967. [58] p. $7.95 ISBN 0–690–15721–5 (lib. ed. $7.49 ISBN 0–690–15722–3)   67–18509
In a volume with the same fully illustrated format as his preceding astronomy books, Branley explains the universe in terms which a young child understands and enjoys. (Gr 3–5)

————. *Gravity Is a Mystery.* Illustrated by Don Madden. New York, Crowell, 1970. 33 p. (Let's-read-and-find-out science books) $5.95 ISBN 0–690–35071–6 (lib. ed. $5.79 ISBN 0–690–35072–4)
70–101922
Lively drawings complement a clear text on what is known about the force of gravity. (Gr 2–4)

————. *Measure with Metric.* Illustrated by Loretta Lustig. New York, Crowell, 1975. 33 p. (Young math books) $5.79 ISBN 0–690–01117–2 (paper $1.45 ISBN 0–690–01265–9)
74–4056
Large illustrations suggest projects showing how to measure in meter, liter, and gram for the reader learning metric as the first language of measurement. (Gr 2–5)

Brenner, Barbara. *A Snake-Lover's Diary.* Illustrated with photographs. New York, Young Scott Books, 1970. 90 p. $5.95. Addison-Wesley, Reading, Mass. ISBN 0–201–09349–9
79–98113
Mark's determination to make a scientific study of snakes and keep a diary of his findings lead to his discovery of a surprising number of species. (Gr 4–6)

Brindze, Ruth. *The Rise and Fall of the Seas; the Story of the Tides.* Illustrated by Felix Cooper. New York, Harcourt, Brace & World, 1964. 96 p. $5.95 ISBN 0–15–267380–6
64–11491
An explanation of tides, and the effect of the moon's and sun's gravity on air, water, and the land masses of earth. Methods for predicting tides, the hazards of tides, and their potential value to man are presented. (Gr 4–up)

Bronowski, Jacob, *and* Millicent E. Selsam. *Biography of an Atom.* Illustrated with pictures by Weimer Pursell and with photographs. New York, Harper & Row, 1965. 43 p. $6.79 ISBN 0–06–020641–1
64–19708
The structure of a carbon atom and the cycle of an atom's life are graphically presented. (Gr 4–up)

Burns, Marilyn. *Good for Me! All about Food in 32 Bites.* Illustrated by Sandy Clifford. Boston, Little, Brown, 1978. 127 p. (A Brown paper school book) $7.95 ISBN 0–316–11749–9 (paper $4.95 ISBN 0–316–11747–1)
78–6727
A book on nutrition which goes beyond usual facts on vitamins and minerals to provide cartoon-illustrated, catchy information on food processing, packaging and marketing, taste differences, junk food, and wise buying. (Gr 4–7)

————. *This Book Is about Time.* Illustrated by Martha Weston. Boston, Little, Brown, 1978. 127 p. (A Brown paper school book) $7.95 ISBN 0–316–11752–8 (paper $4.95 ISBN 0–316–11750–1)
78–6614

Time zones, biorhythms, and jet lag are among topics discussed in this engrossing compendium on time. (Gr 6–7)

Busch, Phyllis S. *Wildflowers and the Stories behind Their Names.* Paintings by Anne Ophelia Dowden. New York, Scribner, 1977. 88 p. $9.95 ISBN 0–684–14820–X
73–1351
Common wildflowers, including chicory, dandelion, milkweed, and jewelweed, have brief descriptions and interesting facts about their nomenclature, with botanical paintings in full color and shaded grays. (Gr 4–6)

Caras, Roger A. *A Zoo in Your Room.* Illustrations by Pamela Johnson. New York, Harcourt Brace Jovanovich, 1975. 96 p. $5.95 ISBN 0–15–299968–X
74–24322
A guide to the care and feeding of more than thirty species of mammals, birds, fish, reptiles, amphibians, insects, and other animals that adapt well to home cages. (Gr 4–6)

Cobb, Vicki. *Science Experiments You Can Eat.* Illustrated by Peter Lippman. Philadelphia, Lippincott, 1972. 127 p. $6.95 ISBN 0–397–31487–6 (paper $3.95 ISBN 0–397–31253–9)
71–151474
Experiments illustrating principles of chemistry and physics utilize such everyday foods as salad dressing, nuts, eggs, cabbage, cookies, and yogurt. Includes thought-provoking questions and practical applications. (Gr 5–8)

Cole, Joanna. *A Chick Hatches.* Photographs by Jerome Wexler. New York, Morrow, 1976. 48 p. $7.25 ISBN 0–688–22087–8 (lib. ed. $6.96 ISBN 0–688–32087–2)
76–29017
Exceptional black-and-white or color photographs on every page detail the progress of a chick from fertilization to hatching. (Gr 2–4)

————. *Cockroaches.* Illustrated by Jean Zallinger. New York, Morrow, 1971. 62 p. $5.52 ISBN 0–688–31177–6
74–128784
Discusses the origin, characteristics, habits, and life cycle of cockroaches, some misconceptions about them, and their value to science.
Another excellent introduction to one of the world's most durable insect species is Laurence P. Pringle's *Cockroaches: Here, There, and Everywhere* (New York, Crowell. 32 p. $5.79 ISBN 0–690–19680–6). (Gr 2–4)

————. *Fleas.* Illustrated by Elsie Wrigley. New York, Morrow, 1973. 62 p. $5.52 ISBN 0–688–31844–4
72–5795
Fascinating information on fleas—biological facts and their role in history (including the circus!). Well illustrated with line drawings. (Gr 3–5)

———, *and* Madeleine Edmondson. *Twins; the Story of Multiple Births*. With drawings by Salvatore Raciti. New York, Morrow, 1972. 64 p. $5.52 ISBN 0–688–31981–5   75–168470

With photographs and drawings, this presents the biology of identical, fraternal, and Siamese births; and the effects of heredity and environment on the psychological and personality development of twins, particularly when they are separated. (Gr 4–7)

Conklin, Gladys P. *The Bug Club Book; a Handbook for Young Bug Collectors*. Illustrated by Girard Goodenow. New York, Holiday House, 1966. 96 p. $5.95 ISBN 0–8234–0017–4   66–31932

For gregarious collectors and their leaders, this guide, by an experienced organizer, offers practical ideas for observing, gathering, raising, and preserving specimens. (Gr 3–6)

Cooper, Elizabeth K. *And Everything Nice; the Story of Sugar, Spice, and Flavoring*. Illustrated by Julie Maas. New York, Harcourt, Brace & World, 1966. 80 p. $5.50 ISBN 0–15–203498–6   66–12588

How, when, and where we have obtained the variety of condiments which give interesting flavors to our food. Suggests simple ways to use vanilla, cocoa, nutmeg, cinnamon, and cloves. (Gr 4–6)

Cooper, Gale. *Inside Animals*. Boston, Little, Brown, 1978. 64 p. (An Atlantic Monthly Press book) $6.95 ISBN 0–316–15618–3   76–50919

Drawings of fourteen animals, from amoeba to clam to guinea pig, clarify specialized parts of their anatomies. (Gr 3–5)

Darling, Lois, *and* Louis Darling. *A Place in the Sun; Ecology and the Living World*. Written and illustrated by Lois and Louis Darling. New York, Morrow, 1968. 128 p. $6.25 ISBN 0–688–21485–1   68–126909

Respect for the land and a conviction of the morality of preserving it for following generations make this study of ecology one of reverence as well as of scientific accuracy. (Gr 7–up)

Dobrin, Arnold. *Gerbils*. Written and illustrated by Arnold Dobrin. New York, Lothrop, Lee & Shepard, 1970. 63 p. $6.00 ISBN 0–688–51636–X   77–82101

A fully illustrated guide to the gerbil, with suggestions for teachers and others interested in studying this appealing little mammal. (Gr 3–6)

Dowden, Anne Ophelia T. *The Blossom on the Bough; A Book of Trees*. New York, Crowell, 1975. 71 p. $8.95 ISBN 0–690–00384–6   74–6192

In a distinctively beautiful volume the importance of forests and forest regions in the United States, the parts and cycles of trees, and the functions of flowers and fruits are described in words and pencil drawings by a well-known botanical artist. (Gr 5–7)

———. *Wild Green Things in the City; a Book of Weeds*. New York, Crowell, 1972. 56 p. $8.50 ISBN 0–690–89067–2   72–158687

Meticulous drawings in jewel-like colors document the accuracy of this study of urban ecology. A useful feature is a grouping of weeds found in Manhattan, in Los Angeles, and in Denver. (Gr 3–up)

Drummond, A. H. *The Population Puzzle; Overcrowding and Stress among Animals and Men*. Reading, Mass., Addison-Wesley, 1973. 143 p. $6.95 ISBN 0–201–01566–8   72–8046

Evidence of psychological and behavioral effects of overpopulation among animals gives the reader food for thought regarding the future human situation. (Gr 6–up)

Ellison, Elsie C. *Fun with Lines and Curves*. With illustrations adapted from the author's drawings by Susan Stan. New York, Lothrop, Lee & Shepard, 1972. 95 p. $6.48 ISBN 0–688–51527–4 (paper $2.95 ISBN 0–688–45527–1)   72–1095

In an imaginative treatment supported by string-art designs, the author challenges readers to explore geometric development from simple line forms to constructions of dramatic art and color. (Gr 3–up)

Elting, Mary, *and* Michael Folsom. *The Mysterious Grain*. Illustrated by Frank Cieciorka. New York, M. Evans; distributed in association with Lippincott, Philadelphia, 1967. 118 p. $4.50 ISBN 0–87131–076–7   67–10832

An exciting story of research conducted by teams of archaeologists and paleobotanists for the origins of domesticated corn. (Gr 6–8)

Facklam, Margery. *Frozen Snakes and Dinosaur Bones; Exploring a Natural History Museum*. New York, Harcourt Brace Jovanovich, 1976. 114 p. $6.95 ISBN 0–15–230275–1   75–41394

Taking the reader behind the scenes in a natural history museum, the author describes the museum's organization and development. (Gr 4–6)

Fenner, Carol. *Gorilla Gorilla*. Illustrations by Symeon Shimin. New York, Random House, 1973. [57] p. $5.99 ISBN 0–394–92069–4   70–136590

Text and illustrations work together to give the reader a clear impression of how it is to be a gorilla in the jungle and, later, in the zoo. (Gr 4–6)

Fisher, James. *Zoos of the World; the Story of Animals in Captivity*. Garden City, N.Y., Published for the American Museum of Natural History by the Natural History Press, 1967. 253 p. $6.95 ISBN 0-385-08723-3   67-14047

Famous zoos and unusual facts about zoo occupants are interestingly introduced by this well-known naturalist. (Gr 5-up)

Flanagan, Geraldine L. *Window into an Egg; Seeing Life Begin*. New York, Young Scott Books, 1969. 71 p. $6.95. Addison-Wesley, Reading, Mass. ISBN 0-201-09405-3   66-11411

A simple text and excellent photographs document the growth of a chick embryo, as observed through a window inserted into the side of a fertile egg. (Gr 5-6)

Fodor, R. V. *Earth in Motion; the Concept of Plate Tectonics*. With diagrams by John C. Holden and photographs. New York, Morrow, 1978. 95 p. $5.95 ISBN 0-688-22135-1 (lib. ed. $5.71 ISBN 0-688-32135-6)   77-12568

An explanation of the theory of continental drift and a description of its importance in locating resources and developing warning systems for earthquakes and volcanoes. (Gr 5-7)

Fox, Michael W. *The Wolf*. Illustrated by Charles Frace. New York, Coward, McCann & Geoghegan, 1973. 95 p. $5.95 ISBN 0-698-20200-7   72-76700

A conservationist's narrative, centered on complex aspects of wolf behavior viewed through study of a family with five cubs. Graphic drawings. (Gr 4-6)

Freedman, Russell, *and* James E. Morriss. *How Animals Learn*. New York, Holiday House, 1969. 159 p. $6.95 ISBN 0-8234-0050-6   77-3492

Instinct, learning, and thought are the themes of chapters on animal IQs, puzzle boxes, and other methods for discerning intelligence. Covers major research from Pavlov to the present. Many photographs. (Gr 6-8)

Freschet, Berniece. *Skunk Baby*. Illustrated by Kazue Mizumura. New York, Crowell, 1973. 41 p. $5.79 ISBN 0-690-74194-4   72-83781

Distinctive illustrations in grays and blacks contribute much to a simple text detailing the life of a young skunk and his neighbors, the beaver and porcupine. (Gr 2-4)

Also notable for illustrations as well as text is *Bear Mouse* ($6.95. Scribner. ISBN 0-684-13320-2) with Donall Carrick's soft-color depiction in picture-book format, of the meadow mouse's struggle to survive. (K-Gr 3)

Froman, Robert. *Angles Are Easy As Pie*. Illustrated by Byron Barton. New York, Crowell, 1976. 33 p. (Young math books) $5.79 ISBN 0-690-00916-X   75-6608

A playful alligator introduces the concept of size for angles and explains their relationship to triangles, quadrangles, polygons, and circles. (Gr 3-up)

————. *Less Than Nothing Is Really Something*. Illustrated by Don Madden. New York, Crowell, 1973. 32 p. (Let's-read-and-find-out science book) $5.95 ISBN 0-690-48862-9   72-7546

A clear presentation of positive and negative numbers, with minimal, but appropriate, arithmetic for the reader to work on his own. Illustrations include the fun of a roving parrot to encourage involvement. (Gr 4-up)

————. *Science, Art, and Visual Illusions*. Drawings by Laszlo Kubinyi. New York, Simon and Schuster, 1970. 127 p. $4.50 ISBN 0-671-65085-8   77-86947

A fascinating treatment of an unusual topic, in which the reader gains insight into what he sees and how it affects the message of art. Many photographs as well as sketches. (Gr 7-9)

Gallant, Roy A. *Beyond Earth; the Search for Extraterrestrial Life*. New York, Four Winds Press, 1977. 208 p. $7.95 ISBN 0-590-07437-7   77-5790

A discussion of creation ranging from ancient myths to modern theories of the universe, the birth and death of stars, molecules of life, and man's recent searches for life in space. Well documented with photographs. (Gr 6-9)

————. *How Life Began: Creation Versus Evolution*. New York, Four Winds Press, 1975. 214 p. $7.95 ISBN 0-590-17363-4   75-12996

A philosophical but readable review of man's primitive beliefs and more recent hypotheses concerning the origin of our planet and its life. Illustrated by black-and-white photographs and reproductions of art. (Gr 6-9)

————. *Man the Measurer; Our Units of Measure and How They Grew*. Garden City, N.Y., Doubleday, 1972. 111 p. $4.95 ISBN 0-385-01898-3   73-160879

An attractive book describes how various kinds of measures became established and points out the advantages of the metric system. Suggests projects. Drawings and black-and-white photographs. (Gr 4-7)

Gallob, Edward. *City Leaves, City Trees*. Photographs and photograms by the author. New York, Scribner, 1972. 64 p. $6.95 ISBN 0-684-12808-X   72-37187

A text describing forty kinds of trees in the Northeast and dramatic black-and-white pictures spur the reader to identify trees around him. (Gr 3–6)

——. *City Rocks, City Blocks and the Moon*. Photographs by the author. New York, Scribner, 1973. 48 p. $6.95 ISBN 0–684–13542–6 73–1333
An engaging look at rocks: age-old, man-made, and lunar. Beautiful black-and-white photographs of what can be seen by any observing child in a city neighborhood convey much of the information here. (Gr 3–6)

Gardner, Martin. *Space Puzzles; Curious Questions and Answers about the Solar System*. Illustrated with diagrams and photographs. Drawings by Ted Schroeder. New York, Simon and Schuster, 1971. 95 p. $4.95 ISBN 0–671–65182–X (lib. ed. $5.70 ISBN 0–671–65183–8) 78–144777
The astronomy of the solar system is made both exciting and wondrous. Short explanations are followed by puzzling questions which vary in difficulty and are answered at the end of the book. Black-and-white photographs. (Gr 3–6)

Gilbert, Sara D. *You Are What You Eat; a Common-sense Guide to the Modern American Diet*. New York, Macmillan, 1977. 144 p. $6.95 ISBN 0–02–736020–2 76–39806
Discussion of balanced diets emphasizing buying and cooking as well as nutritional values, government protection of food processing, and the world food crisis. Includes charts for nutrition and additives. (Gr 5–8)

Grillone, Lisa, *and* Joseph Gennaro. *Small Worlds Close Up*. New York, Crown, 1978. [64] p. $7.95 ISBN 0–517–53289–1 77–15860
An introduction to the recently devised scanning electron microscope, used in 3-D photographs of salt crystals, the worn tip of a pin, leaf stomates, and such. Each micrograph is paired with a usual photograph. (Gr 5–8)

Gross, Ruth B. *Alligators and Other Crocodilians*. New York, Four Winds Press, 1978. 58 p. $5.95 ISBN 0–590–07556–X (paper $0.95 ISBN 0–590–00185–X) 77–18310
Awesomely realistic black-and-white photographs accompany a simple text about four basic groups of aquatic reptiles, their living habits and predators. (Gr 2–4)

——. *Snakes*. New York, Four Winds Press, 1975. 63 p. $6.95 ISBN 0–590–07385–0 74–13227

Striking black-and-white photographs add much to this brief introduction to the habits and behavior of some common snakes found in the United States and Canada (including four poisonous species). Concludes with a full-color pictorial summary of twenty-three snakes. (Gr 3–5)

Haines, Gail K. *Natural and Synthetic Poisons*. Illustrated by Giulio Maestro. New York, Morrow, 1978. 96 p. $5.95 ISBN 0–688–22157–2 (lib. ed. $5.71 ISBN 0–688–32157–7) 78–18886
Discusses specific poisons—from animals, plants, bacteria, and the environment (primarily pollutants)—and the science of toxicology. Black-and-white drawings. (Gr 4–6)

Halacy, Daniel S. *Nuclear Energy*. New York, Watts, 1978. 64 p. illus. (A First book) $4.90 ISBN 0–531–01492–4 78–4659
An introduction to atomic theory, from early discoveries to current technology for producing nuclear energy, includes the operation of nuclear power plants and controversy regarding the promise and hazards of nuclear energy. (Gr 5–7)

Harker, Ronald. *Digging Up the Bible Lands*. Illustrated with photographs and maps, and with drawings by Martin Simmons. New York, Walck, 1973. 127 p. (A Walck archaeology) $9.95 ISBN 0–8098–3111–2 72–6954
Biblical history from Abraham to Jesus is interwoven with the history of archaeological findings at eight sites including Babylon, Jerusalem, and Masada.
Other volumes in the publisher's excellent archaeology series are *The Archaeology of Minoan Crete*, by Reynold A. Higgins (ISBN 0–8098–3528–2); *The Archaeology of Ancient Egypt*, by T. G. H. James (ISBN 0–8098–3110–4); and two by Magnus Magnusson—*Introducing Archaeology* (ISBN 0–8098–3109–0) and *Viking Expansion Westwards* (ISBN 0–8098–3529–0). (Gr 6–up)

Harris, Susan. *Reptiles*. Illustrated by Jim Robins. New York, Watts, 1978. 48 p. (An Easy-read fact book) $4.90 ISBN 0–531–01335–9 77–8042
A simple text about many kinds of reptiles, with photographically clear paintings on each page. (Gr 1–4)

Hawes, Judy. *Ladybug, Ladybug, Fly Away Home*. Illustrated by Ed Emberley. New York, Crowell, 1967. [40] p. $5.95 ISBN 0–690–48383–X (lib. ed. $5.97 ISBN 0–690–48384–8; paper $1.45 ISBN 0–690–00200–9) 67–15399
A simple science text filled with sprightly sketches that show the beneficent ladybug in farm and garden activities. (K–Gr 2)

————. *Why Frogs Are Wet*. New York, Crowell, 1968. 35 p. Paper $1.45 ISBN 0–690–00640–3
68–21605
Frog facts, gaily illustrated by Don Madden, for very young naturalists. (K–Gr 2)

Helfman, Elizabeth S. *Wheels, Scoops, and Buckets; How People Lift Water for Their Fields*. Illustrated by Eva Cellini. New York, Lothrop, Lee & Shepard, 1968. 64 p. $5.75 ISBN 0–688–41154–1 68–27709
The uses of ancient and modern tools and devices for securing water for crops are related to world food needs. (Gr 2–4)

Hess, Lilo. *Animals That Hide, Imitate, and Bluff*. Story and photographs by Lilo Hess. New York, Scribner, 1970. 64 p. $6.95 ISBN 0–684–12525–0
71–106530
An introductory look at types of defense that enable animals to evade enemies by camouflage or mimicry. (Gr 3–5)

————.*The Curious Raccoons*. Story and photos by Lilo Hess. New York, Scribner, 1968. 46 p. $5.95 ISBN 0–684–12459–9 68–29363
In a life-cycle picture book, based on this naturalist-photographer's own observations, photographs capture the charm of infant raccoons, dextrous parents, and lessons in a tree "classroom." (Gr 1–3)

Hirsch, S. Carl. *Guardians of Tomorrow; Pioneers in Ecology*. Illustrated by William Steinel. New York, Viking Press, 1971. 192 p. $4.95 ISBN 0–670–35646–8 76–136818
This companion to the author's *The Living Community* (1966) tells of eight men and women, begining with Thoreau, whose persistent efforts created the foundation of ecological understanding we are trying to build on today. (Gr 6–up)

————. *The Living Community: A Venture into Ecology*. Illustrated by William Steinel. New York, Viking Press, 1966. 128 p. $5.95 ISBN 0–670–43492–2 66–14415
An introductory study of the interrelationships among plants and animals and aspects of their environment, interpreted in large, soft-pencil drawings. (Gr 6–8)

Hoke, John. *Terrariums*. New York, F. Watts, 1972. 90 p. (A First book) $4.90 ISBN 0–531–00777–4
70–189761
Illustrated by photographs and drawings, this gives directions for building three sizes of terrariums, including types which can contain animal life, and points out important requirements in terms of ecology. Includes a helpful list of materials and sources of supply. (Gr 4–up)

————. *Turtles and Their Care*. Illustrated with photographs [and] drawings by Barbara Wolff. New York, Watts, 1970. 89 p. (A First book) $4.90 ISBN 0–531–00696–4 78–98669
A helpful book on turtle care, with general notes on turtles and descriptions of common species. (Gr 5–8)

Hopf, Alice L. *Animal and Plant Life Spans*. New York, Holiday House, 1978. 142 p. $6.95 ISBN 0–8234–0320–3 77–17571
Entertaining descriptions and photographs of animal and plant species and three human societies which are notable for longevity. Contains chapters about recent research on heredity, behavior, and environment. (Gr 5–8)

Hussey, Lois J., *and* Catherine Pessino. *Collecting Small Fossils*. Illustrated by Anne Marie Jauss. New York, Crowell, 1971. 57 p. $5.95 ISBN 0–690–19733–0 77–101932
An explanation of the origin of fossils, description of places where they can be found, and suggestions for beginning and organizing a fossil collection. (Gr 3–6)

Hutchins, Ross E. *The Amazing Seeds*. Photographs by the author. New York, Dodd, Mead, 1965. 159 p. $5.95 ISBN 0–396–06478–7 65–19215
The naturalist-photographer offers a graphically illustrated text interpreting the mysteries of seeds and their importance to mankind through the ages. (Gr 5–8)

————. *A Look at Ants*. New York, Dodd, Mead, 1978. 48 p. $4.95 ISBN 0–396–07539–8 77–16867
The author's singular black-and-white photographs amplify a simple text about the physical characteristics, fascinating adaptations, and natural environments of various kinds of ants. (Gr 3–4)

————. *Plants without Leaves; Lichens, Fungi, Mosses, Liverworts, Slime-Molds, Algae, Horsetails*. New York, Dodd, Mead, 1966. 152 p. $5.95 ISBN 0–396–06653–4 66–5679
In this volume, illustrated with the author's own evocative photographs, the naturalist succeeds in making nature lore a fascinating subject. (Gr 4–7)

————. *Scaly Wings; a Book about Moths and Their Caterpillars*. New York, Parents' Magazine Press, 1971. 64 p. (A Stepping-stone book) $5.41 ISBN 0–8193–0440–9 78–131257
Identifies and classifies thirty-seven of the most important moths, including some that are harmful or destructive. Many clear photographs by the author. (Gr 3–8)

Isenbart, Hans-Heinrich. *A Foal Is Born*. Photographs by Hanns-Jörg Anders. Translated by Catherine Edwards. New York, Putnam, 1976. [40] p. $5.95 ISBN 0–399–20517–9   76–2605

Sharp black-and-white photographs with a brief text detail the birth of a foal and its first hours. (Gr 2–4)

James, Elizabeth, *and* Carol Barkin. *The Simple Facts of Simple Machines*. Photographs by Daniel Dorn, Jr. Diagrams by Susan Stan. New York, Lothrop, Lee & Shepard, 1975. 64 p. $5.28 ISBN 0–688–51685–8   74–20664

A fully illustrated explanation of how six basic machines are utilized to make work easier: the lever, pulley, wedge, screw, inclined plane, and wheel and axle. (Gr 3–5)

Johnson, Eric W. *V.D.* With a foreword by King Holmes. Medical consultant, Rob Roy MacGregor. Clinic and operation venus photographs by Eric E. Mitchell. Philadelphia, Lippincott, 1973. 127 p. New and rev. $6.95 ISBN 0–397–31811–1   78–8666

A thorough but succinct discussion of veneral disease, covering the topic from all aspects, including sources of help for today's youth. (Gr 6–up)

Kaufmann, John. *Birds in Flight*. Written and illustrated by John Kaufmann. New York, Morrow, 1970. 96 p. $6.00 ISBN 0–688–31100–8   79–101587

Bird anatomy and basic aerodynamic principles of bird flight are explained lucidly in words and drawings. (Gr 5–8)

Kavaler, Lucy. *Cold against Disease*. New York, J. Day Co., 1971. 158 p. (The Wonders of cold) $7.95 ISBN 0–381–99773–1   69–10810

An explanation of the science of cryobiology which tells how cold temperatures make possible blood and sperm banks, unusual operations, and other medical applications. (Gr 7–9)

———. *Dangerous Air*. Illustrated by Carl Smith. New York, John Day Co., 1967. 143 p. $6.95 ISBN 0–381–99772–3   67–10819

A timely summary of case histories and research on air pollution, with a challenging discussion of political and industrial aspects. (Gr 7–up)

———. *The Wonders of Fungi*. Illustrated with photographs and with drawings by Richard Ott. New York, Day, 1964. 128 p. $5.79 ISBN 0–381–99770–7   64–10450

Describes molds, mushrooms, and yeasts and their effects on food, crops, soil, and the world of medicine. Experiments are suggested. (Gr 5–8)

Kelly, James E., *and* William R. Park. *The Dam Builders*. Drawings by Herbert E. Lake. Reading, Mass., Addison-Wesley, 1978. [47] p. $5.95 ISBN 0–201–05727–1   77–5406

Detailed, but not difficult, information on how dams are built, with explicit drawings emphasizing the big machines used. (Gr 3–5)

———. *The Tunnel Builders*. Drawings by Herbert E. Lake. Reading, Mass., Addison-Wesley, 1976. [48] p. $5.95 ISBN 0–201–03721–1   74–5076

Ample drawings and diagrams in both color and black-and-white explain graphically the complex processes of tunnel construction. (Gr 2–5)

Kettelkamp, Larry. *A Partnership of Mind and Body; Biofeedback*. New York, Morrow, 1976. 96 p. $6.25 ISBN 0–688–22088–6 (lib. ed. $6.00 ISBN 0–688–32088–0)   76–24818

The author's explanations of how instrument feedback can aid conscious control of skin temperature, heart rate, muscle tension, and even brain waves are accompanied by black-and-white photographs. (Gr 5–7)

Knight, David C. *Colonies in Orbit; the Coming Age of Human Settlements in Space*. New York, Morrow, 1977. 94 p. $6.25 ISBN 0–688–22096–7 (lib. ed. $6.00 ISBN 0–688–32096–1)   76–56086

A vision of how humans might build and colonize space stations, with discussion of how life might differ. Proposes various station shapes and locations and sources of materials. Illustrated with diagrams and black-and-white photographs of artists' conceptions. (Gr 4–7)

———. *Eavesdropping on Space; the Quest of Radio Astronomy*. New York, Morrow, 1975. 128 p. $6.00 ISBN 0–688–32019–8   74–19285

An accurate and thorough discussion introduces technical background on the electromagnetic spectrum and describes major types of radio telescopes and their uses in exploring not only the solar system but the universe. (Gr 4–8)

Kohl, Judith, *and* Herbert Kohl. *The View from the Oak; the Private Worlds of Other Creatures*. Illustrated by Roger Bayless. San Francisco, Sierra Club Books/Scribner, 1977. 110 p. $8.95 ISBN 0–684–15016–6 (paper $4.95 ISBN 0–684–15017–4)   76–57680

An attractively illustrated introduction to zoology presents intriguing facts about the environment learned from observing the sensory discoveries of such varied creatures as the ant, bee, and dolphin. (Gr 6–8)

Kondo, Herbert. *Adventures in Space and Time; the Story of Relativity.* Illustrated by George Solonevich. New York, Holiday House, 1966. 93 p. $4.95 ISBN 0–8234–0000–X   66–8849

An introduction to Einstein's thinking about puzzles in the physical universe followed by statements of theories of gravitation, space, time, motion, and relativity. (Gr 7–9)

Langone, John. *Bombed, Buzzed, Smashed, or . . . Sober; a Book about Alcohol.* Boston, Little, Brown, 1976. 212 p. $7.95 ISBN 0–316–51424–1   76–8490

In his account of the history, use, and abuse of alcohol, the author gives serious consideration to the formation of responsible habits in youth. (Gr 7–up)

————. *Death Is a Noun; a View of the End of Life.* Boston, Little, Brown, 1972. 228 p. $5.95 ISBN 0–316–51420–9   70–189261

The biological meaning of death, such related topics as euthanasia, abortion, and immortality, and society's attitudes toward these are surveyed in a dispassionate yet philosophical fashion. (Gr 7–up)

————. *Human Engineering; Marvel or Menace?* Boston, Little, Brown, 1978. 158 p. $6.95 ISBN 0–316–51427–6   77–26030

A lucid, up-to-date, and provocative treatment of "science's attempts to alter, control, and prolong—indeed, even create—life." (Gr 7–up)

Laycock, George. *Animal Movers; a Collection of Ecological Surprises.* Garden City, N.Y., Published for the American Museum of Natural History [by] the Natural History Press, 1971. 107 p. $4.50 ISBN 0–385–08827–2   71–141689

Relates clearly many cases in which animals transplanted into new environments have unexpectedly upset the ecological balance. (Gr 4–6)

————. *Squirrels.* New York, Four Winds Press, 1975. 102 p. $5.95 ISBN 0–590–07376–1   74–28478

An account of the characteristics and behavior of major American squirrels and such cousins of theirs as the chipmunk, woodchuck, sik-sik, and prairie dog. Many black-and-white photographs. (Gr 4–6)

Leen, Nina. *The Bat.* New York, Holt, Rinehart and Winston, 1976. 79 p. $6.95 ISBN 0–03–015581–9   75–32252

In an alluring picture album, nearly a hundred striking black-and-white photographs by the author identify twenty-two species of bats and their activities. (Gr 4–7)

————. *Snakes.* New York, Holt, Rinehart and Winston, 1978. 80 p. $6.95 ISBN 0–03–039926–2   77–13917

Unusual photographs of snakes are arranged according to such aspects as locomotion, eating habits, and defense, with minimal but informative text. (Gr 4–6)

Linn, Charles F. *Probability.* New York, Crowell, 1972. 33 p. (Young math books) $5.79 ISBN 0–690–65602–5   79–171006

Wendy Watson's friendly and articulate mice enliven the introductions here to such concepts as data gathering, frequency counts, and ratios. Searching questions and descriptions of practical experiments add to the effectiveness. (Gr 3–up)

Lubell, Winifred, *and* Cecil Lubell. *Birds in the Street; the City Pigeon Book.* New York, Parents' Magazine Press, 1971. 64 p. (A Stepping-stone book) $5.41 ISBN 0–8193–0438–7   71–131258

A fascinating, short account of the ubiquitous pigeon—city pest, wild pigeon, and related birds—its nesting, food-getting, and other habits. (Gr 1–4)

Macaulay, David. *Underground.* Boston, Houghton Mifflin, 1976. 109 p. $9.95 ISBN 0–395–24739–X   76–13868

The subterranean network which supports a twentieth-century city is presented in meticulous, imaginative drawings and diagrams. (Gr 4–up)

MacClintock, Dorcas. *A Natural History of Giraffes.* Pictures by Ugo Mochi. New York, Scribner, 1973. 134 p. $7.95 ISBN 0–684–13239–7   72–9580

The striking black paper cutouts of Ugo Mochi make this book a thing of beauty, and the full text leaves few, if any, questions about giraffes unanswered. (Gr 7–9)

McClung, Robert M. *Caterpillars and How They Live.* Illustrated by [the author] New York, Morrow, 1965. 63 p. $6.00 ISBN 0–688–31152–0   65–20949

A profusion of clear, soft-pencil drawings of caterpillars, in all stages of the life cycle, enhance the scientific value of this simply written study. (Gr 3–6)

————. *Hunted Mammals of the Sea.* Illustrated by William Downey. New York, Morrow, 1978. 191 p. $7.95 ISBN 0–688–22146–7 (lib. ed. $7.63 ISBN 0–688–32146–1)   77–25388

Well-illustrated chapters on great whales, dolphins, sea otters, walrus, polar bears, and other sea mammals stress current conservation efforts, describe life habits, and discuss the history of their interaction with man. (Gr 6–8)

———. *Lost Wild America; the Story of Our Extinct and Vanishing Wildlife.* Illustrated by Bob Hines. New York, Morrow, 1969. 240 p. $7.75 ISBN 0–688–21464–9   69–13397

Readable, attractively illustrated documentation of the conditions of North American wildlife from the arrival of the first Europeans to the present. Also, *Lost Wild Worlds: The Story of Extinct and Vanishing Wildlife of the Eastern Hemisphere* ($9.25 ISBN 0–688–22090–8). (Gr 6–9)

McCoy, Joseph J. *In Defense of Animals.* New York, Seabury Press, 1978. 192 p. (A Clarion book) $8.95 ISBN 0–8164–3196–5   76–58508

Human cruelty to animals is documented in this detailed, chilling, but balanced report. Black-and-white photographs. (Gr 7–up)

Manchester, Harland F. *New Trail Blazers of Technology.* Illustrated with photographs. New York, Scribner, 1976. 214 p. $7.95 ISBN 0–684–14718–1   76–16760

In calling attention to ten creative minds behind such twentieth-century inventions as the Xerox copier, cable TV, and wankel engine, the science writer points out how much education is required today and how difficult it is for a scientist to achieve recognition. (Gr 6–9)

Milne, Lorus J., *and* Margery J. G. Milne. *Because of a Flower.* Drawings by Kenneth Gosner. New York, Atheneum, 1975. 152 p. $6.95 ISBN 0–689–30452–8   74–19292

In an ecological study alive with intriguing facts, such plants as the blackberry, orchid, and milkweed are shown to provide centers for small communities of animal life attracted by their flowers, fruits, and seeds. Meticulously detailed drawings. (Gr 5–8)

Mims, Forrest M. *Number Machines; an Introduction to the Abacus, Slide Rule, and Pocket Calculator.* New York, McKay, 1977. 54 p. $5.95 ISBN 0–679–20401–6   76–30777

Clear explanations of these three instruments, plus instructions for making and using the abacus and slide rule. Diagrams and black-and-white photographs. (Gr 4–6)

Mizumura, Kazue. *The Blue Whale.* New York, Crowell, 1971. 32 p. (Let's-read-and-find-out science books) $5.79 ISBN 0–690–14994–8 70–139107

Appealing soft watercolor paintings effectively illustrate comparative sizes and habits of the giant of the sea and complement a simple, direct text. (K–Gr 3)

———. *Opossum.* New York, Crowell, 1974. 33 p. (Let's-read-and-find-out science books) $6.79 ISBN 0–690–00397–8   73–13514

The artist, who provides text as well as drawings for this easily read nature story, depicts in a most appealing manner the world of an opossum and her pouch-nurtured babies. (K–Gr 2)

Morris, Robert A. *Dolphin.* Pictures by Mamoru Funai. New York, Harper & Row, 1975. 64 p. (A Science I can read book) $5.95 ISBN 0–06–024337–6   75–6292

The year's adventures of a newborn dolphin, in a simple narrative which incorporates natural history with the description of escapades. Two- and three-color drawings. (Gr 1–3)

———. *Seahorse.* Pictures by Arnold Lobel. New York, Harper & Row, 1972. 60 p. (A Science I can read book) $4.95 ISBN 0–06–024338–4 70–146004

An informative, amply illustrated introduction to a fascinating fish, describes its growth, habits, and marine environment. (K–Gr 2)

Myrick, Mildred. *Ants Are Fun.* Pictures by Arnold Lobel. New York, Harper & Row, 1968. 63 p. $4.79 ISBN 0–06–024356–2   68–10205

A science "I Can Read" book tells a fascinating story of ants and ant farms, with interested children creating a new colony home and observing ant activity in it. (Gr 2–3)

Papy, Frédérique, *and* Georges Papy. *Graph Games*, by Frédérique and Papy. Illustrated by Susan Holding. New York, Crowell, 1971. 33 p. (Young math books) $5.79 ISBN 0–690–34965–3   72–157647

Graphs are introduced as imaginative maps to unravel puzzling relationships. A functional use of color and lucid style make the concepts accessible to very young mathematicians.

Among other titles in the Young Math series published this year is *The Ellipse* by Mannis Charosh, illustrated by Leonard Kessler ($5.95 ISBN 0–690–25857–7). The author's treatment develops important ideas and encourages his readers' active participation. (K–Gr 3)

Parish, Peggy. *Dinosaur Time.* Pictures by Arnold Lobel. New York, Harper & Row, 1974. 30 p. (An Early I can read book) $4.95 ISBN 0–06–024653–7 (lib. ed. $4.79 ISBN 0–06–024654–5)   73–14331

Realistic, full-page drawings and a simple text describe eleven kinds of dinosaurs. Pronunciations are indicated. (Gr 1–3)

Patent, Dorothy H. *Frogs, Toads, Salamanders and How They Reproduce.* Illustrations by Matthew Kalmenoff. New York, Holiday House, 1975. 142 p. $6.95 ISBN 0–8234–0255–X   74–26567

A natural history of amphibians centers on adaptations to and away from water. Many species are discussed and illustrated in black-and-white drawings. (Gr 4–6)

Paysan, Klaus. *Aquarium Fish from around the World*. Minneapolis, Lerner Publications Co., 1971. 106 p. $6.95 ISBN 0–8225–0561–4   73–102892
Large, color photographs of over 100 fish species are accompanied by concise descriptions and brief information on food and water temperature requirements. (Gr 3–up)

Prescott, Gerald W. *The Diatoms; a Photomicrographic Book*. New York, Coward, McCann & Geoghegan, 1977. 47 p. $5.96 ISBN 0–698–30631–7   76–16582
An introduction to a plentiful but little-known group of algae which are valuable for food, oil, oxygen, and vitamin D. Discusses their structure and methods of reproduction, as well as how to collect them. (Gr 5–7)

Prince, Jack H. *Animals in the Night; Sense in Action after Dark*. New York, Nelson, 1971. 142 p. $5.95 ISBN 0–8407–6142–2   71–145917
A study of how animal sensory organs have adapted to life at night, with emphasis on sight and hearing and much detail not usually found in children's books. Black-and-white photographs and drawings. (Gr 6–8)

Pringle, Laurence P. *Death Is Natural*. New York, Four Winds Press, 1977. 54 p. $5.95 ISBN 0–590–07440–7   76–48923
A text in simple language gives perspective of death by discussing the recycling of atoms, nature's overproduction of offspring, the role of predators and microorganisms, and the extinction of species. Black-and-white photography by the author. (Gr 3–5)

————. *Discovering Nature Indoors; a Nature and Science Guide to Investigations with Small Animals*. Garden City, N.Y., Published for the American Museum of Natural History [by] the Natural History Press, 1970. 128 p. illus. $4.95 ISBN 0–385–01000–1   70–103134
Provocative ideas for home and school study of fish and water animals in aquariums; directions for building and using a simple microscope, an ant farm, and a maze for worms. (Gr 5–8)

————. *Estuaries; Where Rivers Meet the Sea*. New York, Macmillan, 1973. 55 p. $5.95 ISBN 0–02–775300–X   72–86506
An easy text and black-and-white photographs introduce the physical characteristics and plant and animal inhabitants of one of earth's most valuable ecosystems—the estuary. (Gr 4–6)

————. *Listen to the Crows*. Illustrated by Ted Lewin. New York, Crowell, 1976. 33 p. $5.79 ISBN 0–690–01069–9   75–43535
An invitation to listen to the language of the ubiquitous crow, this book presents both facts and theories (plainly identified as such) about how these birds communicate. Handsomely illustrated with black-and-white drawings. (Gr 4–7)

————. *The Only Earth We Have*. New York, Macmillan, 1969. 86 p. $5.95 ISBN 0–02–775210–0 (paper $0.95 ISBN 0–02–044880–5)   71–78076
A concise, not overstated view of man's abuse of his planet—the converting of wildlands, air pollution, use of insecticides, and waste—documented with striking photographs. Also, *Our Hungry Earth; the World Food Crisis* ($6.95 ISBN 0–02–775290–9). (Gr 5–8)

————. *Pests and People; the Search for Sensible Pest Control*. New York, Macmillan, 1972. 118 p. $5.95 ISBN 0–02–775270–4   71–165104
The continuing quest for biological methods to control pests—as opposed to the use of pesticides that have been indicted as biocidal—is examined and reported, with a final chilling caveat concerning "roadblocks" created by growers, insecticide manufacturers, the government, and the public. Many black-and-white photographs augment the text. (Gr 5–up)

————. *Wild Foods; a Beginner's Guide to Identifying, Harvesting and Cooking Safe and Tasty Plants from the Outdoors*. Text and photographs by Laurence Pringle. Illustrations by Paul Breeden. New York, Four Winds Press, 1978. 182 p. $9.95 ISBN 0–590–07511–X   78–1910
With many a cautionary note the ecologist identifies nineteen wild plants which may well serve as foods and adds directions for cooking them. (Gr 5–8)

Quinn, John R. *Nature's World Records*. New York, Walker, 1977. 96 p. $5.95 ISBN 0–8027–6290–5   76–57059
A collection of maximal data for the smallest, tallest, and even leggiest, with figures substantiating claims given in an entertaining text, and the author's lively drawings on every page. (Gr 4–6)

Rahn, Joan E. *Watch It Grow, Watch It Change*. New York, Atheneum, 1978. 88 p. $6.95 ISBN 0–689–30665–2   78–6287
With the author's own detailed line drawings, this discusses the formation and growth of plant parts such as stems, leaves, roots, flowers, tubers, and buds and the germination of seeds. (Gr 4–6)

Rau, Margaret. *The Gray Kangaroo at Home.* With drawings by Eva Hülsmann. New York, Knopf [distributed by Random House], 1978. 89 p. $5.95 ISBN 0–394–83451–2 (lib. ed. $5.99 ISBN 0–394–93451–8) 77–14942
A great forester kangaroo of Australia and her "young-at-foot" joey struggle against predators, storm, and bushfire. (Gr 5–8)

Rhine, Richard. *Life in a Bucket of Soil.* Illustrated by Elsie Wrigley. New York, Lothrop, Lee & Shepard, 1972. 96 p. $6.00 ISBN 0–688–51514–2 72–155756
A description of hundreds of soil creatures, including ideas for raising some for purposes of study. Contains much information not readily found elsewhere in one source. Line drawings. (Gr 3–6)

Robertson, Alden. *The Wild Horse Gatherers.* San Francisco, Sierra Club Books; New York, [trade distribution by Scribner], 1978. 95 p. $10.95 ISBN 0–684–15589–3 (paper $6.95 ISBN 0–684–15591–5) 77–17512
The author's action-filled photographs and first-person narrative give a sense of immediacy to this account of rounding up wild horses for adoption. (Gr 4–up)

Rockwell, Anne F., *and* Harlow Rockwell. *Machines.* New York, Macmillan, 1972. [23] p. $5.95 ISBN 0–02–777520–8 72–185149
The simplest of books to illustrate sources of energy-efficient machines, and machine parts such as ball bearings and gears. Clear, direct color illustration. (K–Gr 2)

Ross, Frank X. *Undersea Vehicles and Habitats; the Peaceful Uses of the Ocean.* New York, Crowell, 1970. 183 p. $7.95 ISBN 0–690–84416–6 76–106577
Traces the history of diving equipment, submarine vehicles, and undersea habitats and describes construction, peaceful uses, and possible future developments. Drawings and photographs. (Gr 7–9)

Rounds, Glen. *Wild Horses of the Red Desert.* Written and illustrated by Glen Rounds. New York, Holiday House, 1969. [48] p. $5.95 ISBN 0–8234–0146–4 77–2897
For horse lovers, a picture book that gives in its pages a sense of the wildness of the great open West. (All ages)

Russell, Franklin. *Hawk in the Sky.* Illustrated by Frederic Sweeney. New York, Holt, Rinehart and Winston, 1965. 61 p. Paper $1.25. Scholastic Book Service. ISBN 0–590–11853–6 65–14149

A scientist shares his observations of the red-tailed hawk from its early survival from predators to the mysterious urges of migration and mating. Many fine drawings of action in nature. (Gr 3–6)

St. John, Glory. *How to Count like a Martian.* New York, Walck, 1975. 66 p. $7.95 ISBN 0–8098–3125–2 74–19714
After studying counting systems from ancient times to the present—including the Egyptian base ten, the Babylonian base sixty, the Hindu system using three symbols, and the abacus and computer systems—the reader is ready to decode a message from Mars which, it is determined, uses the number system base four. (Gr 5–7)

Sarnoff, Jane, *and* Reynold Ruffins. *A Great Aquarium Book; the Putting-It-Together Guide for Beginners.* New York, Scribner, 1977. 47 p. $7.95 ISBN 0–684–14589–8 (paper $3.95 ISBN 0–684–14630–4) 75–39298
Practical guidance for the creation of a basic aquarium, from choosing fish to providing a comfortable and healthful environment for them. Reynold Ruffins's illustrations are in full color, realistic as biological drawings, and humorous for the directives on fish care. (Gr 4–up)

Schaeffer, Elizabeth. *Dandelion, Pokeweed, and Goosefoot; How the Early Settlers Used Plants for Food, Medicine, and in the Home.* Illustrations by Grambs Miller. Reading, Mass., Addison-Wesley, 1972. 94 p. (Young Scott books) $5.95 ISBN 0–201–09304–9 72–1836
Although not intended as a field book, this meticulously illustrated volume contains a mine of information about plants of woodland, pasture, and swamp—their origins and uses for medicine, food, and the household. Suggestions are included for making an herb garden, collecting and drying, making teas and salads, and dyeing cloth. (Gr 4–up)

Schaller, George B., *and* Millicent E. Selsam. *The Tiger! Its Life in the Wild.* New York, Harper & Row, 1969. 71 p. $6.89 ISBN 0–06–025280–4 69–14447
A study of tiger behavior made fascinating by the authors' revelation of personal involvement in field research. (Gr 5–8)

Schick, Alice. *The Peregrine Falcons.* Pictures by Peter Parnall. New York, Dial Press, 1975. 83 p. $5.95 ISBN 0–8037–4971–6 (lib. ed. $5.47 ISBN 0–8037–4972–4) 74–18599
In addition to explaining natural history in the life cycle of this rare hawk, the absorbing text describes

efforts made to save falcons from extinction by breeding them in captivity. Line drawings magnify interest. (Gr 4–6)

Schlein, Miriam. *Giraffe, the Silent Giant.* Illustrated by Betty Fraser. New York, Four Winds Press, 1976. 58 p. $6.95 ISBN 0–590–07421–0   76–7922

Giraffes and their discovery, natural history, and interaction with humans are presented with charming black-and-white drawings. (Gr 3–5)

Schwartz, George I. *Life in a Drop of Water.* Garden City, N.Y., Published for the American Museum of Natural History [by] the Natural History Press, 1970. 174 p. $4.95 ISBN 0–385–01548–8 71–92177

Particularly interesting for young people using microscopes is this descriptive and analytical text, plus photographs, which presents the interrelationships of marine organisms and their effect on bodies of fresh and salt water. (Gr 7–9)

Scott, Jack D. *Canada Geese.* Photographs by Ozzie Sweet. New York, Putnam, 1976. 64 p. $6.95 ISBN 0–399–20492–X   76–871

Excellent photographs and a poetically written but accurate text reveal such activities typical of the Canada goose as migrating, courting, preening, and feather loss. (Gr 4–7)

The author's *Discovering the American Stork*, with photographs by Ozzie Sweet (New York, Harcourt Brace Jovanovich. 62 p. $6.50 ISBN 0–15–203055–7), discusses habits and habitats and conservation efforts to save this unusual bird. (Gr 5–up)

————. *City of Birds; and Beasts; Behind the Scenes at the Bronx Zoo.* With photographs by Ozzie Sweet. New York, Putnam, 1978. 120 p. $8.95 ISBN 0–399–20633–7   77–13888

An all-day tour of the 252-acre Bronx Zoo reveals its organization and daily operation. Many unusual animal portraits. (Gr 5–8)

————. *Little Dogs of the Prairie.* Photographs by Ozzie Sweet. New York, Putnam, 1977. 62 p. $7.95 ISBN 0–399–20561–6   76–56217

An examination of the habits of the busy and attractive prairie dog, a vanishing form of American wildlife. Provides basic biological facts and projects the flavor of their life in colonies. Animated photographs distinguish this book, as well as the author's *The Gulls of Smuttynose Island* ($6.95 ISBN 0–399–20618–3). (Gr 4–6)

Selsam, Millicent E. *Birth of a Forest.* Illustrated by Barbara Wolff. New York, Harper & Row, 1964. 54 p. $5.79 ISBN 0–06–025276–6   63–17281

Photographs are combined with the artist's explicit drawings for a simple text to show how a lake turns into a forest. (Gr 4–6)

————. *Bulbs, Corms, and Such.* Photographs by Jerome Wexler. New York, Morrow, 1974. 48 p. $7.25 ISBN 0–688–21822–9 (lib. ed. $6.96 ISBN 0–688–31822–3)   74–5939

Excellent photographs of blossoms in full color and revealing cross sections show how bulbs, rhizomes, tubers, and corms grow and divide to produce more daffodils, dahlias, and other blooms. (Gr 3–5)

————. *The Harlequin Moth: Its Life Story.* New York, Morrow, 1975. 48 p. $6.95 ISBN 0–688–22049–5 (lib. ed. $6.43 ISBN 0–688–32049–X)   75–17862

Striking photographs by Jerome Wexler—including enlargements for the four stages of a moth and a detailed series for transition stages—make this study a beautiful book. (Gr 3–5)

————. *Land of the Giant Tortoise; the Story of the Galapagos.* New York, Four Winds Press, 1977. 64 p. $7.95 ISBN 0–590–07416–4   77–4897

A text, liberally furnished with handsome color and black-and-white photographs by Les Line and the author, describes unique fauna and flora of these volcanic islands. Clearly shows how Darwin derived from observations there the basis for his theory of evolution. (Gr 4–6)

————. *Popcorn.* Photographs by Jerome Wexler. New York, Morrow, 1976. 48 p. $6.25 ISBN 0–688–22083–5 (lib. ed. $6.00 ISBN 0–688–32083–X)   76–26627

Black-and-white or color photographs on every page portray corn growth from germination to new seeds, with a concise text that also describes pollinating one's own plants and the value of corn products. (Gr 2–4)

————. *The Tomato and Other Fruit Vegetables.* Photographs by Jerome Wexler. New York, Morrow, 1970. 47 p. $6.00 ISBN 0–688–31493–7 70–117225

Enlarged photographs illustrate the growth and structure of the tomato, cucumber, snap bean, and eggplant. (Gr 3–5)

————. *Tyrannosaurus Rex.* New York, Harper & Row, 1978. 41 p. $5.95 ISBN 0–06–025423–8 (lib. ed. $5.79 ISBN 0–06–025424–6)   77–25677

Using the 1902 discovery of *Tyrannosaurus* as an example, the author describes searching the area, plastering bones, museum reconstruction of the skeleton, and deductions about the creature's way of life. Black-and-white photographs, old and new. (Gr 3–5)

————, and Jerome Wexler. *The Amazing Dandelion*. New York, Morrow, 1977. 46 p. $6.25 ISBN 0–688–22129–7 (lib. ed. $6.00 ISBN 0–688–32129–1)   77–9029
Wexler's close-up photographs (a few in color) of the dandelion and its various parts enhance the clarity of Selsam's brief text about the structure, pollination, seed dispersal, and nutritional value of this common wildflower. Also, *Mimosa, the Sensitive Plant* ($6.95 ISBN 0–688–22167–X; lib. ed. $6.67 ISBN 0–688–32167–4). (Gr 2–5)

Shaw, Evelyn S. *Elephant Seal Island*. Pictures by Cherryl Pape. New York, Harper & Row, 1978. 62 p. (A Science I can read book) $4.95 ISBN 0–06–025603–6 (lib. ed. $5.79 ISBN 0–06–025604–4)   77–25649
An imaginative story of seal life—a simple text with informative, three-color pictures. (Gr 1–2)

————. *Octopus*. Pictures by Ralph Carpentier. New York, Harper & Row, 1971. 61 p. (A Science I can read book) $4.79 ISBN 0–06–025559–5 74–135779
An easy-to-read description of the habitat, characteristics, habits, and life cycle of the octopus. (Gr 1–2)

Shuttlesworth, Dorothy E. *Animals That Frighten People; Fact Versus Myth*. New York, Dutton, 1974. 122 p. $6.95 ISBN 0–525–25745–4 73–77458
An appealing topic, with a wide range of material on wolves, bears, bats, snakes, tarantulas, and such. Black-and-white photographs add both information and eyecatching interest. (Gr 4–7)

————. *Clean Air, Sparkling Water; the Fight against Pollution*. Garden City, N.Y., Doubleday, 1968. 95 p. $4.95 ISBN 0–385–03052–5   68–17788
Discussion of the causes and dangers of air and water pollution and present and future efforts to combat them. (Gr 3–5)

————. *The Story of Ants*. Illustrated by Su Zan N. Swain. Garden City, N.Y., Doubleday, 1964. 60 p. $4.95 ISBN 0–385–06676–7   63–11388
Colorful drawings and diagrams amplify this fascinating discussion of many kinds of ants. (Gr 5–up)

Silverstein, Alvin, *and* Virginia B. Silverstein. *Alcoholism*. With an introduction by Gail Gleason Milgram, consulting editor. Philadelphia, Lippincott, 1975. 128 p. $6.95 ISBN 0–397–31648–8 (paper $2.95 ISBN 0–397–31649–6)   75–17938
A nonmoralizing, broad discussion covers the effects of alcohol on the body, the causes, stages, and treatments of alcoholism, teenage drinking, and life with an alcoholic parent. (Gr 6–9)

————. *Cats; All about Them*. With photographs by Frederick J. Breda. New York, Lothrop, Lee & Shepard, 1978. 224 p. $6.95 ISBN 0–688–41841–4 (lib. ed. $6.67 ISBN 0–688–51841–9)   77–25182
Domestication, breeds, pet care, cats in literature and history, experimentation, and wild species are topics covered, with many excellent photographs. (Gr 3–5)

————. *Rabbits; All about Them*. Photographs by Roger Kerkham. New York, Lothrop, Lee & Shepard, 1973. 128 p. $6.48 ISBN 0–688–51564–9   73–4952
Captivating photographs of varying kinds of *Lagomorpha* of all ages—from engaging "kittens" to alert mature adults—accompany discussion of rabbits in the wild and in the laboratory, their ecological significance, and the pervasive role of "rabbits in lore and legends," plus notes on care of pets. (Gr 4–up)

————. *Rats and Mice; Friends and Foes of Man*. Illustrated by Joseph Cellini. New York, Lothrop, Lee & Shepard, 1968. 96 p. $6.25 ISBN 0–688–41617–9   68–27715
Describes these rodents from many points of view: their general biology, role as enemy of man, value to science, and appearance in legend and language. (Gr 4–6)

Simon, Hilda. *Partners, Guests, and Parasites; Coexistence in Nature*. New York, Viking Press, 1970. 127 p. $5.95 ISBN 0–670–54086–2   71–106924
A description in text and four-color illustrations of temporary and permanent alliances made between animals or plants for mutual survival. (Gr 7–9)

————. *Snakes; the Facts and the Folklore*. New York, Viking Press, 1973. 128 p. $6.95 ISBN 0–670–65315–2   73–5154
Not merely an identification guide, but an absorbing discussion of many of the world's snakes, their characteristics and habits. The author's illustrations show to great advantage their beautiful colors and patterns. (Gr 5–8)

Simon, Seymour. *Killer Whales*. Philadelphia, Lippincott, 1978. 96 p. $6.95 ISBN 0–397–31784–0 (paper $3.95 ISBN 0–397–31792–1)   77–20187
A description of the physical characteristics, habits, natural environment, and behavior in captivity of the killer whale, seen as obedient and friendly in contrast to earlier reports. Black-and-white photographs. (Gr 3–6)

————. *Pets in a Jar; Collecting and Caring for Small Wild Animals*. Illustrated by Betty Fraser. New York, Viking Press, 1975. 95 p. $6.95 ISBN 0–670–55060–4   74–14905

How to find and maintain insects and small fresh- and salt-water animals such as planaria, hydras, toads, and starfish. Observations and experiments are suggested. Attractive line drawings. (Gr 3–6)

Sitomer, Mindel, *and* Harry Sitomer. *What Is Symmetry?* New York, Crowell, 1970. 33 p. (A Young math book) $5.95 ISBN 0–690–87612–2 (lib. ed. $5.79 ISBN 0–690–87613–0; paper $1.45 ISBN 0–690–87618–1)   70–101933

Ed Emberley's engaging alligator drawings encourage the reader to create as well as observe designs with matching elements, to help develop sophisticated notions about line symmetry, point symmetry, and plane symmetry.

Another book in this Young Math Book series, *Weighing & Balancing* by Jane Jonas Srivastava ($5.95 ISBN 0–690–87114–7), also demands reader participation. Aliki's pictures enliven and clarify the conceptual development. (Gr 5–8)

Sobol, Harriet L. *Jeff's Hospital Book.* Photographs by Patricia Agre. New York, Walck, 1975. [47] p. $6.95 ISBN 0–8098–1229–0   74–25982

A supportive presentation of hospital procedures describes Jeff's preparation for an eye operation and his recovery. (PreS–Gr 3)

Sootin, Harry. *Easy Experiments with Water Pollution.* Drawings by Lucy Bitzer. New York, Four Winds Press, 1974. 109 p. $6.95 ISBN 0–590–07334–6   73–88082

Imaginative, safe experiments with chlorination, water softening, aeration, and pollutants are well illustrated, with easy-to-follow directions. (Gr 5–8)

Soucie, Anita H. *Plant Fun: Ten Easy Plants to Grow Indoors.* Illustrated by Grambs Miller. New York, Four Winds Press, 1974. 125 p. $7.95 ISBN 0–590–07323–0   73–88079

Novice gardeners will gain confidence from this guide in which simple directions and clear pictures suggest the fun of growing cacti, African violets, avocados, and other popular house plants for windowsills and terrariums. (All ages)

The Spider's Web. By Oxford Scientific Films. Photographs by John Cooke. New York, Putnam, 1978. [28] p. $5.95 ISBN 0–399–20621–3   77–8322

Close-up photographs reveal how two different species of spiders spin webs and catch their prey. A simple caption for each picture adds information to details in the four-page text. In the same picture-book series, and similarly exceptional for its blown-up color pictures, is *House Mouse* ($5.95 ISBN 0–399–20620–5). (Gr 3–6)

Srivastava, Jane J. *Statistics.* Illustrated by John J. Reiss. New York, Crowell, 1973. 32 p. (Let's-read-and-find-out science book) $5.79 ISBN 0–690–77300–5   72–7559

Just the beginning of a look at the subject, raising awareness of such principles as sampling and counting; a book most effective when used by a teacher. (Gr 4–up)

Stein, Sara B. *How to Raise Mice, Rats, Hamsters, and Gerbils.* Photographs by Robert Weinreb. New York, Random House, 1976. 48 p. (A Child's book of pet care) $5.99 ISBN 0–394–93224–2) (paper $3.95 ISBN 0–394–83224–8)   76–8138

This book and two companion handbooks, also illustrated with black-and-white color photographs—*How to Raise a Puppy* (ISBN 0–394–93223–4) and *How to Raise Goldfish and Guppies* (ISBN 0–394–93225–0)—offer helpful advice on the selection and care of pets and counter the child's anthropocentric views by describing an animal's capabilities. (Gr 3–5)

Stevens, Carla. *The Birth of Sunset's Kittens.* Photographs by Leonard Stevens. New York, Young Scott Books, 1969. [44] p. $5.95. Addison-Wesley, Reading, Mass. ISBN 0–201–21698–5   69–14569

Appealing photographs record the birth process of a litter of kittens while a quiet, childlike text explains it. (All ages)

————. *Insect Pets; Catching and Caring for Them.* Illustrated by Karl W. Stuecklen. New York, Greenwillow Books, 1978. 96 p. (A Greenwillow read-alone guide) $5.95 ISBN 0–688–80121–8 (lib. ed. $5.49 ISBN 0–688–84121–X)   77–9940

An easy-to-read text and line drawings give directions for capturing and caring for seven insects: praying mantises, ladybugs, crickets, whirligigs, water striders, fireflies, and antlions. Experiments are suggested. (Gr 1–3)

Tunis, Edwin. *Chipmunks on the Doorstep.* New York, Crowell, 1971. 69 p. $7.95 ISBN 0–690–19044–1 (lib. ed. $6.79 IBSN 0–690–19045–X)   73–132305

Lovingly described in minute detail are the physical characteristics and habits of the chipmunk. The many pictures scattered over the pages are delicate in color and small in size. (Gr 4–7)

Walters, John F. *Carnivorous Plants.* Illustrated with photographs. New York, Watts, 1974. 60 p. (A First book) $4.90 ISBN 0–531–02700–7   73–21976

Bladderwort, Venus flytrap, sundew, and pitcher plant are among the species of insect-eating plants shown here in photographs and reproductions of old prints. Directions are included for growing them in terrariums. (Gr 5–7)

Weber, William J. *Wild Orphan Babies; Mammals and Birds: Caring for Them and Setting Them Free*. New York, Holt, Rinehart & Winston, 1975. 159 p. $5.95 ISBN 0–03–014211–3   74–23811
For foster parents, a veterinarian's expert instructions on animal care, not to be readily found elsewhere. Black-and-white photographs by the author. (Gr 5–7)

Weiss, Harvey. *Motors and Engines and How They Work*. New York, Crowell, 1969. 62 p. $7.95 ISBN 0–690–56478–3   69–11828
An introductory explanation of motors and engines with directions for building models of a water wheel, sailboat, windmill, and a "gravity engine." (Gr 2–5)

Weiss, Malcolm E. *666 Jellybeans! All That? An Introduction to Algebra*. Illustrated by Judith Hoffman Corwin. New York, Crowell, 1976. 33 p. (Young math books) $5.79 ISBN 0–690–00914–3   75–9528
As if approaching a game, the author shows the reader, step by step, how to find unknown numbers from clues given in this introduction to algebra. Three-color pictures enliven the account. (Gr 3–4)

———, *and* Ann E. Weiss. *The Vitamin Puzzle*. Illustrated by Pat De Aloe. New York, Messner, 1976. 96 p. $7.29 ISBN 0–671–32777–1   75–45293

With a nonscientific approach and cartoon drawings, an engaging story is told of how vitamins were discovered and important aspects of nutrition recognized, with a warning against junk foods. (Gr 3–5)

Wohlrabe, Raymond A. *Exploring the World of Leaves*. Photographs by the author; diagrams by John F. McTarsney. New York, Crowell, 1976. 150 p. $8.95 ISBN 0–690–00511–3   75–15865
A description of leaf classification and types, structure, functions, and importance to plant and animal life includes suggestions for experiments and science projects. (Gr 6–up)

Wolberg, Barbara J. *Zooming In; Photographic Discoveries under the Microscope*. Photographs by Lewis R. Wolberg. New York, Harcourt Brace Jovanovich, 1974. 64 p. $7.75 ISBN 0–15–299970–1   73–18631
More than fifty black-and-white photomicrographs —of rocks, metals, plant and animal tissue cells—with informative captions that indicate observable parts and processes. (Gr 5–8)

Zim, Herbert S. *Caves and Life*. Illustrated by Richard Cuffari. New York, Morrow, 1978. 62 p. $5.95 ISBN 0–688–22112–2 (lib. ed. $5.71 ISBN 0–688–32112–7)   77–337
Fascinating facts about cave formation, cave wildlife, and man's use of caves. Many clear drawings and diagrams. (Gr 3–6)

Psychology and Sociology

Ancona, George. *Growing Older.* New York, Dutton, 1978. [48] p. $7.95 ISBN 0–525–31050–9
78–7605
Revealing reminiscences denote the vitality of persons advancing in age. Photographs show them in old age and also in childhood. (Gr 4–6)

Burns, Marilyn. *I Am Not a Short Adult; Getting Good at Being a Kid.* Illustrated by Martha Weston. Boston, Little, Brown, 1977. 125 p. (A Brown paper school book) $7.95 ISBN 0–316–11745–5 (paper $4.95 ISBN 0–316–11746–3)   77–24486
A compendium on "kidhood" for browsing and stimulating discussion. Provides background information and raises questions about children's legal rights and relation to school, work, parents, and TV. (Gr 4–6)

Hall, Elizabeth. *Why We Do What We Do: a Look at Psychology.* Boston, Houghton Mifflin, 1973. 183 p. illus. $6.95 ISBN 0–395–17516–X   73–8844
Reports of laboratory studies add to the interest of this straightforward discussion of such psychological matters as personality, motivation, and the emotions. (Gr 7–up)

LeShan, Eda J. *Learning to Say Good-By: When a Parent Dies.* Illustrated by Paul Giovanopoulos. New York, Macmillan, 1976. 85 p. $6.95 ISBN 0–02–756306–X   76–15155
The author's frank discussion of emotions that accompany grieving and of a child's hidden concerns about death makes this a positive book for children to read or adults to use. (Gr 3–up)

——. *What's Going To Happen to Me? When Parents Separate or Divorce.* Illustrated by Richard Cuffari. New York, Four Winds Press, 1978. 134 p. $6.95 ISBN 0–590–07535–7   78–4340
A reassuring explanation of divorce—prelude, experience, and aftermath—written calmly and directly for the young reader, citing specific and typical reactions of children and parents. (Gr 4–6)

Peterson, Jeanne W. *I Have a Sister—My Sister Is Deaf.* Pictures by Deborah Ray. New York, Harper & Row, 1977. [32] p. $4.95 ISBN 0–06–024701–0 (lib. ed. $5.79 ISBN 0–06–024702–9)   76–24306
An older sister's affectionate description of a little sister's deafness explains that her ears don't hurt but her feelings often do when she is not understood. Expressive soft-pencil drawings. (K–Gr 3)

Sobol, Harriet L. *My Brother Steven Is Retarded.* Photographs by Patricia Agre. New York, Macmillan, 1977. 26 p. $5.95 ISBN 0–02–785990–2
76–46996

In an informal essay eleven-year-old Beth describes how a retarded brother affects her life, both in the family and in the community. Well illustrated with black-and-white photographs. (Gr 3–5)

Wolf, Bernard. *Anna's Silent World.* Philadelphia, Lippincott, 1977. 48 p. $6.95 ISBN 0–397–31739–5
76–52943

The author describes the special training and electronic equipment used to extend Anna's hearing and ability to talk, read, and write. Both specific and objective with photographs by the author depicting many activities. (Gr 2–5)

———. *Connie's New Eyes.* Philadelphia, Lippincott, 1976. 95 p. $8.95 ISBN 0–397–31697–6 (paper $1.25. Pocket Books, New York. ISBN 0–671–29897–6)
76–17014

In a striking photographic essay, blind Connie trains a golden retriever to be her seeing-eye dog and after college becomes a teacher of handicapped children. (Gr 4–6)

Children's Books
1979

A List of Books for Preschool Through Junior High School Age

Compiled by *Virginia Haviland,* Chief of the Children's Literature Center, Library of Congress, with the assistance of the following committee:

Office of Education, U. S. Department of Health, Education, and Welfare— Mary Billings, Educational Materials Specialist, Educational Materials Review Center (EDMARC).

*Arlington County, Virginia—*Deborah Weilerstein, Coordinator of Children's Services, and Elizabeth Goebel, Head, Central Children's Room, Department of Libraries.

*District of Columbia—*Elizabeth B. Murphy, Coordinator, Children's Service, Public Library, and Sarah E. Gagne, Science Teacher, Public Schools.

*Library of Congress—*Margaret N. Coughlan, Reference Specialist in Children's Literature, Children's Literature Center.

*Montgomery County, Maryland—*Ann Friedman and Laurie Mielke, Assistant Coordinators, Children's Services, Department of Public Libraries.

*Prince George's County, Maryland—*Katherine Ann Cima, Media Specialist, Northern Area Administrative Office, Public Schools, and Mary Elizabeth Wildberger, Media Specialist, Phyllis E. Williams School.

Note: International Standard Book Number is given after price, Library of Congress card number follows bibliographic information, and grade level appears at end of annotation.

PICTURE AND PICTURE—STORY BOOKS

Anno, Mitsumasa. *The King's Flower*. New York, Collins. [30] p. $7.95 ISBN 0-529-05458-2 (lib. ed. $7.91 ISBN 0-529-05459-0)   78-9596
Pictures strong in line and color, with imaginative, sometimes humorous, details, support an easily read text in telling about a king "who had to have everything bigger and better than anyone else." (K-Gr 2)

Ahlberg, Janet, *and* Allan Ahlberg. *Each Peach Pear Plum, an "I Spy" Story*. New York, Viking Press. [32] p. (An I-spy-book) $8.95 ISBN 0-670-28705-9   78-16726
Cheerfully colored paintings invite the reader to play "I Spy" with various characters from nursery lore. Winner of the 1979 Kate Greenaway Medal. (PreS-Gr 1)

Aruego, Jose, *and* Ariane Dewey. *We Hide, You Seek*. New York, Greenwillow Books. [32] p. $7.95 ISBN 0-688-80201-X (lib. ed. $7.63 ISBN 0-688-84201)   78-13638
Bright and lavish paintings in a nearly wordless picture book reveal how forest animals can camouflage themselves and hide from each other. (PreS-Gr 1)

Calhoun, Mary. *Cross-Country Cat*. Illustrated by Erick Ingraham. New York, Morrow. [40] p. col. illus. $6.95 ISBN 0-688-22186-6 (lib. ed. $6.67 ISBN 0-688-32186-0)   78-31718
In this effectively illustrated animal fantasy, Harry, a somewhat grumpy seal-point Siamese cat, effects his own rescue on skiis, after being accidently abandoned by his human family. (K-Gr 3)

Cohen, Miriam. *Lost in the Museum*. Pictures by Lillian Hoban. New York, Greenwillow Books. [32] p. $7.25 ISBN 0-688-80187-0 (lib. ed. $6.96 ISBN 0-688-84187-2)   78-16765
Vivid drawings in pleasing colors capture the spirit of first-graders who get lost in a museum. (K-Gr 2)

Cole, Brock. *The King at the Door*. Garden City, N.Y., Doubleday. [32] p. illus. (part col.) $7.95 ISBN 0-385-14718-X (lib. ed. $8.90 ISBN 0-385-14719-8)   78-20064
The author-illustrator's lusty, animated drawings underscore the tongue-in-cheek humor of a folklike tale about the comeuppance of an innkeeper at the hands of a chore boy "brighter than a burnt match." (K-Gr 2)

Hall, Donald. *Ox-Cart Man*. Pictures by Barbara Cooney. New York, Viking Press. [40] p. $8.95 ISBN 0-670-53328-9   79-14466
The 1979 Caldecott Medal winner presents in detailed full-page, full-color paintings executed in American Primitive style the journeying of an early nineteenth-century New England farmer with his goods and produce for market. (K-Gr 3)

Hoban, Tana. *One Little Kitten*. New York, Greenwillow Books. [24] p. $6.95 ISBN 0-688-80222-2 (lib. ed. $5.71 ISBN 0-688-84222-4)   78-31862
Faithful to the charms of kitten stances and playfulness is a sequence of black-and-white photographs which follow a very young one's explorations. (PreS-K)

Hughes, Shirley. *Moving Molly*. Englewood Cliffs, N.J., Prentice-Hall. [32] p. $7.95 ISBN 0-136-04587-1   78-16732
After moving to the country Molly is lonely until she meets the twins Kathy and Kevin and three cats in their jungle of a garden. Full-color paintings. (K-Gr 1)

Hutchins, Pat. *One-Eyed Jake*. New York, Greenwillow Books. [32] p. $7.25 ISBN 0-688-80183-8 (lib. ed. $6.96 ISBN 0-688-84183-X)   78-18346
Colorful, detailed illustrations and vigorous text tell how One-Eyed Jake receives a just reward for all his awful deeds. (K-Gr 2)

Isadora, Rachel. *Ben's Trumpet*. New York, Greenwillow Books. [32] p. $6.95 ISBN 0-688-80194-3   78-12885
In varied black-and-white art deco illustrations Isadora recreates the music of the Jazz Age, focusing on young Ben who longs passionately to play a real trumpet. (Gr 1-4)

Kalan, Robert. *Blue Sea*. Illustrated by Donald Crews. New York, Greenwillow Books. [24] p. $6.95 ISBN 0-688-80184-6 (lib. ed. $6.67 ISBN 0-688-84184-8)   78-18396

Figures in a variety of clear colors on cerulean pages make a spatial-concept book as, in humorous scenes, big fish repeatedly get trapped in apertures through which a little fish easily escapes. (PreS-K)

Levitin, Sonia. *A Sound to Remember*. New York, Harcourt Brace Jovanovich. [32] p. $6.95 ISBN 0-15-277248-0   79-87522
The story of how Jacov, slow and clumsy, deals with his problematical honor of blowing the shofar (ram's horn) on the Jewish High Holy Days. With Gabriel Lisowski's soft-pencil drawings. (K-Gr 2)

Lobel, Arnold. *A Treeful of Pigs*. Pictures by Anita Lobel. New York, Greenwillow Books. [32] p. $7.95 ISBN 0-688-80177-3 (lib. ed. $7.35 ISBN 0-688-84177-5)   78-1810
A fresh bit of pictorial nonsense in color presents a lazy farmer who must fulfill the pact he made with his wife to help her with the farm work when "pigs grow in the trees like apples." (K-Gr 2)

Massie, Diane R. *Chameleon Was a Spy*. New York, Crowell. [40] p. illus. (part col.) $6.95 ISBN 0-690-03909-3 (lib. ed. $6.79 ISBN 0-690-03910-7)   78-19510
Chameleon becomes a spy in order to recover for the Pleasant Pickle Company its stolen formula for the world's best pickles. (K-Gr 3)

Mother Goose. *James Marshall's Mother Goose*. New York, Farrar, Straus & Giroux. [39] p. $8.95 ISBN 0-374-33653-9   79-2574
Pastel wash drawings in green, yellow, and brick fully extract the humor in a selection of familiar and not-so-familiar nursery rhymes. (PreS-Gr 1)

Noble, Trinka H. *The King's Tea*. New York, Dial Press. [32] p. $6.95 ISBN 0-8037-4529-X (lib. ed. $6.40 ISBN 0-8037-4530-3)   79-50749
In a gently humorous cumulative tale, with equally humorous pastel pictures, it is clear that buttercups are to blame for the state of the King's tea. (K-Gr 2)

Oakley, Graham. *The Church Mice at Bay*. New York, Atheneum. [36] p. $8.95 ISBN 0-689-30629-6   78-62260
The well-known church mice revolt, successfully, against a hippy new curate who cuts out their cheese ration and replaces Sampson, their benign church cat, with a cruel mouser. Full-color, action-packed pictures. (K-Gr 2)

Peet, Bill. *Cowardly Clyde*. Boston, Houghton Mifflin. 38 p. $8.95 ISBN 0-395-27802-3   78-24343
Boldly comic color drawings show timorous Clyde, a war-horse, defeating an "owl-eyed monster." (Gr 2-4)

Shulevitz, Uri. *The Treasure*. New York, Farrar, Straus & Giroux. [31] p. col. illus. $7.95 ISBN 0-374-37740-5   78-12952
Luminous illustrations capture the flavor of the town and country background for this variant of a well-known Eastern European folktale in which a poor man traveling to find a treasure learns that it is in his own home. (K-Gr 2)

Stevenson, James. *Monty*. New York, Greenwillow Books. [32] p. $7.95 ISBN 0-688-80209-5 (lib. ed. $7.63 ISBN 0-688-84209-7)   78-11409
Droll illustrations in pastel wash are well integrated with the words of an amusing text for this approach to a transportation problem faced by a rabbit, a duck, and a frog. (PreS-Gr 1)

Van Allsburg, Chris. *The Garden of Abdul Gasazi*. Boston, Houghton Mifflin. [31] p. $8.95 ISBN 0-395-27804-X   79-17610
To be admired for its eerily atmospheric drawings, this almost surreal black-and-white picture book is about a boy and a dog that trespass on the grounds of a retired magician. (K-Gr 3)

Watanabe, Shigeo. *How Do I Put It On?; Getting Dressed*. New York, Collins. 28 p. (An I can do it all by myself book) $6.95 ISBN 0-529-05555-4 (lib. ed. $5.91 ISBN 0-529-05557-0)   79-12714
The efforts of a bumbling young bear to dress himself will appeal to the equally young child. Engagingly illustrated with Yasuo Ohtomo's simple, soft-color drawings. (PreS)

Watson, Jane W. *Which Is the Witch?* By W. K. Jasner [*pseud.*] Pictures by Victoria Chess. New York, Pantheon Books. [46] p. (An I am reading book) $3.95 ISBN 0-394-83978-1 (lib. ed. $4.99 ISBN 0-394-93978-6)   78-31407
Young Jenny in holiday costume is terrified when a real witch trades places with her on Halloween. (GR 1-3)

Williams, Jay. *The City Witch & the Country Witch*. New York, Macmillan. [43] p. $8.95 ISBN 0-02-793050-5   78-11333

When a city witch who makes traffic move smoothly trades places with a country witch who encourages things to grow, they find that they must adapt their individual magic to circumstances. Ed Renfro's cartoons are colorful and amusing. (K-Gr 3)

Yeoman, John. *The Wild Washerwomen, a New Folk Tale*. With pictures by Quentin Blake. New York, Greenwillow Books. [31] p. col. illus. $7.95 ISBN 0-688-80219-2 (lib. ed. $7.63 ISBN 0-688-84219-4)   78-32147

Blake gives rambunctious characterizations to seven washerwomen tired of scrubbing who on a rampage are confronted by seven grubby woodcutters. (K-Gr 2)

FIRST READING

Hoff, Sydney. *Slugger Sal's Slump*. New York, Windmill Books and E. P. Dutton. 48 p. $5.95 ISBN 0-525-61590-3   78-26338

Typical Hoff cartoons show Slugger Sal slumping so badly that he appears washed up as a ballplayer—until a last-minute reversal. (Gr 1-3)

Kent, Jack. *Hoddy Doddy*. New York, Greenwillow Books. 56 p. (Greenwillow read-alone) $5.95 ISBN 0-688-80192-7 (lib. ed. $5.71 ISBN 0-688-84192-9)   78-23635

Three chuckle-inducing Danish noodlehead stories in which lobsters are mistaken for a ship's crew, the town clock is buried at sea, and a proud citizen aids the local cuckoo in a contest with a foreign bird. Color drawings border on a cartoon style. (K-Gr 2)

Krasilovsky, Phyllis. *The Man Who Tried to Save Time*. Garden City, N.Y., Doubleday. (A Reading-on-my-own book) $4.95 ISBN 0-385-12998-X (lib. ed. $5.90 ISBN 0-385-12999-8)   77-74304

A man attempts unsuccessfully to speed up his orderly life by shaving in bed and eating breakfast at night. As droll as the story are Marcia Sewall's many full-color drawings. (Gr 1-3)

Lobel, Arnold. *Days with Frog and Toad*. New York, Harper & Row. 64 p. (An I can read book) $6.95 ISBN 0-06-023963-8 (lib. ed. $6.79 ISBN 0-06-023964-6)   78-21786

Five fresh episodes about the two friends, who find sometimes that it's good to be alone. Soft-color paintings. (K-Gr 2)

Rice, Eve. *Once in a Wood; Ten Tales from Aesop*. Adapted. New York, Greenwillow Books. 64 p. (Greenwillow read-alone) $5.95 ISBN 0-688-80191-9 (lib. ed. $5.71 ISBN 0-688-84191-0)   78-16294

Retaining an appropriate traditional flavor and made beguiling by the adaptor's stippled drawings, these retellings are accessible to the youngest reader. (K-Gr 3)

Seuss, Dr. *Oh Say Can You Say?* New York, Beginner Books. [40] p. col. illus. (I can read it all by myself) $3.50 ISBN 0-394-84255-3 (lib. ed. $4.39 ISBN 0-394-94255-8)   78-20716

Tongue-twisting verses describe such ludicrous characters as a book-reading parrot named Hooey, The Fuddnuddler Brothers, and a walrus which whispers "through tough rough wet whiskers." (Gr 1-3)

Sharmat, Marjorie W. *Griselda's New Year*. Pictures by Normand Chartier. New York, Macmillan. 63 p. (Ready-to-read) $6.95 ISBN 0-02-782420-9   79-11375

Griselda Goose's attempts to carry out her New Year's resolutions bring nothing but trouble to her friends. Three-color anthropomorphic drawings. (Gr 1-2)

Shub, Elizabeth. *Seeing Is Believing*. Pictures by Rachel Isadora. New York, Greenwillow Books. 63 p. (Greenwillow read-alone) $5.95 ISBN 0-688-80211-7 (lib. ed. $5.71 ISBN 0-688-84211-9)   78-12378

Two stories—one about a Cornish pisky, the other about an Irish leprechaun—exude the flavor and mood of fairy adventure. (Gr 1-3)

Stevenson, James. *Fast Friends; Two Stories*. New York, Greenwillow Books. 64 p. col. illus. (Greenwillow read-alone) $6.95 ISBN 0-688-80197-8 (lib. ed. $6.67 ISBN 0-688-84197-X)   78-14828

Amusingly illustrated by the author, two winsome read-alone stories tell how a turtle and a snail and then a mouse and another turtle become "fast friends" in unusual situations. (Gr 1-3)

Van Leeuwen, Jean. *Tales of Oliver Pig*. Pictures by Arnold Lobel. New York, Dial Press. 64 p. col. illus. (Dial easy-to-read) $5.89 ISBN 0-8037-8736-7 (paper $1.95 ISBN 0-8037-8737-5)
79-4276
Five short tales of fun and affection—about Oliver Pig and his little sister Amanda. (Gr 1-3)

STORIES FOR THE MIDDLE GROUP

Bawden, Nina. *The Robbers*. New York, Lothrop, Lee & Shepard Books. 155 p. $6.95 ISBN 0-688-41902-X (lib. ed. $6.67 ISBN 0-688-51902-4)
79-4152
A reaction against injustice causes Philip and his friend Darcy to steal an objet d'art from a miserly old woman. (Gr 5-7)

Blaine, Marge. *Dvora's Journey*. Illustrated by Gabriel Lisowski. New York, Holt, Rinehart, and Winston. 126 p. $6.95 ISBN 0-03-048306-9
78-26349
Fugitives from anti-Semitism in prerevolutionary Russia, Dvora and her family journey to Hamburg to discover that there is money to send only two of them to America. (Gr 3-5)

Beatty, Patricia. *Lacy Makes a Match*. New York, Morrow. 222 p. $7.95 ISBN 0-688-22183-1 (lib. ed. $7.63 ISBN 0-688-32183-6)
79-9813
A rollicking story set in turn-of-the-century mining country tells of a thirteen-year-old foundling's search for her roots and success in marrying off her foster brothers. (Gr 4-6)

Bowden, Joan C. *Why the Tides Ebb and Flow*. Illustrated by Marc Brown. Boston, Houghton Mifflin. [40] p. $6.95 ISBN 0-395-28378-7 79-12359
In a rhythmic, strikingly illustrated traditional-style story, an old woman threatens to pull the rock from the hole in the ocean floor if Sky Spirit does not honor his promise to give her shelter. (Gr 1-4)

Byars, Betsy C. *Good-bye, Chicken Little*. New York, Harper & Row. 101 p. $5.95 ISBN 0-06-020907-0 (lib. ed. $5.79 ISBN 0-06-020911-9)
78-19829

The perceptive story of Jimmie who calls himself "chicken" but copes sensibly when his uncle drowns on a dare-driven walk over the river's thin ice. (Gr 4-6)

Callen, Larry. *Sorrow's Song*. Illustrated by Marvin Friedman. Boston, Little, Brown. 150 p. (An Atlantic Monthly Press book) $7.95 ISBN 0-316-12497-4
78-31789
A sequel to *Pinch* ($6.95 ISBN 0-316-12495-8) and *The Deadly Mandrake* ($6.95 ISBN 0-316-12496-6) in which Sorrow Nix, a mute child, persuades Pinch to help hide and protect an injured whooping crane from would-be profiteers. (Gr 4-6)

Chaikin, Miriam. *I Should Worry, I Should Care*. Drawings by Richard Egielski. New York, Harper & Row. 103 p. $7.95 ISBN 0-06-021174-1 (lib. ed. $7.89 ISBN 0-06-021175-X)
78-19480
Her loving Jewish family helps resentful Molly adjust to living in a new Brooklyn neighborhood, just before Hitler's rise to power. (Gr 3-5)

Cleary, Beverly. *Ramona and Her Mother*. Illustrated by Alan Tiegreen. New York, Morrow. 207 p. $6.75 ISBN 0-688-22195-5 (lib. ed. $6.48 ISBN 0-688-32195-X)
79-10323
A humorous, thoroughly satisfying sequel to the 1978 Newbery Honor winner, *Ramona and Her Father* ($6.50 ISBN 0-688-22114-9; lib. ed. $6.01 ISBN 0-688-32114-3) . (Gr 2-4)

Clifton, Lucille. *The Lucky Stone*. Illustrated by Dale Payson. New York, Delacorte Press. 64 p. $6.95 ISBN 0-440-05121-5 (lib. ed. $6.46 ISBN 0-440-05122-3)
78-72862
A great-grandmother tells three short stories about a lucky stone and its owners (one being a runaway slave) and Granddaughter Sweet Tee tells the fourth. Set in large type with many full-page drawings. (Gr 3-5)

Constant, Alberta W. *Does Anybody Care about Lou Emma Miller?* New York, Crowell. 278 p. $6.95 ISBN 0-690-01335-3 (lib. ed. $6.79 ISBN 0-690-03890-9)
78-4774
A pleasant picture of pre-World War I small-town America, when Lou Emma of *Those Miller Girls* and *The Motoring Millers* sheds her self-pitying timidity to push for the establishment of the town's first public library. (Gr 5-7)

Ellison, Lucile W. *Butter on Both Sides*. Illustrated by Judith Gwyn Brown. New York, Scribner. 150 p. $7.95 ISBN 0-684-16281-4   79-15808
In this warm family chronicle Lucy experiences, among other pleasures, a steamboat ride and a Fourth of July Christmas. (Gr 4-6)

Erickson, Russell E. *Warton and the Traders*. Pictures by Lawrence Di Fiori. New York, Lothrop, Lee & Shepard. 95 p. $5.95 ISBN 0-688-41886-4 (lib. ed. $5.71 ISBN 0-688-51886-9)   78-25689
Rollicking, sometimes tense adventures of Warton Toad as he endeavors to secure help for his Aunt Toolie and the wounded fawn she is tending. (Gr 1-3)

Fleischman, Albert Sidney. *The Hey Hey Man*. Illustrated by Nadine Bernard Westcott. Boston, Little, Brown. 31 p. (An Atlantic Monthly Press book) $7.95 ISBN 0-316-26001-0   78-31702
Virgorous words and amusing soft-color paintings tell of the thwarting by a tree spirit of a thief who steals a farmer's gold. (Gr 3-6)

Geras, Adèle. *The Girls in the Velvet Frame*. New York, Atheneum. 149 p. $6.95 ISBN 0-689-30729-2   79-12352
How five sisters in Jerusalem before World War I conspire to have their photograph sent to America in their hope of finding their brother, from whom they have not heard for one year. (Gr 5-7)

Greene, Constance C. *Your Old Pal, Al*. New York, Viking Press. 149 p. $7.95 ISBN 0-670-79575-5   79-12350
A humorous exploration of the vicissitudes of adolescent friendships; a sequel to *A Girl Called Al* (ISBN 0-670-34153-3) and *I Know You, Al* (ISBN 0-670-39048-8). (Gr 5-7)

Hanson, June A. *Summer of the Stallion*. Illustrated by Gloria Singer. New York, Macmillan. 108 p. $7.95 ISBN 0-02-742620-3   78-24212
Janey looked forward to her summer at the ranch as Grandpa's number one hand, but a beautiful and powerful stallion came between them. (Gr 4-6)

Howe, Deborah, *and* James Howe. *Bunnicula; a Rabbit-Tale of Mystery*. Illustrated by Alan Daniel. New York, Atheneum. 98 p. $7.95 ISBN

0-689-30700-4   78-11472
Was the foundling baby bunny a vampire? Chester the cat thought so; Harold the dog scoffed. (Gr 3-5)

Landis, James D. *The Sisters Impossible*. New York, Knopf; distributed by Random House. 171 p. $6.95 ISBN 0-394-84190-5   78-32148
To nine-year-old Lily's astonishment, her beginning ballet classes draw her into a new relationship with her haughty older sister, already an advanced dancer. (Gr 4-6)

Lowry, Lois. *Anastasia Krupnik*. Boston, Houghton Mifflin. 113 p. illus. $6.95 ISBN 0-395-28629-8   79-18625
Anastasia's fast-changing lists of "Things I Love!" and "Things I Hate!" reflect aptly the ups-and-downs of a sensitive, likable, and sometimes laughable ten-year-old. (Gr 4-6)

Pinkwater, Daniel M. *Yobgorgle, Mystery Monster of Lake Ontario*. New York, Houghton Mifflin/ Clarion Books. 156 p. (A Clarion book) $7.95 ISBN 0-395-28970-X   79-11364
A typically zany Pinkwater invention, with Eugene getting caught up in a search for Yobgorgle, the monster of Lake Ontario. (Gr 5-up)

Rabinowitz, Sholom. *Holiday Tales of Sholom Aleichem*. Selected and translated by Aliza Shevrin. New York, Scribner. 145 p. $8.95 ISBN 0-684-16118-4   79-753
Retold from the Yiddish in rich, humorous language—superb for reading aloud—and illustrated handsomely with Thomas di Grazia's strong full-page drawings are seven stories from the holiday life of a Ukrainian Jewish community. (Gr 4-up)

Roach, Marilynne K. *Presto; or, the Adventures of a Turnspit Dog*. Boston, Houghton Mifflin. 148 p. $7.95 ISBN 0-395-28269-1   79-11746
How a turnspit dog escapes enslavement in an eighteenth-century London inn and finds a new life with a puppeteer. Charming black-and-white drawings. (Gr 4-6)

Skurzynski, Gloria. *What Happened in Hamelin*. New York, Four Winds Press. 177 p. $7.95 ISBN 0-590-07625-6   79-15233

A possible solution to the mystery of the lost children of Hamelin is created in this recounting of the Pied Piper legend by the baker's fourteen-year-old assistant. (Gr 5-7)

Snyder, Zilpha K. *The Famous Stanley Kidnapping Case*. Frontispiece by Alton Raible. New York, Atheneum. 212 p. $8.95 ISBN 0-689-30728-4
79-12308
A sequel to *The Headless Cupid* ($8.95 ISBN 0-689-20687-9) finds the Stanleys in Italy, where the children are kidnapped—by amateurs. (Gr 4-6)

Stolz, Mary S. *Go and Catch a Flying Fish*. New York, Harper & Row. 213 p. (An Ursula Nordstrom book) $7.95 ISBN 0-06-025867-5 (lib. ed. $7.89 ISBN 0-06-025868-3)
78-21785
A perceptive story set on a Florida island where thirteen-year-old Taylor and her younger brother Jem pursue their hobbies of bird-watching and fish-collecting while their parents' marriage moves toward separation. (Gr 4-6)

Strete, Craig. *When Grandfather Journeys into Winter*. Illustrated by Hal Frenck. New York, Greenwillow Books. 86 p. $6.95 ISBN 0-688-80193-5 (lib. ed. $6.67 ISBN 0-688-84193-7)
78-14830
With incredible strength and determination Tayhua rides and wins for his grandson the great black stallion, only to make his "journey into winter." (Gr 4-6)

Talbot, Charlene J. *An Orphan for Nebraska*. New York, Atheneum. 208 p. $7.95 ISBN 0-689-30698-9
78-12179
A vivid slice of history in the story of Kevin, an Irish orphan, who in 1872 finds himself en route to Nebraska where he will work as a printer's devil. (Gr 4-6)

Thompson, Jean. *Don't Forget Michael*. Illustrated by Margot Apple. New York, Morrow. 64 p. $6.95 ISBN 0-688-22196-3 (lib. ed. $6.67 ISBN 0-688-32196-8)
79-16637
Seven-year-old Michael finds that being the smallest—and the quietest—member of a large, noisy family sometimes leads to trouble for him. (Gr 1-3)

Tolle, Jean B. *The Great Pete Penney*. New York, Atheneum. 90 p. (A Margaret K. McElderry book) $7.95 ISBN 0-689-50145-5
79-14603
A lighthearted baseball story centers on Priscilla "Pete" Penney who can call up a leprechaun and throw a perfect curve ball. (Gr 3-5)

Williams, Jay. *The Magic Grandfather*. Illustrated by Gail Owens. New York, Four Winds Press. 149 p. $7.95 ISBN 0-590-07588-8
78-22285
A droll fantasy in which TV-addicted Sam proves to his sorcerer-grandfather that he can develop the imagination and concentration necessary for a magician. (Gr 4-6)

Wolkstein, Diane. *White Wave; a Chinese Tale*. [Illustrated by] Ed Young. New York, Crowell. [32] p. $6.95 ISBN 0-690-03893-3 (lib. ed. $6.79 ISBN 0-690-03894-1)
78-4781
In Taoist tradition is this poetic tale of a young Chinese farmer befriended by the moon goddess White Wave whom he finds living in a snail shell. Large soft-pencil drawings are strikingly animated. (Gr 3-6)

Zeē, Alkē. *The Sound of the Dragon's Feet*. By Alki Zei. Translated from the Greek by Edward Fenton. New York, Dutton. 113 p. $8.50 ISBN 0-525-39712-4
79-14917
Ten-year-old Sasha, a doctor's daughter in pre-revolutionary Russia, witnesses the sorrows of the poor who are doomed to face injustices and even terror. (Gr 4-6)

Zhitkov, Boris S. *How I Hunted the Little Fellows*. Translated from the Russian by Djemma Bider. New York, Dodd, Mead. [64] p. $6.95 ISBN 0-396-07692-0
79-11738
Fascinated by a miniature steamship on his grandmother's shelf, Boris becomes convinced that there are little people inside it. Animated soft-pencil drawings by Paul O. Zelinsky. (Gr 2-4)

FICTION FOR OLDER READERS

Blos, Joan W. *A Gathering of Days; a New England Girl's Journal*. New York, Scribner. 144 p. $7.95 ISBN 0-684-16340-3
79-16898
Winner of the 1980 Newbery Medal: a story in ingenuous diary form about home and school in early nineteenth-century New England. (Gr 5-7)

Bosse, Malcolm J. *The 79 Squares*. New York, Crowell. 185 p. $7.95 ISBN 0-690-03999-9 (lib. ed. $7.89 ISBN 0-690-04000-8)   79-7591
Fourteen-year-old Eric on probation for breaking school windows learns from an octogenarian ex-convict how all-engrossing the study of a garden can become. (Gr 7-8)

Bridgers, Sue E. *All Together Now; a Novel*. New York, Knopf; distributed by Random House. 238 p. $7.95 ISBN 0-394-84098-4 (lib. ed. $7.99 ISBN 0-394-94098-9)   78-12244
Richly textured with humor and poignancy are events of Casey's summer at her grandparents after she meets Dwayne, a thirty-three-year-old with the mind of a twelve-year-old. (Gr 8-up)

Cleaver, Vera, *and* Bill Cleaver. *A Little Destiny*. New York, Lothrop, Lee & Shepard Books. 152 p. $7.95 ISBN 0-688-41904-6 (lib. ed. $7.63 ISBN 0-688-51904-0)   79-10322
A stark narrative set in Georgia shows Lucy and her all-but-destitute family facing a formidable adversary—their father's murderer? (Gr 5-7)

Cohen, Barbara. *The Innkeeper's Daughter*. New York, Lothrop, Lee & Shepard Books. 159 p. $6.95 ISBN 0-688-41906-2 (lib. ed. $6.67 ISBN 0-688-51906-7)   79-2421
Helping her mother run a small inn in New Jersey, Rachel is also adjusting to the hurtful problems of growing up. (Gr 6-8)

Conford, Ellen. *We Interrupt This Semester for an Important Bulletin*. Boston, Little, Brown. 176 p. $7.95 ISBN 0-316-15309-5   79-9133
A breezy sequel to *Dear Lovey Hart, I Am Desperate* ($6.95 ISBN 0-316-15306-0) features school newspaper editor Carrie Wasserman as she confronts the hazards of investigative reporting and a Southern belle who is after her boyfriend. (Gr 6-8)

Cummings, Betty Sue. *Now, Ameriky*. New York, Atheneum. 175 p. $8.95 ISBN 0-689-30705-5   79-11750
The experiences of nineteen-year-old Brigid Ni Clery who journeys alone to "Ameriky" to try to salvage her family's fortunes. Mature. (Gr 8-up)

Greenberg, Jan. *A Season In-between*. New York,

Farrar, Straus & Giroux. 149 p. $7.95 ISBN 0-374-36564-4   79-17997
The discovery that her father has cancer alters drastically Carrie's stable home life and her seventh-grade preoccupation with growing up. (Gr 5-7)

Hinton, S. E. *Tex*. New York, Delacorte Press. 194 p. $7.95 ISBN 0-440-08641-8   78-50448
In their small Oklahoma town fourteen-year-old Tex lives, loves, and fights with his older brother while their father roams the rodeo circuit. (Gr 7-9)

Konigsburg, E. L. *Throwing Shadows*. New York, Atheneum. 151 p. $8.95 ISBN 0-689-30714-4   79-10422
Five masterfully written short stories—differing in theme and setting—focus on interpersonal relations. (Gr 8-up)

McIlwraith, Maureen M. H. M. *The Third Eye*. By Mollie Hunter [*pseud*.] New York, Harper & Row. 276 p. $7.95 ISBN 0-06-022676-5 (lib. ed. $7.89 ISBN 0-06-022677-3)   78-22159
Jinty's intuitive sense—her "third eye"—brings her close to the old Earl as he struggles with the "Ballingford doom." Told in flashbacks. (Gr 6-8)

Mazer, Harry. *The Last Mission; a Novel*. New York, Delacorte Press. 182 p. $7.95 ISBN 0-440-05774-4   79-50674
A tender, sobering chronicle about a teenaged Jewish boy who joins the Air Force with his older brother's ID card because he is determined to fight Hitler. (Gr 7-up)

Myers, Walter D. *The Young Landlords*. New York, Viking Press. 197 p. $8.95 ISBN 0-670-79454-6   79-13264
When an "Action Group" of enterprising Harlem teenagers unexpectedly, for one dollar, become owners of a rundown tenement, they learn to deal warily and imaginatively with their eccentric tenants. (Gr 6-8)

O'Dell, Scott. *The Captive*. Boston, Houghton Mifflin. 224 p. $8.95 ISBN 0-395-27811-2 79-15809
The first volume of a projected trilogy relates the experiences of a sixteen-year-old idealistic seminarian who accompanies a Spanish nobleman to the

New World, only to find himself having to choose between death and godhood. (Gr 7-9)

Pascal, Francine. *My First Love & Other Disasters.* New York, Viking Press. 186 p. $7.95 ISBN 0-670-49952-8   78-25720
Wish-fulfillment, first love, and the hyperbole of adolescence are captured in this first-person account of Victoria's summer at the beach. (Gr 6-8)

Peyton, K. M., *pseud. A Midsummer Night's Death.* Cleveland, Collins. 138 p. $6.95 ISBN 0-529-05453-1   78-9822
Set in a boy's school, a superior whodunit in which Jonathan, stunned by the death of his English teacher, has reasons to doubt the verdict of suicide. (Gr 6-8)

Pinkwater, Daniel M. *Alan Mendelsohn, the Boy from Mars.* New York, Dutton. 248 p. $8.95 ISBN 0-525-25360-2   78-12052
A satisfyingly detailed account of the way two classmates at Bat Masterson Junior High School use a mind control system to accomplish zany tricks. (Gr 5-7)

Say, Allen. *The Ink-Keeper's Apprentice.* New York, Harper & Row. 185 p. $7.95 ISBN 0-06-025208-1 (lib. ed. $7.79 ISBN 0-06-025209-X)   78-20264
In postwar Tokyo fourteen-year-old Kiyoi joins two famous cartoonists as an apprentice and experiences an expanding new life there, until his father decides to emigrate to America. (Gr 7-8)

Sebestyen, Ouida. *Words by Heart.* Boston, Little, Brown. 162 p. (An Atlantic Monthly Press book) $7.95 ISBN 0-316-77931-8   78-27847
Before 1910 no black child had entered the Kansas scripture-reciting contest won by Lena: would the town's anger die down and could Lena follow her father's commitment to forgiveness? (Gr 5-7)

Sutcliff, Rosemary. *Song for a Dark Queen.* New York, Crowell. 192 p. $7.95 ISBN 0-690-03911-5 (lib. ed. $7.89 ISBN 0-690-03912-3)   78-19514
A vividly drawn life of Britain's Queen Boadicea, who led a valiant but futile revolt against the Romans in 62 A.D. (Gr 7-9)

Thrasher, Crystal. *Between Dark and Daylight.* New York, Atheneum. 251 p. $8.95 (A Margaret K. McElderry book) ISBN 0-689-50150-1 79-12423
This sequel to *The Dark Didn't Catch Me* ($7.95 ISBN 0-689-50025-4; paper $1.95 ISBN 0-689-70465-8) shows courageous Seely and her uprooted family finding friendships as well as violence and poverty in a new community. (Gr 6-up)

Von Canon, Claudia. *The Moonclock.* Boston, Houghton Mifflin. 159 p. illus. $6.95 ISBN 0-395-27810-4   79-1076
Letters between Jacob and his "dear wife" in Vienna during 1683, plus other epistles from this young bride, chronicle in vivid manner both domestic and political affairs during the Turkish siege. (Gr 7-up)

Yep, Laurence. *Sea Glass.* New York, Harper & Row. 208 p. $7.95 ISBN 0-06-026744-5 (lib. ed. $7.89 ISBN 0-06-026745-3)   78-22487
When Craig Chin, of San Francisco's Chinatown, fails to achieve his father's dream for him of playing in All-American sports, elderly Uncle Quail helps him to find himself. (Gr 6-8)

FOLKLORE

Barth, Edna. *Balder and the Mistletoe; a Story for the Winter Holidays.* Retold. New York, Seabury Press. 64 p. (A Clarion Book) $7.95 ISBN 0-8164-3215-5   78-4523
An attractive retelling of the Norse legend, profusely illustrated with Cuffari's sweeping line-and-wash drawings in three colors. (Gr 3-6)

The Cat on the Dovrefell; a Christmas Tale. Translated from the Norse by Sir George Webbe Dasent. New York, Putnam. [32] p. $8.95 ISBN 0-399-20680-9 (paper $3.95 ISBN 0-399-20685-X)   78-26340
Tomie de Paola's brilliant blues, greens, and whites evoke the Norwegian setting of this Christmas Eve folktale about a man from Finnmark, his great white bear, and a pack of trolls. (K-Gr 4)

Domanska, Janina. *King Krakus and the Dragon.* New York, Greenwillow Books. [36] p. $8.95 ISBN 0-688-80189-7 (lib. ed. $8.59 ISBN 0-688-84189-9)   78-12934
Richly illustrated in European folk art style is a

Polish legend about Dratevka the shoemaker who contrives to slay the dragon threatening the peace of Krakow. (K-Gr 3)

Fritz, Jean. *Brendan the Navigator; a History Mystery about the Discovery of America.* New York, Coward, McCann & Geoghegan. 31 p. col. illus. $6.95 ISBN 0-698-20473-5   78-13247
Lively line drawings by Enrico Arno suit a jocular retelling of the "history mystery" of St. Brendan's voyage to America. (Gr 3-5)

Gág, Wanda. *The Sorcerer's Apprentice.* New York, Coward, McCann & Geoghegan. [32] p. illus. (part col.) $6.95 ISBN 0-698-20481-6
77-23990
A comfortable little volume, illustrated with fitting drollery by Margot Tomes, contains Wanda Gág's retelling of the folk story about an apprentice who learns a spell but not the secret of how to stop it. (Gr 2-4)

Kendall, Carol, *and* Yao-wen Li. *Sweet and Sour; Tales from China.* Retold. New York, Seabury Press. 111 p. (A Clarion book) $7.95 ISBN 0-8164-3228-7   78-24349
Two dozen tales from both oral tradition and specified dynasties deal with human foibles and magic. Delicately limned drawings by Shirley Felts. (Gr 4-6)

North American Legends. Edited by Virginia Haviland. New York, Collins. 214 p. $7.95 ISBN 0-529-05457-4   78-26999
An anthology of tall tales indigenous to America, tales of European and African immigrants, and folklore of American Indians and Eskimos. Strikingly illustrated by Ann Strugnell. (Gr 5-up)

The Old Woman and Her Pig & 10 Other Stories. Told and illustrated by Anne Rockwell. New York, Crowell. 87 p. $10.95 ISBN 0-690-03927-1 (lib. ed. $10.79 ISBN 0-690-03928-X)   78-13901
Copiously illustrated in soft, flat colors are eleven favorite folktales and fables retold simply in a companion to the author's earlier *The Three Bears and 15 Other Stories* ($9.95 ISBN 0-690-00597-0). (PreS-Gr 3)

Riordan, James. *Tales from Tartary.* Retold. Illus-

trated by Anthony Colbert. London, Kestrel Books; New York, Viking Press. 170 p. (*His Russian tales,* v. 2) $12.50 ISBN 0-670-69156-9
77-27871
Humor, wit, and elements of magic enliven these thirty-nine tales traditional to much of Central Asia. A companion to *Tales from Central Russia,* illustrated by Krystyna Turska (ISBN 0-670-69154-2). (Gr 5-8)

The Talking Stone; an Anthology of Native American Tales and Legends. Edited by Dorothy de Wit. With decorations by Donald Crews. New York, Greenwillow Books. 213 p. $8.95 ISBN 0-688-80204-4 (lib. ed. $8.59 ISBN 0-688-84204-6)
79-13798
Arranged in nine geographic divisions are twenty-seven examples of myths, hero tales, and trickster stories, some of them retold here by the compiler. (Gr 4-6)

Yellow Robe, Rosebud. *Tonweya and the Eagles, and Other Lakota Indian Tales.* Retold. New York, Dial Press. 118 p. $7.95 ISBN 0-8037-8973-4 (lib. ed. $7.45 ISBN 0-8037-8974-2)
78-72470
Within a framework of the Lakota Indian boyhood of the storyteller's father are animal tales illustrated with Jerry Pinkney's vividly animated soft-pencil drawings. (Gr 4-6)

POETRY, RHYMES, AND SONGS

Coletta, Irene, *and* Hallie Coletta. *From A to Z; the Collected Letters of Irene and Hallie Coletta.* Englewood Cliffs, N.J., Prentice-Hall. [57] p. illus. $6.95 ISBN 0-13-331678-5   78-21263
Humorous rebus rhymes make a brain-teasing alphabet book. (Gr 1-4)

Dinosaurs and Beasts of Yore. Verses selected by William Cole. Cleveland, Collins. 62 p. $8.50 ISBN 0-529-05511-2   78-31619
Light verse celebrating prehistoric creatures has Susanna Natti's equally lighthearted black-and-white line drawings. (Gr 1-4)

Farber, Norma. *How Does It Feel to Be Old?* Illustrated by Trina Schart Hyman. New York, Dutton. [32] p. (A Unicorn book) $7.95 ISBN

0-525-32414-3   79-11516

A discerning illustrator catches nuances of the poet's delight in sharing with her granddaughter a sense of the rewards, privileges, and other pleasures that have come to her in her later years. (Gr 5-up)

Fiddle-I-Fee, a Traditional American Chant. Illustrated by Diane Stanley. Boston, Little, Brown. [32] p. col. illus. $7.95 ISBN 0-316-81040-1
79-14117

A cumulative folk rhyme describes a little girl's special tea party for her animal friends, all depicted in a humorous anthropomorphic manner. (PreS-Gr 1)

Starbird, Kaye. *The Covered Bridge House and Other Poems.* New York, Four Winds Press. 53 p. $6.95 ISBN 0-590-07544-6   79-11418

A New England poet's reflections on everyday matters are enlivened by Jim Arnosky's evocative silhouettes and pen-and-ink sketches. (Gr 3-5)

ARTS AND HOBBIES

Asch, Frank, *and* Jan Asch. *Running with Rachel.* Photographs by Jan Asch and Robert Michael Buslow. New York, Dial Press. 64 p. $7.28 ISBN 0-8037-7553-9 (paper $3.95 ISBN 0-8037-7552-0)
78-72471

Action photographs and an informal text convey the pleasure young Rachel receives from jogging. (Gr 3-5)

Bierhorst, John. *A Cry from the Earth; Music of the North American Indians.* New York, Four Winds Press. 113 p. $8.95 ISBN 0-590-07533-0
78-21538

A handsomely illustrated introduction to Indian music and dance includes a discussion of instruments and of the structure and uses of the music. (Gr 6-up)

Bradley, Duane. *Design It, Sew It, and Wear It; How to Make Yourself a Super Wardrobe without Commercial Patterns.* Illustrated by Judith Hoffman Corwin. New York, Crowell. 145 p. $8.95 ISBN 0-690-01297-7 (lib. ed. $8.79 ISBN 0-690-03839-9)
76-55732

Explicit instructions, with helpful drawings, for making simple tops, skirts, and dresses. (Gr 7-up)

Brown, Marcia. *Listen to a Shape.* New York, Watts. [32] p. $4.95 ISBN 0-531-02383-4 (lib. ed. $7.90 ISBN 0-531-02930-1)
78-31616

For this and two companion volumes—*Touch Will Tell* (ISBN 0-531-02384-2; lib. ed. ISBN 0-531-02931-X) and *Walk with Your Eyes* (ISBN 0-531-02385-0; lib. ed. ISBN 0-531-02925-5)—the artist-photographer has provided succinct lines of text and evocative color pictures. (K-Gr 3)

Davis, Edward E. *Into the Dark; a Beginner's Guide to Developing and Printing Black and White Negatives.* New York, Atheneum. 210 p. illus. $9.95 ISBN 0-689-30676-8   78-11284

A practical step-by-step guide to darkroom work and equipment includes instructions on devolping negatives and printing photographs in color as well as in black and white. (Gr 7-up)

Fogel, Julianna A. *Wesley Paul, Marathon Runner.* Photographs by Mary S. Watkins. Philadelphia, Lippincott. 39 p. $7.95 ISBN 0-397-31845-6 (lib. ed. $7.89 ISBN 0-397-31861-8)   78-23649

An account of a young Chinese American runner highlights his record-breaking performance in the New York City Marathon and his dream of competing in the Olympics. (Gr 4-up)

Krementz, Jill. *A Very Young Skater.* New York, Knopf; distributed by Random House. [109] p. $9.95 ISBN 0-394-50833-5   79-2209

Described in a photo essay similar to *A Very Young Dancer* (ISBN 0-394-40885-3) are the hours of practice and study (including ballet) a young skater must undertake before reaching stardom. Also published this year in the same series is *A Very Young Circus Flyer,* with full-color and black-and-white photographs (ISBN 0-394-50574-3). (Gr 4-up)

Lasker, David. *The Boy Who Loved Music.* Illustrated by Joe Lasker. New York, Viking Press. [48] p. $9.95 ISBN 0-670-18385-7   79-14651

Pictured in a panoramic pageant of rich color is the history of Joseph Haydn's "Farewell" Symphony, which he composed when stubborn Prince Nicolaus Esterhazy refused to allow his court musicians to return to Vienna at summer's end. (Gr 5-up)

Laycock, George. *The Complete Beginner's Guide to Photography.* Garden City, N.Y., Doubleday.

149 p. (The Complete beginner's guide series) $7.95 ISBN 0-385-13264-6 (lib. ed. $8.90 ISBN 0-385-13265-4)   78-1207

A practical introduction to photography discusses with well-reproduced pictures the selection and care of cameras, composition, darkroom techniques, and photography as a business. (Gr 5-8)

Norvell, Flo Ann H. *The Great Big Box Book.* Photographs by Richard Mitchell. New York, Crowell. 90 p. $8.79 ISBN 0-690-03939-5 (lib. ed. $8.79 ISBN 0-690-03940-9)   78-22500

Explicit instructions for creating a wide variety of things from boxes, such as a log cabin, walkie-talkie space helmets, and giant building blocks. (Gr 5-up)

Pettit, Florence H. *The Stamp Pad Printing Book.* New York, Crowell. 87 p. $7.95 ISBN 0-690-03967-0 (lib. ed. $7.89 ISBN 0-690-03968-9)   78-22504

How to use a stamp pad for printing bookmarks, notepaper, posters, greeting cards, wrappings, and other useful items. Illustrated by the author and Robert M. Pettit. (Gr 3-up)

Price, Christine. *Dance on the Dusty Earth.* New York, Scribner. 60 p. $8.95 ISBN 0-684-16088-9   78-25714

A graphic success with its abundance of charcoal drawings is this presentation of folk dances significant in the cultures of African, Polynesian, Thai, and other peoples. (Gr 5-up)

Purdy, Susan G. *Jewish Holiday Cookbook.* New York, Watts. 96 p. (A Holiday cookbook) $6.90 ISBN 0-531-02281-1 (paper $2.95 ISBN 0-531-03430-5)   79-4462

Recipes for traditional Jewish holiday foods, for kosher and nonkosher cooks. (Gr 4-6)

Sandler, Martin W. *The Story of American Photography, an Illustrated History for Young People.* Boston, Little, Brown. 318 p. $16.95 ISBN 0-316-77021-3   78-24025

A profusely illustrated history of photography in the United States from 1840 to the present. (Gr 7-up)

Walker, Barbara M. *The Little House Cookbook; Frontier Foods from Laura Ingalls Wilder's Classic*

Stories. Illustrations by Garth Williams. New York, Harper & Row. 240 p. $8.95 ISBN 0-06-026418-7 (lib. ed. $8.79 ISBN 0-06-026419-5)   76-58733

Recipes based on the pioneers' food described in the "Little House" books by Laura Ingalls Wilder, together with quotes from the books and description of how the food was prepared. (Gr 4-up)

BIOGRAPHY

Blassingame, Wyatt. *Thor Heyerdahl, Viking Scientist.* New York, Elsevier/Nelson Books. 100 p. $7.95 ISBN 0-525-66626-5   79-1002

An account of the 1947 trans-Pacific journey from Peru to Polynesia in the balsa raft *Kon-Tiki* and also of the later journeys of *Ra I* and *Ra II* to study pollution in the Atlantic. (Gr 5-up)

Fritz, Jean. *Stonewall.* With drawings by Stephen Gammell. New York, Putnam. 152 p. $7.95 ISBN 0-399-20698-1 (paper $3.95 ISBN 0-399-20699-X)   79-12506

Stonewall Jackson's idiosyncratic personality and a sense of the fearful waste of war both emerge in this account of his Civil War career. (Gr 6-8)

Greenfield, Eloise, *and* Lessie Jones Little. *Childtimes; a Three-Generation Memoir.* With material by Pattie Ridley Jones. Drawings by Jerry Pinkney and photographs from the authors' family albums. New York, Crowell. 176 p. $8.95 ISBN 0-690-03874-7 (lib. ed. $8.79 ISBN 0-690-03875-5)   77-26581

Reminiscences of three generations of black women spanning the 1880s through the 1950s give a sometimes sad, sometimes humorous view of this period of black history. (Gr 5-up)

Haskins, James. *Andrew Young, Man with a Mission.* New York, Lothrop, Lee & Shepard Books. 192 p. illus., ports. $7.50 ISBN 0-688-41896-1 (lib. ed. $7.20 ISBN 0-688-51896-6)   79-1046

Young's life as a clergyman, civil rights worker, legislator, and U.S. ambassador to the United Nations. (Gr 6-up)

Kherdian, David. *The Road from Home; the Story of an Armenian Girl.* New York, Greenwillow

Books. 238 p. map. $8.95 ISBN 0-688-80205-2 (lib. ed. $8.59 ISBN 0-688-84205-4)   78-72511

The 1979 Newbery Medal honor book recounts the early childhood in Turkey of the author's mother, her agony of deportation, and her arrival in America as a "mail-order bride." (Gr 6-8)

HISTORY, PEOPLE, AND PLACES

Aliki. *Mummies Made in Egypt*. New York, Crowell. [32] p. $6.95 ISBN 0-690-03858-5 (lib. ed. $6.79 ISBN 0-690-03859-3)   77-26603

A description of the practice of mummification in ancient Egypt, with detailed full-color paintings and black-and-white drawings. (Gr 3-6)

Greenfeld, Howard. *Rosh Hashanah and Yom Kippur*. [Illustrated by Elaine Grove. New York, Holt, Rinehart, and Winston] 31 p. $5.95 ISBN 0-03-044756-9   79-4818

A meaningful interpretation of two important holidays in the Jewish calendar emphasizes the sense of awe and feeling of repentance that the High Holy Days can invoke. (Gr 3-6)

Karen, Ruth. *Feathered Serpent; the Rise and Fall of the Aztecs*. New York, Four Winds Press. 184 p., illus. $8.95 ISBN 0-590-07413-X   78-22129

A well-documented examination of the culture and history of the Aztecs, from their creation myths to the coming of the conquistadores. (Gr 6-9)

Lawson, Don. *FDR's New Deal*. New York, Crowell. 152 p. $7.95 ISBN 0-690-03953-0   78-4775

An account of the administration, legislation, and personalities behind Roosevelt's New Deal in its attempt to lead the United States out of a severe economic depression. Illustrated with photographs. (Gr 6-8)

Mangurian, David. *Children of the Incas*. New York, Four Winds Press. 73 p. $8.95 ISBN 0-590-07500-4   79-12186

Thirteen-year-old Modesto, a Quechua Indian boy, describes his family, home, and day-to-day activities in a Peruvian village near Lake Titicaca, views enhanced by the author's revealing photographs. (Gr 3-6)

Poynter, Margaret. *Gold Rush!, the Yukon Stam-*

pede of 1898. New York, Atheneum. 91 p. $6.95 ISBN 0-689-30694-6   78-14503

An account of greed and heroism in the Klondike gold rush of 1896-98, illustrated with photographs and a map. (Gr 7-9)

Wolf, Bernard. *In This Proud Land; the Story of a Mexican American Family*. Philadelphia, Lippincott. 95 p. $8.95 ISBN 0-397-31815-4   78-9680

A sensitive photo-essay about a closely knit family of Mexican-American migrants who struggle against great odds to become part of the American mainstream. (Gr 5-8)

NATURE AND SCIENCE

Allison, Linda. *The Wild Inside; Sierra Club's Guide to the Great Indoors*. San Francisco, Sierra Club Books/Scribner. 144 p. (A Yolla Bolly Press book) $8.95 ISBN 0-684-16108-7 (paper $4.95 ISBN 0-684-16119-2)   79-937

Objects inside a house illustrate principles of geology, electricity, meteorology, natural history, and so on. Amusing ink line drawings by the author. (Gr 5-7)

Ancona, George. *It's a Baby!* New York, Dutton. [48] p. $7.95 ISBN 0-525-32598-0   79-10453

Evocative black-and-white photographs accompanied by a simple text document an infant's first twelve months of development. (PreS-Gr 3)

Barry, Scott. *The Kingdom of Wolves*. New York, Putnam. 63 p. $8.95 ISBN 0-399-20657-4   78-9895

A photographic essay on the wolf contains a plea for its protection. (Gr 4-6)

Branley, Franklyn M. *Columbia and Beyond; the Story of the Space Shuttle*. New York, Collins. 88 p. illus. (part col.) $12.95 ISBN 0-529-05525-2   78-26891

A well-documented account of the space shuttle, with many photographs. For the same audience is Frank X. Ross, Jr.'s *The Space Shuttle* (Lothrop, Lee & Shepard Books. $6.50 illus. ISBN 0-688-41882-1; lib. ed. $6.24 ISBN 0-688-51882-6) which adds to a similar coverage a bit of history and directions for making a paper model. (Each, Gr 7-up)

Caras, Roger A. *On Safari with Roger Caras*. Photographs by Barclay Caras. New York, Windmill Books. 48 p. $7.95 ISBN 0-525-61600-4   79-13778
The naturalist and his son share dangers and thrills on a Kenya safari. Many excellent photographs. (Gr 3-up)

Cobb, Vicki. *More Science Experiments You Can Eat*. Illustrated by Giulio Maestro. New York, Lippincott. 126 p. $7.95 ISBN 0-397-31828-6 (lib. ed. $7.89 ISBN 0-397-31878-2; paper $3.95 ISBN 0-397-31853-7)   78-12732
Experiments involving common foods and kitchen equipment are presented with attractive, and generally informative, illustrations. A welcome sequel to the popular *Science Experiments You Can Eat* ($7.95 ISBN 0-397-31487-6; paper $4.95 ISBN 0-397-31253-9) . (Gr 4-7)

Englebardt, Stanley L. *Miracle Chip; the Microelectronic Revolution*. New York, Lothrop, Lee & Shepard Books. 128 p. illus. $6.95 ISBN 0-688-41908-9 (lib. ed. $6.67 ISBN 0-688-51908-3)   79-13235
An explanation of microprocessors, now the basis of a new technology as evidenced in minicomputers, pocket calculators, digital wrist watches, and numerous other devices. (Gr 6-up)

Facklam, Margery, *and* Howard Facklam. *From Cell to Clone; the Story of Genetic Engineering*. Illustrated with diagrams by Paul Facklam and with photographs. New York, Harcourt Brace Jovanovich. 128 p. $7.95 ISBN 0-15-230262-X   79-87515
A look at cloning, its beginnings and its future, with discussion of its morality. (Gr 7-up)

Haines, Gail K. *Brain Power; Understanding Human Intelligence*. New York, Watts. 117 p. illus. (An Impact book) $5.45 ISBN 0-531-02287-0   78-10805
Fascinating facts on human intelligence: how the brain works, brain anatomy, creativity, and possible future brain alterations. (Gr 7-9)

Hewett, Joan. *Watching Them Grow; Inside a Zoo Nursery*. Photographs by Richard Hewett. Boston, Little, Brown. 64 p. $7.95 ISBN 0-316-35968-8   79-13345
Photographs of engaging baby apes in a zoo nursery show how an attendant cares for them—bottle feeding, diapering, and providing gentle discipline and affection. (Gr 3-6)

Kettelkamp, Larry. *Lasers, the Miracle Light*. New York, Morrow. 126 p. $6.95 ISBN 0-688-22207-2 (lib. ed. $6.67 ISBN 0-688-32207-7)   79-17486
The laser—an acronym for "light amplification by stimulated emission of radiation"—is described as used in medicine, research, holography, and communications. Helpful diagrams and photographs. (Gr 7-up)

Kiefer, Irene. *Energy for America*. New York, Atheneum. 199 p. $9.95 ISBN 0-689-30713-6   79-14656
Convincing discussion of the use of energy derived from finite quantities of fossil fuels and the need to develop alternate energy sources. Photographs, diagrams, charts, and maps. (Gr 7-9)

Lambert, David. *The Earth and Space*. [Editorial consultant, James Muirden; editor, Angela Wilkinson] New York, Warwick Press. 93 p. $7.90 ISBN 0-531-09155-4   78-68539
An introduction to geology and astronomy includes sections about life on earth and the exploration of space, with informative color photographs and drawings. (Gr 4-7)

Lauber, Patricia. *What's Hatching Out of That Egg?* New York, Crown. [64] p. $7.95 ISBN 0-517-53724-9   79-12054
Text and illustrations introduce eleven kinds of eggs and the animals that hatch out of them: the ostrich, python, bullfrog, monarch butterfly, and others. (Gr 3-5)

Laycock, George. *Tornadoes, Killer Storms*. New York, McKay. 58 p. $6.95 ISBN 0-679-20979-4   78-20326
Scientific description of the emergence and damaging strength of tornadoes—"storms of mystery"—through details of historical incidents. (Gr 6-8)

Limburg, Peter R. *The Story of Your Heart*. Illustrations by Ellen Going Jacobs. New York, Coward, McCann & Geoghegan. 96 p. $6.49 ISBN 0-698-30705-4   78-24308
A sound introduction to the heart: its structure,

functions, and malfunctions and techniques used to repair it. Line drawings. (Gr 5-7)

McClung, Robert M. *America's Endangered Birds: Programs and People Working to Save Them.* Illustrated by George Founds. New York, Morrow. 160 p. $7.95 ISBN 0-688-22208-0 (lib. ed. $7.63 ISBN 0-688-32208-5)   79-9241
An informal report on the state of six endangered species—the ivory-billed woodpecker, whooping crane, American bald eagle, brown pelican, California condor, Kirtland's warbler—with documentation of conservation measures. (Gr 5-9)

McDearmon, Kay. *Gorillas.* New York, Dodd, Mead. 59 p. $4.95 ISBN 0-396-07645-9   78-11292
An attractive, easy-to-read introduction to the gorilla, in the wild and in captivity. Engaging photographs. (Gr 3-5)

Math, Irwin. *Morse, Marconi and You.* [Diagrams by Hal Keith] New York, Scribner. 80 p. $8.95 ISBN 0-684-16081-1   79-1351
An explanation of basic principles accompanies instructions for the young radio amateur in the making of models from readily available materials. (Gr 7-up)

Patent, Dorothy H. *Sizes and Shapes in Nature— What They Mean.* New York, Holiday House. 160 p. $7.95 ISBN 0-8234-0340-8   78-12554
A discussion, with diagrams and photographs, of factors which determine the great variety of sizes and shapes of plants and animals. (Gr 5-7)

Pringle, Laurence P. *Natural Fire; Its Ecology in Forests.* New York, Morrow. 63 p. $5.95 ISBN 0-688-22210-2 (lib. ed. $5.71 ISBN 0-688-32210-7)   79-13606
Excellent black-and-white photographs share in an explanation of the ecological desirability of periodic forest fires. (Gr 6-8)

Pringle, Laurence P. *Nuclear Power; from Physics to Politics.* New York, Macmillan. 133 p. (Science for survival series) $7.95 ISBN 0-02-775390-5   78-27180
This scientist's antinuclear bias becomes clear in his well-illustrated survey of the technical development and political aspects of nuclear power. (Gr 6-up)

Roever, Joan M. *Snake Secrets.* New York, Walker. 155 p. $7.95 ISBN 0-8027-6332-4 (lib. ed. $7.85 ISBN 0-8027-6333-2)   78-4318
Attractive pencil drawings accompany a great amount of information on snakes, including the keeping of them as pets. (Gr 6-up)

Selsam, Millicent E., *and* Joyce Hunt. *A First Look at Sharks.* Illustrated by Harriett Springer. New York, Walker. 32 p. (A First look at series) $7.95 ISBN 0-8027-6372-3 (lib. ed. $7.85 ISBN 0-8027-6373-1)   79-2200
Evocatively illustrated in grays and blacks is this introduction for beginning readers to various species of sharks, their physical characteristics, habits, and environments. (Gr 1-3)

Simon, Seymour. *Deadly Ants.* Illustrations by William R. Downey. New York, Four Winds Press. 49 p. $7.95 ISBN 0-590-07610-8   79-14705
Eye-catching fine-line drawings accompany a short text on the life habits of harmful ants, chiefly of fire ants and army ants, and consideration of their interaction with man. (Gr 4-6)

Simon, Seymour. *The Long View into Space.* New York, Crown. [48] p. $7.95 ISBN 0-517-53659-5   79-11388
A photographic essay with an explanatory text and sharp black-and-white pictures that allow the viewer to look far into the universe. (Gr 3-5)

Simon, Seymour. *The Secret Clocks; Time Senses of Living Things.* Illustrated by Jan Brett. New York, Viking Press. 74 p. $8.95 ISBN 0-670-62892-1   78-31910
Facts on biological clocks and rhythms of plants and animals; clearly illustrated and with suggestions for readers' projects. (Gr 4-6)

Van Woerkom, Dorothy. *Hidden Messages.* New York, Crown. [32] p. $6.95 ISBN 0-517-53520-3   78-10705
This account of the discovery of pheromones and their role in insect communication includes Benjamin Franklin's experiments with ants and Fabre's study of moths. Colorful illustrations by Lynne Cherry. (Gr 1-4)

Weber, William J. *Care of Uncommon Pets.* New

York, Holt, Rinehart, and Winston. 222 p. $7.95 ISBN 0-03-022731-3   78-14093
A basic guide for the selection and care of some twenty animal pets, including gerbils, ducks, toads, salamanders, and tortoises. With black-and-white photographs. (Gr 6-up)

PSYCHOLOGY AND SOCIOLOGY

Seixas, Judith S. *Living with a Parent Who Drinks Too Much*. New York, Greenwillow Books. 116 p. $6.95 ISBN 0-688-80196-X (lib. ed. $6.67 ISBN 0-688-84196-1)   78-11108

Practical advice for children who live with alcoholic parents. (Gr 6-8)

Sullivan, Mary Beth, *and others. Feeling Free*. Illustrations, Marci Davis, Linda Bourke; photographs, Alan J. Brightman. Reading, Mass., Addison-Wesley. 186 p. $9.95 ISBN 0-201-07479-6 (paper $5.95 ISBN 0-201-07485-0)   79-4315
What it's like to be different: to be blind, to be a dwarf, to have dyslexia, or to use crutches—problems explored by children themselves. Games, cartoons, plays, and stories help create understanding. (Gr 4-7)

Title Index

Author Index*

Aardema, Verna, 1, 38
Acquaye, Saka, 49 (M)
Adams, Richard G., 29
Adkins, Jan, 53
Adoff, Arnold, 45 (C), 61
Aesop, 93
Afanasev, Alexei, 1, 44
Ahlberg, Allen, 91
Ahlberg, Janet, 91
Aiken, Conrad, 45
Aiken, Joan, 17, 29, 45
Ajayi, Afolabi, 49 (M)
Alegria, Ricardo E., 38
Aleichem, Sholom, 95
Aleksin, Anatolii G., 17
Alexander, Lloyd, 17
Alexander, Martha G., 1
Alexander, Ray P., 61 (C)
Alger, Leclaire, 38 (X)
Aliki, 73, 102
Allison, Linda, 102
Allport, Alan J., 53
Almedingen, E. M., 29
Almedingen, Martha E., 29, 67
Amon, Aline, 53, 73
Ancona, George, 54, 89, 102
Andersen, Hans Christian, 1, 17
Angrist, Stanley W., 73
Anno, Mitsumasa, 1
Antonacci, Anthony J., 53
Antonacci, Robert J., 53
Armour, Richard, 46
Armstrong, Tom, 53 (X)
Armstrong, William H., 29
Arthur, Lee, 73
Aruego, José, 1, 91
Asbjornsen, P. C., 43
Asch, Frank, 2, 100
Asch, Jan, 100
Asimov, Isaac, 73
Atkinson, Linda, 61
Atwood, Ann, 74
Aylesworth, Thomas G., 74 (C)

Babbitt, Natalie, 2, 18
Bacon, Margaret H., 17
Baker, Betty, 18
Baldwin, Gordon C., 67
Bang, Molly G., 38
Bangs, Edward, 2
Barker, Albert, 67
Barkin, Carol, 80
Baron, Virginia O., 46 (C)
Barry, Scott, 102
Barsam, Richard Meram, 10 (X)
Barth, Edna, 38, 53, 98
Bason, Lillian, 38
Batterberry, Ariane R., 43
Batterberry, Michael, 53
Baumann, Hans, 67
Bawden, Nina, 18, 94
Baylor, Byrd, 2, 54, 74
Bealer, Alex W., 67
Beatty, Patricia, 18, 94
Behn, Henry, 46 (T)
Bell, Anthea, 34, 35 (T)
Bellairs, John, 18
Belloc, Hilaire, 46, 47
Belpré, Pura, 38
Benchley, Nathaniel, 2, 29
Berends, Polly B., 18
Berger, Gilda, 74
Berger, Melvin, 54, 74
Bergman Sucksdorff, Astrid, 67
Berloquin, Pierre, 74
Bernheim, Evelyne, 68
Bernheim, Marc, 68
Bernstein, Margery, 39
Bider, Djemma, 96 (T)
Bierhorst, John, 39 (E), 46 (C), 100
Blackburn, G. Meredith, 46 (C)
Blackburn, John Brenton, 50 (C)
Blaine, Marge, 94
Blake, Quentin, 54 (C)
Blassingame, Wyatt, 101
Blos, Joan W., 96
Bodecker, N. M., 2, 46

Bodker, Cecil, 18
Bogan, Louise, 46 (E)
Bond, Michael, 18
Bond, Nancy, 18
Bonsall, Crosby N., 2
Bosse, Malcolm J., 97
Boston, Lucy, 19
Bowden, Joan C., 94
Bradbury, Bianca, 19
Bradley, Duane, 100
Brady, Irene, 74
Brancato, Robin F., 29
Branley, Franklyn M., 68, 74, 102
Breissberg, Petronella, 2
Brenner, Barbara, 75
Brewton, John E., 46 (C), 50 (C)
Brewton, Sara W., 46 (C), 50 (C)
Bridgers, Sue E., 97
Briggs, Katherine M., 19
Briggs, Raymond, 2
Brindze, Ruth, 75
Broekel, Ray, 43 (C)
Bronowski, Jacob, 75
Brown, John Sebastian, 45 (M)
Brown, Marcia, 3, 100
Brown, Palmer, 19
Bryan, Ashley, 39 (C), 46 (C)
Bulla, Clyde R., 19
Burch, Robert, 19
Burgess, Gellett, 47
Burnett, Constance B., 61
Burnford, Sheila E., 29
Burningham, John, 3
Burns, Marilyn, 75, 89
Burton, Hester, 30
Busch, Phyllis S., 75
Byars, Betsy C., 19, 94

Calhoun, Mary, 91
Callen, Larry, 19, 94
Cameron, Eleanor, 20
Campbell, Elizabeth A., 68
Caras, Roger A., 75, 103

*This index includes editors, translators, and others. They are designated as follows: (C) compilers, selectors, adapters; (E) editors; (M) musicians; (T) translators; and (X) all others—advisors, researchers, contributors, etc.

Illustrator Index*

*This index includes book designers and photographers as well as illustrators. In cases where illustrators are also the authors of their own books, they are listed in the author index.